TOYS, GAMES, AND MEDIA

TOYS, GAMES, AND MEDIA

Edited by

Jeffrey Goldstein
University of Utrecht

David Buckingham
University of London

Gilles Brougère
University of Paris-Nord

 LAWRENCE ERLBAUM ASSOCIATES, PUBLISHERS
2004   Mahwah, New Jersey   London

Lawrence Erlbaum Associates, Inc., Publishers
10 Industrial Avenue
Mahwah, New Jersey 07430

Cover design by Kathryn Houghtaling Lacey

Library of Congress Cataloging-in-Publication Data

Toys, games, and media / edited by Jeffrey Goldstein, David Buckingham, Giles Brougère.
    p. cm.
    Includes bibliographical references and index.
    ISBN 0-8058-4903-3 (cloth : alk. paper)
    1. Media programs (Education). 2. Media literacy. 3. Play. I. Goldstein, Jeffrey H. H.
Buckingham, David, 1954– . III. Brougère, Gilles.

LB1028.4.T69 2004
371.33–dc22
                                                                    2004046975
                                                                    CIP

Books published by Lawrence Erlbaum Associates are printed on acid-free paper,
and their bindings are chosen for strength and durability.

Printed in the United States of America
10 9 8 7 6 5 4 3 2 1

Contents

Foreword

Brian Sutton-Smith
University of Pennsylvania

The exciting thing about this book is that one greets it as the latest news about what is happening with the development of media literacy for children. What we want to know is how are the children making out with television, video games, the Internet, computers, and, of course, toys, games, and books? None of us adults older than middle age went through any massive hybridization such as this. The oldest of us had only radio, not many toys, but many books and plenty of street games. What we learn in this volume is that there is an increasing integration of all these processes in the lives of the children being studied. Whether we are talking about homes or schools, education or entertainment, playground play or media play, commercial or public investments, or children or adults, a melding is going on that is having varying combinations of effects on how children develop in contemporary society. Yet if we read these chapters carefully, we find two major messages: The one is largely negative about the failure of various "educationally loaded" media to absorb children, and the other is largely positive about the success of play to continue its existence within the new context of these multiple media.

NEGATIVE MESSAGES

A careful reading of these chapters gives the impression that most of them see the current educational media situation as doing an inadequate service to the play life of children. No one denies that media socialization is inevitable in some way in a global world, but everyone seems to find many currently available forms of computer play defective in their ability to promote the best kind of play life for children. Of course, one has to be careful here because all the writers are of an older generation, and as such may be well biased in favor of their older ways of playing. But there is documentation here

- of the limited fun that children have with the idiosyncrasies of smart toys such as robots
- of the limited use children make of all the computer educational programs available to them
- of the relative unimportance of these media phenomena, as compared with the importance to the children of their own more varied everyday play lives
- of commercial exploitation of children by advertisers, even in cases wherein the children do find the Internet play forms highly attractive.

All of these findings seem to carry a veridical message that all is not well in these particular communicational and educationally oriented cauldrons of toys, games, and media. Different countries are involved, but there are no exceptions to this strain of negativity about the relations of such media and play throughout the chapters.

POSITIVE MESSAGES

When the focus is on children in their own playground, although there still is an impact of popular media figures on play and games, whether from books (Harry Potter) cards (*Pokémon*), or media singing contests, the children assimilate them as the kinds of contests and central person games that have always been an essential part of their peer play. They are forbidden to bring the *Pokémon* cards to schools, so instead, they enact the characters on the cards. Again, what was once the exhibitive girls' game of being voted the best "statue" now becomes a similar exhibitive game of being the best contest singer. For boys, Harry Potter already has so many of the attacks, escapes, and magic that have always been a part of children's traditional imaginative contestive play forms that it is easy to assimilate it into playground social play. See *Children's Games of Street and Playground* by Iona and Peter Opie (1969), which is very much a Potter book. In addition, there are chapters pointing out that the most important thing about games, including computer games, is their own microsystemics. What the children are doing in this kind of play is primarily learning how to interact and perform within this complex field of events. There is always intrinsic game socialization to games. This is one part of the larger metaphysical fact that all kinds of play are alternative ways of living, which are maintained primarily for their own sake throughout life, as for example, devotion to football as participant and spectator. More people in the world watched final world cup soccer 2002 than have ever done anything in common at the same time before in world history. All of this makes it difficult for those who wish to use play primarily for some other educational purpose to succeed in their intentions, as the considerable history of research on play as sociodrama and play as literacy makes clear.

THE PROBLEM WITH PLAY THEORY

So what is happening? It seems to me that the negative conclusions in some of this research, whatever their empirical worth (and that is considerable in most cases), derive primarily from the parlous state of play theory in modern social science. There has never been a consensus about the theoretical meaning of play, so it has become a veritable Rorschach inkblot in modern social science. In the first place, there is the continued dominance of the work ethic, formed in the puritan and industrial labor excesses for former eras. Second, there is the Enlightenment in accord with rationalistic varieties of Darwinism adaptive theory. Currently, this results in the continued implicit belief that for play to be accepted, it needs itself to be a form of behavior useful to the acquisition of ever more complex rational processes, and therefore to school work in general. In several of the studies reported in this book, the children in effect refuse to use the smart toys provided with their implied conceptual enrichments, and instead use them in terms of their own preexisting more simplified play predilections. Part of the problem here is that despite the increasingly high prestige of the idea of play in the modern intellectual ontological mythology, very little research has ever been given to a discovery of what the children actually are doing and achieving with their play for themselves, although several chapters in this volume contrarily and wonderfully do just that. Instead, there is a great and prestigious noise about play as

flexibility (Bruner)
improvisation (Sawyer)
metacommunications (Bateson/Garvey)
emotional regulation (Carson/Parks)
conflict mediation (Freud)
enhancing imagination (Singer)
increasing ego mastery (Erikson)

facilitating abstraction (Vygotsky)

consolidating cognitions (Piaget)

Some, or all, of these processes might well occur and be facilitated during play, but none of them have anything centrally to do with the essential character of play itself. If play is to be understood, we need to know why play is sometimes about hazing, sometimes about winning and losing, sometimes about risk taking, sometimes nonsense, and sometimes festive. This is just to mention several of the major kinds of play that I have dealt with in my book *The Ambiguity of Play* (1997), and that have yet to be integrated into a master theory. Why has play taken these forms so strongly throughout history? Why does it still take these forms? What is going on when you are in the midst of one of these games? What are you trying to do quite realistically and so repetitively within the play frame? I prefer the view that these all are forms of survival. These are older forms of adaptation that still are with us, and that is why they are so exciting and at the same time safe. Another reason is that they also are a reflective parody upon themselves.

Having offered this critique let me emphasize that I would have had no idea of the plight of these current media–play interactions without the benefit of this volume. It brings the reader up to date concerning the current situation for these forms of play/media research with both their limitations and aspirations.

List of Contributors

ABOUT THE EDITORS

Jeffrey Goldstein teaches at the University of Utrecht, the Netherlands. His books include *Sports, Games, and Play* (Lawrence Erlbaum Associates), *Toys, Play, and Child Development* (Cambridge University Press), *Why We Watch: The Attractions of Violent Entertainment* (Oxford University Press), and *Handbook of Computer Game Studies* (MIT Press). He is cofounder of the International Toy Research Association and chairman of the National Toy Council (London).

David Buckingham is director of the Center for Children, Youth, and Media at the Institute of Education, University of London. He is author or editor of 15 books, including *Children Talking Television* (Falmer), *Moving Images* (Manchester University Press), *The Making of Citizens* (Routledge), and *After the Death of Childhood* (Polity).

Gilles Brougère is professor of science of education at the University of Paris-Nord. He is the author of *Jeu et Education* (Paris, L'Harmattan) and editor of *Traditions et Innovations Dans L'éducation Préscolaire: Perspectives Internationales* (Paris, INRPP). He is past president of the International Toy Research Association.

ABOUT THE AUTHORS

Magdalena Albero-Andrés, Universidad Autónoma de Barcelona, Spain

Mikael Alexandersson, University of Gothenberg, Sweden

Mark Allen, Brunel University, Surrey, United Kingdom

Doris Bergen, Miami University of Ohio, Oxford, Ohio

Maria Costa, Spanish Toy Research Institute, Ibi-Alicante, Spain

Malena Fabregat, Spanish Toy Research Institute, Ibi-Alicante, Spain

Elizabeth Grugeon, De Montfort University, Bedford, England

Waltraut Hartmann, University of Vienna, Vienna, Austria

Stephen Kline, Simon Fraser University, Burnaby, BC, Canada

Jonas Linderoth, University of Gothenberg, Sweden

Berner Lindström, University of Gothenberg, Sweden

Lydia Plowman, University of Stirling, Stirling, Scotland

Alan Powers, Pollock's Toy Museum, London, England

M. Romero, Spanish Toy Research Institute, Ibi-Alicante, Spain

Ellen Seiter, University of California, Los Angeles, California

Gisela Wegener-Spöhring, University of Cologne, Cologne, Germany

Christine R. Yano, University of Hawaii, Honolulu, Hawaii

1

Introduction:
Toys, Games, and Media

Jeffrey Goldstein
David Buckingham
Gilles Brougère

Toys, games, and media are merging inexorably into a seamless blend of entertainment, information, education, and play. Although traditional toys and play have not lost their appeal, technology is increasingly applied to the pursuit of pleasure. And pleasure in the form of computer-mediated activities and games is increasingly applied in the pursuit of more purposeful goals such as education in the form of "edutainment" or, more directly, as educational toys and computer games. In *Toys, Games, and Media*, the focus is on the interplay, so to speak, between traditional toys and play and those mediated by or combined with digital technology. The discussion considers how traditional and technology-enhanced toys are used in traditional play and in new ways of playing, and how these are woven into children's lives.

The astute reader will notice that this book is not divided neatly into independent sections labeled "toys," "games," and "media." The 14 chapters in *Toys, Games, and Media* began as papers at a conference with this theme in August 2002. The meeting was jointly organized by the International Toy Research Association (www.he.se/ide/ncfl/ITRA.html) and the Centre for the Study of Children, Youth, and Media at the University of London Institute of Education (www.ccsonline.org.uk/mediacentre/home.html). More than 150 delegates from nearly 30 countries participated in the London conference. The editors invited a dozen contributors to elaborate and update their conference papers for this book. The contributors include long-established scholars as well as young scientists and educators from Europe and North America. Their disciplines involved communications and media studies, education, history, psychology, and sociology. The result is a look at the past, present, and near future of toys, games, and play based on cutting-edge research, sometimes with prototype and new hybrid toys.

UNDERSTANDING CONVERGENCE

This book, based on the aforementioned conference, reflects the increasing convergence of toys, games, and media, both in the commercial marketplace and in children's daily lives. This convergence of media—print, television, film, computer games, toys, and collectibles—occurs almost seamlessly. This development is far from new. A look back to the early days of Disney will show instances of how movies were used as an opportunity for merchandising toys and other commodities, particularly, though by no means exclusively, to children. Even in the early days of television, children's programming generated spin-offs, and shows that now are recollected with sentimental nostalgia (e.g., BBC's *Muffin the Mule* and *Sooty* from the 1950s) were money-spinning franchises in their day. As this latter example suggests, and as the subsequent success of *Sesame Street* confirms, "educational" media produced by public service broadcasters can prove just as profitable in this respect as the apparently more "exploitative" productions of commercial companies. Indeed, in the past few years, public service productions such as *Barney* and *Teletubbies* have been among the most profitable media phenomena, not the least in terms of global toy merchandising.

Toys, games, and media today are increasingly enmeshed in webs of "integrated marketing," which depend on what marketers call the "synergy" between different types of products. Books, movies, and TV shows are tied in with games (not just computer games, but also more traditional games such as cards and board games) and with toys of many kinds, ranging from the plastic models contained in fast-food "happy meals" to the more elaborate and expensive interactive toys considered in the third section of this book.

Play is not always media driven. Harry Potter famously began life in a book—indeed in one with a very short print run. Pokemon started out as a computer game. The Ninja Turtles first appeared in an obscure alternative comic, whereas it appears that Beyblades began as a toy. Yet the companies responsible for these properties were quick to capitalize on their success by translating them to other media.

In the world of media, merchandising is no longer an afterthought or a lucky accident, but an integral part of the commercial strategy. In cultural terms, this has ambiguous consequences. Children's culture is now highly intertextual: Every "text" (including commodities such as toys) effectively draws upon and feeds into every other text. When children play with

Pokemon cards or toys, for example, they draw on knowledge and expertise they have derived from watching the TV shows and movies, or from playing the computer games: Each play event is part of a broader flow of events that crosses from one medium or "platform" to another. This is play that involves an energetic form of activity (children who want to succeed in the game), or in the broader peer-group culture that surrounds it, there must be energetic seekers of information, honing their skills in a disciplined way and working flexibly across different media and modes of communication.

THE MEANINGS OF ACTIVITY

Many critics argue that children are no longer able to engage in authentic, spontaneous play, that the narratives, symbols, and scenarios of their play have been taken over by the media, depriving children of the opportunity to develop their imagination and autonomy. Yet much research, including many of the studies contained in this book, suggests that children are far from being the passive victims proposed by this kind of pessimistic critique. In their play, children actively appropriate cultural commodities, making their own discriminations and judgments, while combining and re-working them in myriad ways. Contemporary children's culture depends not on passive consumption, but on the energetic activity of the child.

This also is a process of learning. Participating in recreational activities and joining game-playing communities means developing the necessary know-how for legitimate participation. To participate, an individual must be ready to learn. Contemporary play objects are, by the virtue of their electronic functions and affordances, vessels of knowledge. It is not surprising that many practices involving these objects arise out of exploration and discovery, heuristic activities par excellence. Discovering an object and its uses, learning the means by which to communicate with others via this object, sharing in and eventually collectively creating new meanings around this object, such is the implicit curriculum of the overall toy culture, of those recreational objects that, beyond the standard toy, include the video game console and the computer.

Yet there also are limits to activity. It may be a mistake to equate activity with agency, or with genuine control or power on the part of the user. Users who are more active may simply be more open to exploitation, as Ellen Seiter's contribution to this volume suggests. Furthermore, the seductive rhetoric of "interactivity" should be considered with caution. There are striking continuities between "interactive" computer games and the board games that preceded them, not just in their thematic concerns, but also in the ways by which they seek to engage the player, as well as in the rewards and pleasures they offer. In both cases, much of the activity derives from the social context of play. On the other hand, much of the "interactivity" of contemporary media is little more than superficial or tokenistic—a matter of e-mailing in the answers to a TV quiz, clicking away at the interface of a Web site or an educational CD-ROM, or prompting the limited repertoire of a talking doll.

Nevertheless, a look across the contemporary media landscape, not just for children, but also for adults, strikingly shows how the metaphor of play has become central to a range of genres. For example, the new hybrids of game shows and documentaries represented by "makeover" shows and "reality" programs can be identified, as well as the use of TV-linked Web sites in shows such as *Big Brother* or in more overtly gamelike programs such as *Fightbox*. For some critics, this merely indicates the terminal "infantilization" of adult culture, whereas others are inclined to celebrate its irreverent, and perhaps even subversive, appeal.

The contributions collected together in this volume cast an interesting light on these issues, and offer a range of contrasting perspectives. For example, the chapters by Grugeon (From Pokemon to Potter), Albero-Andres (The Internet and Adolescents), and Seiter (The Internet Playground) provide evidence of the aforementioned activity, although as Seiter and also Kline (Learners, Spectators, or Gamers?) imply, there are limits on the extent of children's "literacy" or competence when it comes to new media. Seiter, along with Powers (The Revival of the English Toy Theater, 1945–2001), Hartmann and Brougere (Toy Culture in Preschool Education and Children's Toy Preferences), Wegener-Spöhring (War Toys in the World of Fourth Graders: 1985 and 2002), and Fabregat, Costa, and Romero (Adaptation of Traditional Toys and Games to New Technologies), also makes the vital point that children's engagement with toys, games, and media needs to be understood in the social and interpersonal contexts wherein they are situated.

AN OUTLINE OF THE BOOK

The chapters in this volume are arranged according to three themes: toy culture, children and digital media, and the influence of technology on play. In part 1, the changing nature of contemporary children's culture is considered. Although new media and developments in information technology have influenced the play, toys, and games of children and adults, traditional forms of play and traditional play objects have not been replaced, even if they have been merged and reshaped.

Because this volume aims to present a dynamic picture of the changing nature of toys, games and media, several chapters deal with comparisons across time (Powers, English toy theater, 1945–2001; Wegener-Spöhring, war toys in 1985 and 2002; Grugeon, media-related play, 2000–2003) and place (Hartmann and Brougere, Australia, Austria, Brazil, France, Sweden; Yano, Japan). Powers considers the evolution of the English toy theater, tracing how it appears to have survived despite commercial pressures by adapting its contents to changing cultural enthusiasms. The toy theater can be seen as an example of an "interactive" toy that long predates the advent of digital technology. It shows how some themes of children's play persist despite historical change.

Hartmann and Brougere, along with colleagues in Australia, Brazil, and Sweden, conducted surveys over a 10-year period to determine the toys available to preschool children in home, preschool, and day-care (crèche) settings. Two opposing toy cultures emerge: preschool toy culture and the more "child-centered" family toy culture. The ensuing tension between adult objectives and child interests is the source of the recreation versus education dilemma.

Yano (Japanese Cute at Home and Abroad) shows that the integrated, multimedia approach described as symptomatic of children's culture also is reflected in adult "toys." As she suggests, the Japanese notion of *kawaii* (or "cute") embodies some of the tensions that surround contemporary conceptions of childhood, but it also is inflected in diverse and sometimes unexpected ways when exported to a global market.

School recess represents an essential area for marketing as well as for criticism and reconstitution of child culture—a place where Harry Potter hangs with Pokémon. In this influential space, conformity and change, tradition and innovation, and acceptance and rejection of the contemporary are found side-by-side. Elizabeth Grugeon asked trainee primary school teachers to observe school breaks on the playgrounds. They recorded jokes, games, and narrative play in an effort to discover the influence of the media. In 2000, Pokemon, Beanie Babies, Game Boys, and the lore of football and wrestling were frowned upon by teachers and banned from classrooms, but enthusiastically welcomed by children on the playground. A year later, the playground repertoire had been extended by text-messaging and Harry Potter. Children incorporate and adapt a variety of media crazes into their narrative play.

These chapters suggest that the boundaries between toys, games, and media are blurring. So perhaps are other boundaries, namely, those between education and entertainment, as observed by Kline (Learners, Spectators, or Gamers?) and Linderoth, Lindstrom, and Alexandersson (Learning With Computer Games); between home and school, as observed by Hartmann and Brougere; between the commercial and the public sector; and perhaps also, as Yano's contribution implies, between adults and children themselves.

Part 2 presents four studies investigating children's uses of digital media from the United States (Ellen Seiter), Canada (Stephen Kline), Spain (Magdalena Albero-Andres), and Sweden (Jonas Linderoth, Berner Lindstrom, and Mikael Alexandersson). These chapters are a rich source of information on how and how often children used computers, the Internet, video games, and mobile telephones in 2002.

Seiter considers how children use the Internet to play. How do games on the Web compare with more traditional forms of children's play? How do issues of access and social communication differ between computers and playgrounds? The findings presented in this chapter are based on a 3-year study of a California after-school computer laboratory for children ages 8 to 11 years. Seiter shows that, whereas the children were very aware of the commercial motivations of other media, they were significantly less attuned to the ways in which advertising, sponsorship, and market research functioned in relation to the Internet.

The chapters by Stephen Kline and Magdalena Albero-Andres paint a complex cultural portrait of interactive media and video games. They contrast the utopian visions built around multimedia as described by Negroponte (1995), Rushkoff (1996), and others, with the commercial, social, and educational realities of today's media diet.

Magdalena Albero-Andres presents the results of a study that investigated how children use the Internet to communicate, play, and learn. Interviews and observation of children ages 12 to 14 years in the city of Barcelona examine how family, peer group, children's culture, urban context, and previous media experience shape the use of the Internet. The results show a natural integration of the Internet into the classic elements of children's culture, and a self-learning process for the acquisition of skills in the use of the Internet itself. Children tended to use the Internet as a source of information only when completing school assignments. Albero-Andres identifies gaps between school proposals for the use of the Internet and the interests, motivations, and knowledge of children using the Web.

Kline explores the impact of interactive media from the vantage point of media theory by tracing how the hybrid between computers and television has changed Canadian children's media preferences and use patterns in the home. Kline characterizes the broad patterns of adolescent media use, their genre preferences, and their stated motives for using different media.

Linderoth, Lindstrom and Alexandersson offer a more sanguine view of new media than Kline, presenting an analysis of video recordings of children ages 6 to 11 playing different computer games in different settings. When children do not have the necessary resources, such as prior experience, for making sense of the represented phenomena, the content of the game stays on a virtual level, and representations obtain their meanings only from the function they have in the game context. These authors describe the implications of games in educational settings, for instance, the educator's need to offer the proper resources to support the learning process. This also has consequences for designers of educational games, who can use different game elements to support or undermine the child's understanding of content.

In part 3, the focus is on how technological developments influence children's play. "Smart toys," those that contain microchips or interface with computers, are investigated in four chapters.

Most toy and game design and development have focused on visuals, audio, and electronics. There is little evidence of "haptic" (touch) design. Mark Allen (Tangible Interfaces in "Smart Toys") observes that the sense of touch and its ability to produce pleasure have been overlooked. Allen observed a group of 20 children ages 5 to 9 years who were given toys with varying degrees of electronic interactivity. Video evidence was combined with structured interviews involving 14 of the children and their teacher. A disparity was found between the child's favorite toy and the one the child found most haptically stimulating. The children did not discover the full functionality of the toys.

Doris Bergen (Preschool Children's Play With Rescue Heroes: Effects of Technology-Enhanced Figures on the Themes of Play) studied prototype prosocial action figures developed by Fisher-Price. Although technology-enhanced "talking" toys have become increasingly popular with parents and children, there is little research on how children play with such toys. Also, little is known about the themes of pretend play in which children engage using realistic replica figures of fire and police personnel, especially with regard to prosocial helping behaviors. This question is of special interest since the September 11 disaster. Preschool boys and girls ages 3½ to 4½ years played with Fisher-Price Rescue Heroes that "talk" (with computer chips) and with similar Rescue Heroes that do not talk.

Lydia Plowman and Rosemary Luckin (Children's Interaction With "Smart" Toys) describe the Cachet Project (Children and Electronic Toys), which aims to explore and map children's interactions with digital interactive toys, in this case Microsoft Actimates. These are free-standing digital toys with a vocabulary of 4,000 words based on popular educational cartoon and storybook characters. These soft "plush" toys have squeezable sensors that provoke the toy into head and arm gestures accompanied by a speech prompt designed to engage the child in interactive games, such as saying the alphabet or timing the child's favorite song. A particularly interesting feature of these toys is their ability to interact with compatible software by means of a radio pack. When linked in this way, the plush toy comments on the child's progress or offers advice as the child tackles thought-provoking activities offered by the software.

M. Fabregat, M. Costa, and M. Romero of the Spanish Toy Research Institute describe how toys can be adapted for children with special needs.

They describe the development of a ride-on vehicle with a global positioning system to prevent collisions, designed for children who are blind or partially sighted. The project is a collaborative effort between engineers, child development experts, and a Spanish toy company.

The chapters by Allen, Bergen, Plowman, and Luckin demonstrate that in the case of interactive toys, children often engage with new media in quite traditional ways, bypassing some of the more innovative technological possibilities. This differs little from the approach of adults who learn how to do what they must with their computer, but do not explore its full range of possibilities.

REFERENCES

Negroponte, N. (1995). *Being digital.* New York: Knopf.
Rushkoff, D. (1996). *Children of chaos.* New York: Harper.

TOY CULTURE

2

The Toy Theater: The Revival and Survival of an English Tradition

Alan Powers

In 1884, Robert Louis Stevenson wrote in his essay, A Penny Plain and Two-pence Coloured, published in the *Magazine of Art*, "That national monument, after having changed its name to Park's, to Webb's, to Redington's, and at last to Pollock's, has now become, for the more part, a memory."[1] Stevenson was the most famous, but not the first nor the last commentator to evoke his own childhood in terms of the English toy theater or "juvenile drama," and to regret its decline, while speaking disparagingly of the alternative toys that had taken its place.[2] He was speaking of a toy originating from the Regency, which reached its height of popularity in the 1830s and 1840s. The publications consisted of printed and hand-colored sheets of characters and scenery based on actual productions, with a text of the play abridged for performance on a wooden theater, for which proscenium fronts and orchestras also were published. After 1850, little new original material was issued, although Webb and Pollock, whom Stevenson names, continued in business in the East End of London into the 1930s, selling new printings off the old plates in nearly adjacent streets, each professing only vague awareness of the other's existence.

---

[1]Robert Louis Stevenson, A Penny Plain and Twopence Coloured. *Magazine of Art*, 1884, pp. 227–232.

[2]Bibliographies are found in George Speaight, *A History of the English Toy Theatre*, London, Studio Vista, 1969, and Peter Baldwin, *Toy Theatres of the World*, London, Zwemmer, 1992.

The theme of decline that gives poignancy to Stevenson's essay was voiced in the 1860s by other writers such as Rosetti. As a literary trope, it combined personal feelings about the loss of childhood with a more general sense of lost folk art vigor in the face of Victorian gentility. There also was a patriotic theme, expressed by Stevenson, because English toy theaters were superseded in the trade by German chromolithographed ones, which were more magnificent, but offered less interaction for the child. The German tradition of toy theater and paper theater is one among several others, but this account is devoted to the English one, and chiefly concerns the successor businesses to that of Benjamin Pollock, based on a stock of printing plates and printed sheets still extant at the time of his death. Independent of the Pollock business, although probably largely stimulated by its survival, there were other manifestations of interest in toy theater, mostly appealing more to adults than to children, so that although never a majority interest, it can claim attention as a constituent part of the culture of childhood in postwar Britain.

There were many stages in the adult appreciation of toy theaters in Britain between Stevenson's and Pollock's deaths in 1937.[3] These divided mainly into two categories. On the one hand, there were newly drawn theaters and plays published in a variety of formats including London Underground posters and breakfast cereal promotions. On the other hand, there were appreciative and scholarly articles by Edward Gordon Craig and others in his journal *The Mask* in 1912, an exhibition of toy theater staged by the publisher Stanley Nott in New York in 1927, and performances by George Speaight at the bookshop, of John and Edward Bumpus in Oxford Street at Christmas in 1932 and 1933, accompanied by sales of theaters and sheets of plays.[4] Born in 1914, Mr Speaight has subsequently contributed more than any other single person to the revival of interest in the toy theater, as a performer and researcher.[5] He organized an 80th birthday exhibition and celebration for Mr. Pollock shortly before his death at the George Inn, Southwark, in association with the British Model Theatre Guild, active since 1925. This attracted commentary in *The Times*, which also awarded an obituary to Mr. Pollock, indicating fertile ground for a revival. A further manifestation of interest was *The Triumph of Neptune*, a ballet choreographed by Georges Balanchine for Serge Diaghilev in 1926, with costumes, scenery, and plot derived from toy theater sheets by Pollock and Webb.[6]

The revival of toy theater after World War II was different from these, in that it tried to use the original material and market it directly for children,

---

[3] See Chapter XV, Revival, in Speaight, op. cit.

[4] A copy of the Stanley Nott catalog is in the British Library 011795.dd.61.

[5] See Barry Clarke and David Powell, *George Speaight, A Life in Toy Theatre*, catalog of an exhibition at Pollock's Toy Museum, 2003.

[6] See *The Triumph of Neptune*, catalog of an exhibition at Pollock's Toy Museum, London, 2003.

placing the nostalgic and antiquarian interest of adults at a remove, although what was offered to children was a strongly historicized toy. The Pollock shop was carried on by Mr. Pollock's two daughters, but there was a concern among enthusiasts that it might be bombed. The shop was indeed hit by a V1 flying bomb in July 1944. Before this occurrence, most of the stock had been removed because it had been bought by an antiquarian bookseller, Alan Keen, for £850.[7] It consisted of printed sheets, lithographic stones, and a large number of copper and zinc printing plates, dating back to 1834. These represented the succession and amalgamation of several earlier toy theater businesses. Keen had been a commercial artist, but in a brief career as an antiquarian bookseller, he struck gold when he discovered a copy of Hall's *Chronicles* with annotations believed to be in Shakespeare's hand. The sale of this book financed the Pollock purchase.

Keen found investors for his business, constituted as Benjamin Pollock Ltd., with the actors Ralph Richardson and Robert Donat among the directors. He rented a shop in the relatively new block of buildings on John Adam Street, off the Strand, that replaced part of the original Adelphi development by the Adam Brothers. Keen's notes for the business indicate that he expected to sell toy theaters for children and also prints from the original plates for collectors, together with spin-off products using the attractive graphic imagery of the Pollock designs.[8]

Only the first of these ambitions was realized to any large extent. Keen believed that "the big money is in mass production which in no wise destroys the charm or tradition."[9] He was quick to get established in business at the end of the war despite the difficulties of production. George Speaight was an obvious candidate to become involved in the business because he not only had performed at Bumpus's, but had worked there as a bookseller. In addition, Keen had responded to a request from the publishers, Macdonald & Co., for an author to write a history of the toy theater, recommending Speaight, who took his research materials with him when posted as a radio operator to Ceylon at the end of the war. Speaight's book, *Juvenile Drama*, published in 1946, was both scholarly and romantic, and has remained the authority in the field.

Benjamin Pollock himself produced wooden theaters in small quantities. It is not clear who designed Keen's new theaters, but his first career would at least have given him insight into design possibilities. His most successful model was the Regency Theatre, with its varnished hardboard stage supported on a bowed orchestra strip held in tension by screws running up

---

[7]The imminent closure of the shop was marked by The End of the Juvenile Drama? written by Anne Scott-James, an article that appeared 25 March 1944 in *Picture Post*, a leading left-wing illustrated weekly. The Misses Pollocks were also recorded on a short Pathé newsreel.

[8]An undated sheet of notes in the records of Benjamin Pollock Ltd. at Pollock's Toy Museum.

[9]Copy of a letter from Keen to Speaight, 29 November 1945, Pollock's Toy Museum.

into the base of the plastic-molded proscenium front. A light grid to hold the scenery, based on the traditional form, completes the theater. Keen's publicity proclaimed that "the long-lost and forgotten Regency prosceniums of J. K. Green are being reprinted, colored and built into a new improved collapsible stage, with a curved apron, . . . altogether an affair of much glamour and grace." The actual number of Regency Theatres manufactured is not available, although Keen left records of his predictions, such as his hope at the end of 1945 of sending "a quarter of a million stages out of the country in February." He forecast 17,000 to be sold in the first half of 1947. These figures undoubtedly exaggerate the actual numbers, but even so, they must reflect some basis of success. A lighting kit run from a transformer was developed for sale with the theaters.

A Regency Theatre was exhibited at the Britain Can Make It exhibition at the Victoria and Albert Museum in 1947 as one among a collection of products approved by the Design Council. With its muted coloring, reflecting late Georgian rather than Victorian taste, it indeed represents the cautious return of decoration within the "contemporary" style of the postwar period. Even more typical of the taste of the time was the alternative abstract front and "orchestra" for the Regency, termed the "Adelphi," designed by the photographer Edwin Smith, who also was involved in creating artwork from the original plays for the abbreviated versions written by George Speaight. The Regency and Adelphi sold for 38s 6d, which was a substantial price for a toy, but evidently not too steep for what one imagines was a middle-class professional market.

In addition to the Regency, there was the Victoria Theatre, based on another of J. K. Green's proscenium fronts and produced as a flat-pack cardboard design. A first order of 1,000 was delivered in July 1946, but because of subsequent problems with production, it had to be offered at a discount. A larger wooden theater was available for schools and clubs.

The republication of plays began with Keen's extravagant gesture of reprinting *The Silver Palace*, a J. K. Green production of 1841. This visually splendid piece in the masque tradition was one of Diaghilev's sources for *The Triumph of Neptune*. Unfortunately, the color printing was crude, the edition far too large, and the original script unsuitable for performance by children. The other play reprinted in its entirety was *The Red Rover*, a pirate drama based on Fennimore Cooper, which was by contrast very finely printed in black and white and much more suitable for performance.

At an early point, Keen approached J. B. Priestley with the proposal that he write a new play to go with characters and scenes on a theme of highwaymen from the Pollock stock. Priestley rejected this, but instead wrote a script, which was illustrated by Doris Zinkeisen, a well-known stage designer with a taste for Regency swagger. There was a long gestation before the play was published as Puffin Cut-Out Book (PC5), in November 1948 by

Penguin Books. Its cover, derived from the Regency proscenium, exhibited the fine standards of color printing and typography that Penguin upheld in the postwar years. *The High Toby* received plenty of publicity with a celebrity performance at Heal's shop in Tottenham Court Road. Keen favored its publication in book form because, considering "the unintelligence of the toy trade," he thought it would sell better this way.

A Theatre You Can Make Yourself, with drawings by Jane Cumming, a larger format hand-lithographed Puffin Cut-Out Book (PC6), was published in the same month as *The High Toby*, but although clearly based on the juvenile drama in concept, it did not seek to imitate it in any detail. This was not a product of the Pollock business, although it indicated the general feeling that toy theater was interesting and could be commercially successful. A toy theater version of *Treasure Island*, by Geoffrey Robinson, with handdrawn lithographed designs by Marian Marsh, was published by Puffin in 1953 (PC11). It included a theater proscenium on the cover. This was the last of this series of publications. Pollock's itself issued a cutout *Hamlet* in the same style as *The High Toby*, based in this case on color stills from the Laurence Oliver film of Shakespeare's play, with financial support from J. Arthur Rank, which also was retailed by Penguin. An independent publication was an insert of a miniature theater in *The Strand* magazine of December 1947 with characters and scenes for Cinderella, by the popular children's illustrator Edward Ardizzone, indicating the popularity of toy theaters at this date.

Cinderella and *Aladdin* both were published in 1947 as reduced versions of Victorian originals, rearranged by Edwin Smith to scripts by George Speaight. Two further plays were published as color-printed inserts in *The Model Stage* magazine, which was a further creation of Benjamin Pollock Ltd. in 1950, based on the format of *The High Toby*. These were *Blackbeard the Pirate* and *Harlequinade*, both prepared in 1947 but held over. The Model Stage No. 3 contained *The Bethlehem Story* in the style of an early Gothic illumination by the artist Sheila Jackson, who has maintained a long-time interest in puppets and toy theater. She also began to prepare artwork for Prokofiev's *Peter and the Wolf*. Another unpublished play, intended for The Model Stage No. 4 in 1950, was *The Atom Secrets*, with a script by George Speaight on a contemporary theme, scenery by Malvina Cheek, and characters by another as yet unidentified hand.[10]

The failure to complete these publishing enterprises indicated the difficulty that Benjamin Pollock Ltd. had surviving in the more stringent financial climate after 1947. The imposition of a 70% import duty on toys coming into the United States was a major blow, indicating that this had previously

---

[10]When Malvina Cheek looked at the artwork in 2003, she recognized the scenes, including a house interior and pictures of canal narrow boats, as her own work, but believed that the figures were by another hand.

been an important market. The shop moved from John Adam Street to 16 Little Russell Street, a back street near the British Museum. George Speaight's salary often was unpaid for long periods, and he left in 1951 to perform marionettes at the Festival Pleasure Gardens, Battersea, as part of the Festival of Britain. Toy theaters were in evidence in Festival exhibitions that year, and fitted well with the patriotic revival of folk art that was one of the Festival's themes. Meanwhile, Benjamin Pollock Ltd. went into insolvency in 1952.

The decline at this moment might have been final, but Pollock's was rescued from receivership by Marguerite Fawdry, who had trained as an actress with Michel St. Denis and had bought a toy theater for her son John.[11] Interested in popular art, she successfully revived the Pollock business at 44 Monmouth Street on the edge of Covent Garden from 1955 onward, creating a toy museum to provide a context for the sale of toy theaters and other traditional toys. In 1969, the shop and museum moved to 1 Scala Street in Fitzrovia, and the museum was established as a charitable trust. The museum and shop have been kept going since Mrs. Fawdry's death in 1995 by a small but dedicated staff.

The publications of Alan Keen's period were taken over as stock by Mrs. Fawdry, and new color-printed and reduced plays were added to the range, in addition to wooden theaters made by a series of different workshops. Two new plays were published in 1956, both with an eye to current children's interests. *The Flying Saucerers* by Reginald Reynolds and Robert Culff was an arch portrayal of Anglo-American cultural relations, with Martians in the place of the Americans. *The Massacre of Penny Plain*, again by Reynolds (a sometime collaborator of George Orwell), with Hugh McLelland as artist, took a lighthearted view of the Western genre.

Whereas the first postwar Pollock company seems to have been able to benefit from a gap in the toy market in its early years, television was seen 10 years later as the chief competition. In 1963, the toy historian Leslie Daiken described Pollock's as "a thriving business . . . catering for a growing demand for theater as against telly, which seemed an inevitable reaction." He went on to suggest that this would indicate some conscious renewal of Victorian values: "Discerning parents who nostalgically remember the role played ancestrally by Toy Theaters in their family circle, now look to the Pollock shop for inspiration."[12] The feeling of nostalgia evoked by Stevenson has spread from toy theaters into other areas of the toy trade that straddle the boundary between adult and child interests. The stock sold in

---

[11]The story is told in Speaight (1969), and in Kenneth Fawdry, *The Story of Benjamin Pollock* and *Pollock's Toy Museum*, London, Pollock's Toy Museum, 1981. See also Alan Powers, Undercover surrealism: the story of Pollock's toy museum. *Things*, 10 (Summer 1999), 6–25.

[12]Leslie Daiken, *World of Toys*. London: Lambarde Press, 1963, p. 146.

the Pollock shop, apart from the toy theaters, mostly had a reference to the past in the form of either direct reproduction or new designs in the spirit of the old.

In *The Stage* in 1946, Ralph Richardson raised the issue of the educational value of the toy theater, explaining it in terms of the skills that could be acquired through its practice:

> Now that Punch and Judy, after being figures of fun for centuries, have been officially approved as a legitimate means of instruction under the new Education Act, the toy theatre will be regarded in a more serious light. Quite apart from the joy children derive from such a pastime, it teaches them to speak correctly and allows them to project themselves into the personalities of their puppets. Never has a toy with such magic in its appeal to the young possessed such cultural value.[13]

Richardson omitted, however, the aspects of art and craft that others have stressed. In 1884, Stevenson understood nostalgia not as a retreat from the difficulties of modern life, but as a form of subversion, believing that it challenged the conformity of late Victorian culture with its evocation of danger and crime through plays about highwaymen and smugglers. Toy theater represented the play of the imagination, in contrast to moralistic literature and didactic games. He described how the pleasure of the toy theater was bound up in anticipation with the detailed work of coloring and cutting out rather than performance. These qualities could be found appropriate to the educational climate of the 1960s, with its emphasis on practical activity and visual aspects of learning. Because Marguerite Fawdry's husband Kenneth was head of educational television at BBC, they were well aware of these issues, and children were encouraged to invent their own plays.

Mrs. Fawdry's revival of Pollock's coincided with John Wright's setting up of The Little Angel Marionette Theatre in Islington in 1961, at a time when British television, ironically perhaps, still used marionettes extensively for children's programs. The first international puppet festival was held in Britain in 1963, and Pollock's also had an international flavor, with toy theaters from traditional sources in France, Spain, and Denmark as well as English sources. The museum collection also reflected an international stance, with representation of many Eastern European and Third World countries.

The aesthetic of Pollock's in the 1960s reflected contemporary design trends, with brighter colors in the color printing and a pop art quality in the catalog designs. These coincided with interest shown in toys by the American designers Charles and Ray Eames, with the photographs selected for

---

[13]*The Stage*, 17 January 1946.

their *House of Cards* (1952), and with films such as *Toccata for Toy Trains* (1957). Indeed, British pop artists occasionally used Pollock imagery. A notable example is the borrowing of a toy theater proscenium in Pauline Boty's painting "BUM" (1966) commissioned by Kenneth Tynan for use on the set of *Oh Calcutta!*[14] A Pollock's toy theater was included in Jasia Reichardt's exhibition, *Play Orbit*, at the Institute of Contemporary Arts in 1969, which combined a pop art view of toys with a presumption that modern artist designers could use abstraction to create effective new toy designs that might also work as pieces of art. The toy theater therefore runs in the background of successive cultural movements, while also exerting a periodic direct influence on stage design.

The toy theater has therefore discovered some surprising new associations since its relaunch in 1945, even if Diaghilev had already made the association between high art and its lowly status. Franco Zefferelli's choice of a Pollock's toy theater as a symbol of the special virtues of an English upbringing in the film *Tea with Mussolini* was a demonstration of its cultural significance. In the current climate of museum education, the toy theater has enormous potential for learning in many areas without losing the quality of strangeness and illogicality that Stevenson valued so highly.

---

[14]See Sue Watling and Alan David Mellor, Pauline Boty, *The Only Blonde in the World*. London: Whitford Fine Art/The Mayor Gallery, 1998, p. 19.

3

War Toys in the World of Fourth Graders: 1985 and 2002

Gisela Wegener-Spöhring

In former centuries, war toys formed an integral part of culture and child education, although they have always been subject to sporadic criticism. After a ban on war toys through the Versailles agreements after World War I, they proved to be a real issue to parents and educators in postwar Western Germany. The Bundestag witnessed debates. Activities and flyers abounded ("Stop the war in children's rooms!"), as did campaigns promoting the exchange of war toys for "pedagogically sound" toys (Wegener-Spöhring, 1995).

Inspired by these developments, the author conducted a study in 1985. The broad reception of this study mirrors the interest in the topic at that time (Wegener-Spöhring, 1985, 1986, 1989a, 1989b, 1989c, 1994). One crucial result was the notion of "balanced aggressiveness," which hypothesized that children are capable of balancing aggressive elements of play such that the aggressive actions are restricted to the level of pretense, thus enabling all parties involved in the play to cope with its aggressive and alarming elements. The follow-up study 17 years later posed the following question: Can this notion still be evidenced in a world of play heavily changed by the media?

NATURE OF THE INVESTIGATIONS

The database for these studies consisted of 20 (1985) and 30 (2002) semistructured interviews about the topic "toys you can fight with" conducted with fourth graders, in which 429 and 634 children, respectively, participated. The age of the children ranged from 9 to 12 years. The vast majority of the children were 9 to 10 years old. The interviews took place in the children's classrooms. The time allotted was one classroom period (45 min). After the interviews, a chiefly multiple-choice questionnaire with 8 to 10 questions was completed. In 2002, two questions about multimedia and PC usage were added.[1]

The protocols were evaluated two times by two evaluators, adopting the method of documentary interpretation. Documentary interpretation, originally developed by Karl Mannheim, aims at "a systematic, methodically verifiable access to context-specific and individual sense worlds" (Bohnsack, 1993, p. 65). Besides investigating the concept of balanced aggressiveness, the study also investigated patterns of play and media behavior as well as the role of media in play. In addition, toy mentions in the interviews and questionnaires were counted.

RESULTS

The interview atmosphere had changed considerably over the 17 years. In 1985, the children were enthusiastic. The interviews were intense, and oscillated vividly between fun and seriousness, between loud onomatopoeia and deep thoughtfulness. Apparently, no adult had ever before asked the children about this topic so crucial to their world. They revealed their intimate and secret play world to the interviewers in an almost touching manner. This had completely changed by 2002. Often, the children showed initial hesitation to talk about their games at all. Not that they wanted to hide something from the interviewers. Rather, the topic did not appear to be of great significance anymore. The researchers confirmed what they knew from childhood research: Children "age" earlier, pretend to be less "childlike." "I don't play," a girl said at the beginning of the interview. "I go for walks with my friends." "I don't play," another said. "I work, I read, I listen to music." In the end, they did tell enough, but, in a number of cases, getting the interviews underway was far from easy (Table 3.1).

Frequency and Popularity of War Toys: 1985 and 2002

In 1985, war toys constituted a widespread and male-dominated phenomenon (Table 3.2). Now, 17 years later, the children own more war toys, and

---

[1]The 2002 study was carried out with the support of the following graduation candidates and student assistants at the University of Cologne: Manfred Gimmler, Nina Krauß, Jenny Lowis, Nastaran Najib, Tanja Müller, Klaus Trautmann.

TABLE 3.1
Possession of War Toys Reported in the 1985 and 2002 Questionnaire[2]

	Own War Toys 1985	Would Like More War Toys 1985	Own War Toys 2002	Would Like More War Toys 2002	Own PC/ Playstations 2002
Boys	n = 218		n = 324		
	165 (76%)	98 (45%)	270 (83%)	178 (55%)	279 (86%)
Girls	n = 211		n = 310		
	61 (29%)	7 (3%)	124 (40%)	34 (11%)	156 (50%)

TABLE 3.2
Possession of "Classic" War Toys 1985

	Mentions (n)	% of 382 Mentions of War Toys	% of 429 Children
Face-to-face combat (i.e., fighting and shooting): pistol, rifle, sword, saber, spear, bow and arrow, knife, weapon, tank	192	50	39
Warlike male characters: soldiers, cowboys and Indians, pirates, men	78	20	18
Star wars/Space travel toys	64	17	15
Other	48	13	11
Total	382	100	89

they would like to possess considerably more.[3] However, "toys you can fight with" now include not only "classic" war toys (7%), but also computer games (46%) (Table 3.3). Gender differences in the answers have more or less stayed the same. The researchers differentiated between PC, game console/gameboy, and games.

The most important feature in 1985 was direct fighting, most often carried out with unreal, fantasy, and fairy tale characters. In 2002 only the following were mentioned: soldiers 15 times, and fewer than 10 each for swords, pistols, bows and arrows, and tanks. This means that war toys in the classic sense hardly play a role any longer.

An overview of all toys listed in the questionnaire and the interview in 2002 (Table 3.3) illustrates the play world of today's children.

According to the questionnaire, play currently is dominated by multimedia toys (28%) and computer and console games (46%). Construction games follow far behind, and war toys of the kind described in the investigation

---

[2]Yes/no answers counted.

[3]The table Wish to Have More War Toys (Questionnaire) 2002 is not reproduced in this paper. Here and subsequently, answers which state the name or content of the toy are counted.

TABLE 3.3
Mentions of Toys in the 2002 Questionnaire and Interview

	Mentions in the Questionnaire (n)	% of 634 Children	Mentions in the Interview (n)	% of 634 Children
Dexterity/conjuring games			7	1
Collectors' objects			8	1
War toys	46	7	16	3
Other			17	3
Painting/handicraft			21	3
Cars/vehicles	8	1	26	4
Animals	4	1	29	5
Books/media/music			31	5
Movies/TV series			44	7
People	8	1	59	9
Action characters/sets	58	9	65	10
Board games	15	2	67	11
Dolls/soft toys	9	1	68	11
Construction games	57	9	76	12
Movement/sports	19	3	189	30
Multimedia toys	179	28	192	30
PC/consoles/games	293	46	413	65
Total	696		1,328	

follow behind these (7%). The same holds true for toy wishes. The interviews, in which the children did not speak strictly about "toys you can fight with," considerably reinforced this trend. War toys (3%) are notably surpassed by movement/sports (30%). Even construction games (12%) and board games (11%) reach greater frequencies, as do dolls/soft toys (11%), and play that involves people (9%).

When asked which toys could be used for fighting, only 3% of the children named classic war toys. Even construction games, they find, are more suitable for fighting (4%), and dolls/soft toys reach the same frequency (3%). Currently, fighting is done primarily through computer games (40%), and the direct fight with unreal and fantasy characters, still enthusiastically described in 1985, has in general been transferred to the screen. This was known before, of course, but the author was not aware of the degree of change. The interviews portrayed this trend more sharply.

One further problem needs to be mentioned: The far-reaching embedding of games in the multimedia context makes it difficult to categorize them. Many exist not only as toys, but also through media representation and as computer games. This also is true for traditional board games and even sports. Only in very few cases is it unambiguously clear what the children have in mind.

War Toys As Seen by Children: 1985 and 2002

In 1985, the interviews generated 492 statements, which were grouped into nine categories (Table 3.4). The chief criteria "What is fun?" and "reasons against war toys" then were differentiated further. In 2002, a total of 1,698 statements were registered. Both the reasons for this and the changes in content for some central categories can be illustrated. Sixteen categories were used. Of course, the categories about computer specifics and multimedia were added in 2002. Table 3.4 presents the relative number of mentions in terms of their significance as analyzed by chi-square.

The Dominance of Computer Games and the Decrease in Play Ideas

The toys named by the children in the 2002 interviews are dominated by computer and console games ($n = 413$), followed by multimedia toys ($n = 192$). Instead of reporting their wonderful games, as they did 17 years before, many of the children replied by merely naming a game title. This fact is reflected in the figures for toy mentions in Table 3.3. Statements for "PC/consoles/games" were counted among the categories during the interviews if children added a description. These resulted in another 158 mentions (9% of all mentions) (Table 3.4). For the category "multimedia," this figure is 65 (4%). Moreover, it is this toy to which the overwhelming majority of mentions in the other categories refer. It can be seen that a significant change in childplay has taken place.

The contents of computer and console games, however, are almost never enacted (i.e., imitated in play behavior without a PC; only 3 children in all). Even for multimedia, this number is only 11, and not more than 11 report the much-feared enactment of TV contents. Thus this problem seems not to exist to the extent feared.

Fantasy play still exists, with 9% of children admitting that they played made-up scenarios. However, this is only 3% of the total mentions. What are these play ideas that exist despite the reported dominance of the computer?

The Children Take Up Something That Then Acts as a Play Arena. "I do, like, tournaments with shoe boxes and dolls. There they must, like, fight against each other again and again" (boy).

The Children Use the Characters From Multimedia in Creative Games. "We sometimes play, like, roller coaster, and then they can be blown out in the curve, also the male ones are blown out" (boy).

TABLE 3.4
Statements About War Toys in 1985 and 2002

	Mentions in 1985 (n)	% of 429 Children in 1985	% of 492 Mentions in 1985	Mentions in 2002 (n)	% of 634 Children in 2002	% of 1698 Mentions in 2002
Distancing/relativizing**	47	11	10	60	9	4
Stereotypes**	12	3	2	1	0	0
Ideas for playing	19	4	4	54	9	3
Irreality/ambivalence**	25	6	5	31	5	2
Realism	2	0	0	23	4	1
Identification with play character				99	16	6
Departure from play level				18	3	1
Internal aggressiveness				46	7	3
External aggressiveness				39	6	2
Criticism: insufficient aggressiveness				7	1	0
TV/cinema						
Describing TV/cinema				18	3	1
Enacting TV/cinema				11	2	1
Computer specifics						
Describing playstations/consoles/PC				158	25	9
Enacting playstations/consoles/PC				3	0	0
Multimedia						
Describing multimedia				65	10	4
Enacting multimedia				11	2	1
Gender-specific statements (total)**	53	12	11	41	6	2
What is fun (total)	185	43	38	701	111	41
Reasons against (total)**	149	35	30	312	49	18
Total	492		100	1,698	100	100

**Significant (<0.01).

Even the Classic Play Idea Still Exists, Although Rarely. "I like making up stories, and then I paint it. Then I cut out cardboard characters. Some are bad" (girl).

Adults Are Ridiculed, Although Also Rarely. "I tie Star Wars characters to a rope and hang them out the window. And the neighbors always wonder what that is. I tease them" (boy).

We see play ideas still exist. Also the old war game—one is almost tempted to say, the 'good old war game'—has not disappeared completely. Its marginalized position, however, cannot be ignored. To relativize, or to distance yourself from such a game ("I play that, but only sometimes"; "I only played that when I was younger"), is hardly ever considered necessary nowadays.

The Disappearance of the Play Features Irreality and Ambivalence

Irreality and ambivalence are two decisive features through which play differs from reality (Wegener-Spöhring, 1978, 1995). The feature of *ambivalence* means that play oscillates between active mastery and discovery of the environment on the one hand and self-detachment and distancing on the other, and also between tension and relief (Heckhausen, 1973) without fully positioning itself. Sutton-Smith (1978) discussed this fact as the "bipolarity" of play, as its dialectic nature. Ambivalence and bipolarity always carry the danger that one of the poles will overpower the other, and thus destroy the game as such. Hence, this context suggests the feature of *balance*, of easing out contradictions. Scheuerl (1975) called this the "always uncertain balance of the course of play" (p. 208). Play, by nature and necessarily, implies a distance from reality (i.e., it is different from "ordinary life" (Huizinga, 1938/1986). It is a "pseudo reality" (Heckhausen, 1973), which is marked off from everyday reality through its rules. American literature uses the term "transformation" in this context: Play transforms the real world into a play world (Sutton-Smith, 1978, 1986, 1997). Thus, the feature of *irreality* is found.

In 1985, 25 mentions (5%) were found in this context (Table 3.4). In some cases, the children were able to verbalize this difficult complex surprisingly well: "It is funny and evil—you can easily imagine that in your thoughts." "Joy and sadness are close together." "On the one hand it's good, on the other it's naff."

The children also verbalized irreality: "It is important to know that it isn't true." "You can live in your imagination." "I find weightlessness in space much better, . . . at home I can break my nasal bone; in space I am weightless; nothing can happen to me there."

The feature of ambivalence was not found at all in the 2002 study. Through the sporadic naming of irreality, a combined counting of both categories results in 31 mentions (1.8%), which appear much less sophisticated than in 1985. One boy said: "I think it's okay as long as it doesn't happen for real." Others said: "The good thing about *Dragonball* is that you can fly and throw bombs with your hands." "I don't remember the war when I'm playing." "It's only computer people that get hurt."

Irreality is emphasized when things get too rough. One boy said, "It's fun when you can kill people, and can also kill yourself." This boy verbalizes the fun–killing on the play level. It is unusual that he includes himself as a victim because this contradicts the practice of combative games. As a reaction, the class uttered an embarrassed and alarmed laughter, and a boy explicitly reestablished irreality by interrupting to say "It's only a game anyway!" For precaution, the class then digressed to a funny topic, and a girl started talking about "Sven," the bonking sheep. And then there was the girl whose father, as she explained, had grown up in a dictatorship. She said, "I play war almost only in my dreams."

Realism, the counterpoint to irreality, was evidenced only to a negligible extent in 1985. The 2002 study did not elicit many mentions of it either, but at least there were more: 23 statements. This means that 4% of the children commented on this, sometimes in a critical manner, but sometimes also as a fun factor. One girl, speaking about a computer game, said, "Sometimes blood leaks out from there." A boy continued, "But that's just what's great about it." At another point, a boy made a critical comment: "I think it's naff that there are, like, these games on the Internet about the World Trade Center where this airplane, like, flies in." This comment finds support with other children.

The Changed Fascination: "What Is Fun" About War Toys

In both studies, children reported experiencing fun with war toys predominantly through fighting (Table 3.5). In 1985, "fighting" chiefly meant a fight with weapons and warlike male figures, with 5% of the children commenting in this vein. This figure was 16% in 2002. If the odd category "fighting with Barbies/fighting with dolls" is added, the figure reaches 18%. Often, however, this refers to fighting on the computer screen. Thus, it is only logical that the "classic" categories of war play including hiding/chasing, destroying/collapsing, and aiming/shooting lose in significance. By contrast, there is a dramatic rise in the categories linked to heightened aggressiveness. This development is treated in a separate section.

Although the typical element of classic war play, onomatopoeia ("making noises"), could be heard from 6% of the children, its total percentage was halved in 2002. Fighting gestures, not categorized in the first study, are be-

TABLE 3.5
What Children Considered Fun About Playing
With War Toys in 1985 and 2002

	Mentions in 1985 (n)	% of 429 Children in 1985	% of 492 Mentions in 1985	Mentions in 2002 (n)	% of 634 Children in 2002	% of 1,698 Mentions in 2002
Fighting	22	5	4	104	16	6
Fighting/Barbie				10	2	1
Hiding/chasing*	10	2	2	10	2	1
Destroying/collapsing*	14	3	3	12	2	1
Aiming/shooting*	17	4	3	30	5	2
Aggressiveness—fun**	5	1	1	109	17	6
Killing**	2	0	0	56	9	3
Making noises*	19	4	4	35	6	2
Gestures				29	5	2
Aesthetics**	17	4	3	11	2	1
Assembling/mounting/technology	18	4	4	39	6	2
Strategy				16	3	1
Independence/feeling strong**	16	4	3	8	1	0
Prestige				26	4	2
Excitement/action	8	2	2	12	2	1
Winning	12	3	2	49	8	3
Rough-and-tumble play	4	1	1	28	4	2
Playing with others	6	1	1	39	6	2
Expelling boredom	5	1	1	9	1	1
Doing forbidden things	2	0	0	15	2	1
Obsession	3	1	1	4	1	0
Fun without a reason*	5	1	1	50	8	3
Total	185		38	701		41

*Significant (<0.05).
**Significant (<0.01).

low even that value. The aesthetics of violence, an element of classic war play, hardly plays a role anymore, and is expressed, in fact, only with reference to "cool" computer graphics. The significance of "assembling/mounting/technology" also halved its overall percentage value. "Independence/ feeling strong," a crucial feature of childplay in which the children themselves are masters and call the shots, has become almost meaningless. In 1985, the children said: "For once, I can simply do what I like, including parents, school." "Because you feel stronger." "You feel like in a movie." This sounds more pragmatic today, if it appears at all. A girl said, "I think everybody should make up their own mind whether they play with this or not!" And a boy said about a nonspecified computer game: "There are loads of levels, you can do what you want."

Winning has increased slightly in significance, whereas "excitement" has decreased slightly. By contrast, more mentions were found for the categories "playing with others" and "rough-and-tumble play" (formerly running about/rollicking) (Wegener-Spöhring, 1995). Although the figures in this context are not large, they nonetheless indicate that children do not necessarily become isolated in front of their PCs. Another reassuring fact is that the category "obsession" (formerly "you can't stop") is just as insignificant as in 1985. It is not a fact that computer game maniacs are growing up today. This was also supported by the high number of references to "movement/sports," which normally are conducted in company with others.

The inability of children to give a reason for their fun was greater in 2002. In reality, this has increased much more than the figures in Table 3.5 reflect. As already hinted, the children often only named the title of a computer game when asked about the fun. Alternatively, the children described the game in a breathtakingly aggressive manner. This is elaborated in the next section.

The Crisis of "Balanced Aggressiveness" and the Increase in Internal and External Aggressiveness

In 1985, there were only two references to the "joy of killing," and these referred only to cowboy and playmobile characters. In 2002, by contrast, there were 56 statements (approximately 3% of all mentions), with 9% of the children commenting that they enjoy the killing. Of course this predominantly concerns the killing of characters, mainly computer characters. Yet it cannot be overlooked that a brutalization of both language and play behavior has taken place. The fact that the "killing" sometimes also occurs in non–computer-based play situations may be taken as somehow reassuring. One boy reported: "Well, I take all my characters outside to my friends. But we don't replay the series. They fly up and also shoot and kill, or they are, like, in a different solar system."

This brutalization becomes even more striking when the values for aggressiveness are examined. These were insignificant in 1985, and the few that manifested concerned contexts for which a playlike embedding still seemed plausible: "We beat each other up with curtain rods. We have fun beating up, don't know why." This had changed completely 17 years later, with one third of the children mentioning aggression (Tables 3.4 and 3.5).

If to the analysis are added those who mention departure from the play level with or without violence and the category of realism (Tables 3.4 and 3.7), then 15% of all the responses expressed by 40% of the children fall into this category. This denotes a completely new development in the past 17 years.

This study differentiated between internal and external aggressiveness, either restricted to or departing from the play frame level, as already explained for the category "departure from play level." This differentiation resulted from the play observations in the studies mentioned earlier, in which the notion of "balanced aggressiveness" was found. Balanced aggression means that children are able to balance aggressive contents of play so that the aggressive actions are restricted to the play level of pretense. The category "departure from the play level" is a newly added one. Admittedly, the drift of play into contention and quarreling is not reported very frequently (18 mentions or 1% of all responses by 3% of the children). A boy said, "I have won, or I'll hit you." A second boy said, "When we make war too brutally, and my friend leaves for home, crying. . . ." Here, balanced aggressiveness is not achieved. The children commented on the course of events without criticizing it. It is different with the 3% of the children who fear that the departure from the play may lead to a heightened potential for violence (16 mentions or 1% of all responses; Table 3.7). A girl said, "I find those games naff because you can enact that for real." Another girl said, "These things are too brutal; I don't like these things. Then you will surely become violent." The number of children making such comments was not great, but the fact was new. Not new, however, was that the children viewed this fact as applying to younger children. In 1985, as in 2002, they were certain that small children should not be given "toys you can fight with" because they certainly would not be able to distinguish between play and reality, and the danger of a future inclination to violence would indeed seem likely. It is interesting that this disapproval was considerably higher in 1985. It is unclear whether this expresses growing tolerance for smaller children's play, a greater tolerance for aggressiveness, or simply increased indifference.

Concretizations of aggressiveness were evidenced in the responses. As a preliminary observation, more than half of the references to aggressiveness ($n = 109$) explicitly stated that aggressiveness is fun. The others ($n = 85$) did not mention this fun factor, nor did they criticize it. Therefore, enjoyment of aggressiveness, or at least tolerance for it, can be assumed. The corresponding figures are grouped together in Table 3.6.

The internal form of aggressiveness, restricted to the play context, frequently came across in a truly ruthless fashion. A boy said, "I have once pulled out somebody's [a play character] arms." A second boy said, "My

TABLE 3.6
References to Aggressiveness in 2002

	Mentions (n)	% of 634 Children	% of 1,698 Mentions	Mentions (n)	% of 634 Children	% of 1,698 Total Mentions
Internal aggressiveness—fun	96	15	6	109	17	6
External aggressiveness—fun	13	2	1			
Internal aggressiveness	46	7	3	85	13	5
External aggressiveness	39	6	2			

friend has one of these Kenny characters" [from *South Park*]. "I tore off its head, then put ketchup in, tore it off again." The brother's McDonald's character gets an arm twist. In *Mortal Kombat*, you can cut off heads, and in a nonspecified computer game, the following events occur: "He makes, like, this sleep. Then he take the hand. Him through the belly." Attention also should be drawn to the statements when Barbies are abused. Despite the ruthlessness displayed here, it has been rated as internal play aggression. Girls made the following statements: "Barbie, there's a series, and I like decapitating them." "I've got a Barbie, but I once tore off her leg." "That soon I won't be able to set fire to Barbies any longer." Although the data show aggressiveness to be predominantly a male affair (Müller, 2002), female aggressiveness shows up here quite uninhibitedly.

The aggressiveness classified as external in this study includes fighting with animals, shocking or "beating up" a little brother, throwing other children's pocket money out the window, and "bashing" the sister "against the wall." This is getting down to business. One boy even mentioned "having broken his arm." All these issues were unheard of 17 years before.

Then there is the description of the contents of computer games. As one girl said, "In *Nuclear Strike* you must shoot other opponents." "In *Star Wars* you have to smash the druids." "In *Resident Evil* you chop off their heads which you then toss around." This girl did not say that she was enjoying it, but we do not hear any criticism either. A boy boasted: "I've got another game, *Alien 3—Genesis*. Blood comes down from the ceiling. There's a, there's a man in the elevator, then you hear a 'Bang'. Even my father gets almost shitless with that." Another said, "In *Playstation 2*, there's a skeleton walking round on level 1; then there's a skeleton coming, and you have to slaughter that." These are only a handful of examples, but I think they show what was meant earlier by "brutalization" of language and play.

The wonderful ability of children to balance aggressiveness on the play level has not disappeared, but has visibly begun to falter. And this means shaking a cornerstone of children's play! The other extreme of this development is that the horrors of war are losing their significance in the child's world.

The Diminishing Horrors of War and Terror:
Reasons Against War Toys

The horrors of war and terror were not investigated. Rather, these concerns materialized as "reasons against war toys" and "what is no fun about war play." This was the same in 1985 as in 2002. Half of the children (49%) offered critical comments in 2002. In 1985, this figure was 35%. On the other hand, these comments reached 30% of all mentions, and therefore the current naming was of a much higher weight than in 2002. The reasons for the increase in 2002 have already been discussed. In this context, a moderately critical statement about computer game elements is rather easy to ascertain. The content-based discussion of the reasons given clarifies this argument (Table 3.7).

By far the largest share of critical comments in 2002 falls within the category of "criticism of war toys/action toys/PC": 129 mentions (8% of the total and 20% of the children). A more decisive finding is the dramatic decrease in statements that reflect awareness of the horrors of war and terror and a pacifist attitude. These three categories account for 13% of the total for 1985. In 2002, however, there are only 42 mentions, which corresponds to 2% of the total. These results are highly significant. As compared with comments 17 years before, these few comments lacked depth in 2002. Some instances demonstrate this.

Here is what the children said 17 years ago: "When a nuclear bomb comes, an air raid shelter will not help. I read in the papers that 700,000 sirens will be wailing. If there is a war, it will be a nuclear war." "We saw pictures from Africa: mother, father, son were lying dead. Nasty!" "In R.I. we saw pictures of Dresden before and after the bombs. There we said, 'War is shit!' " "I find war detestful because many people have to die in it, and everything gets destroyed." "I don't like people shooting at each other, and then lying there with big wounds, still living for a little bit, and then dying."

What do their peers have to say today? "Fighting is stupid! Every fight can be ended by peace." "Toys you can fight with are not good. Because war is a serious matter." "I find this war junk simply harmful." These were three statements typically made by girls. Further statements confined themselves to calling war and violence "senseless" or "naff": "I think it's naff to fight, because mostly you kill everybody." "Sometimes war is senseless." "I find war toys senseless, who, if any, finds killing is good?" "I find it naff to kill other people. Even if it's only a game." This is not very illuminating.

The terrorist acts in New York, which at the time of the 2002 study were only 2 to 4 months old, also were the subject of criticism, although in a similarly trivial manner: A girl said, "Like with the World Trade Center." "And that is also senseless, because it is no use." Another continued, "It's no use to the terrorists either." Yet another said, "It's no use to the terrorists either, because they are dead too now." Still another girl said, "Yes, but they believe in it."

This completes the knowledge about these terrible geopolitical events. A bit of criticism for related games and movies also exists, but again, it is rather weak. A boy said, "I don't like those movies that imitate terror action." Gone are the heartrending antiviolence statements of 17 years earlier. Furthermore, if the terrorist acts had not occurred shortly before, very likely even fewer relevant statements would be on record.

The connection to aggressiveness has already been discussed. In 1985, no child established it, and 17 years later, again, none established a connec-

TABLE 3.7
Reasons Against War Toys in 1985 and 2002

	Mentions in 1985 (n)	% of 429 Children in 1985	% of 492 Mentions in 1985	Mentions in 2002 (n)	% of 634 Children in 2002	% of 1,698 Mentions in 2002
Knowledge about war/violence	6	1	1	8	1	0
War toys and war/violence**	37	9	8	14	2	1
Pacifist attitude**	20	5	4	20	3	1
Departure from play level—violence*	12	3	2	16	3	1
External aggressiveness—war/violence	0	0	0	0	0	2
Is no fun**	29	7	6	34	5	2
Injuries**	13	3	3	7	1	0
Psychic dangers/educational aspects	2	0	0	15	2	1
Criticism of war toys/action toys/PC*	18	4	4	129	20	8
Criticism of excessive aggressiveness				69	11	4
Television	10	2	2			
Preference of gender-specific games	2	0	0			
Total**	149	35	30	312	49	18

Knowledge about war and violence/pacifism (the first three categories): 63 mentions (15% of children and 13% of all mentions in 1985).**
Knowledge about war and violence/pacifism (the first three categories): 42 mentions (7% of children and 2% of all mentions in 2002).**
*Significant (<0.05).
**Significant (<0.01).

tion between war toys and violence external to play. In both studies, 3% of the children feared a violent departure from the level of play. The criticism of "toys you can play with" has considerably increased. In view of the computer game contents familiar to children, this comes as no surprise. It was found that 2% of children see the danger of psychic threats, chiefly in fear, addiction, and nightmares. This was hardly mentioned at all 17 years earlier. However, even today, there still is a small group (1% of the children) for whom all this is not brutal enough. A boy said, "You can't see enough blood in this" (criticism: insufficient aggressiveness in Table 3.4).

CONCLUSION: PLAYING WITH WAR TOYS AND COMPUTER GAMES: STILL "PLAY"?

The author has always taken a liberal attitude toward play, never thinking much about regimentation and exaggerated nervousness regarding aggressive elements. Play has always been wild and rebellious, contrafactual, and liberal. Play constitutes the world of children, and its purpose is not to please adults. This also is true of toys. This view has been put forward with special emphasis by play researcher and theorist Brian Sutton-Smith (1986).

Moreover, the concept of balanced aggressiveness had convinced the author that play could overcome the limitations and definitions inherent to the toy. In light of the research reported here, the author must admit to becoming doubtful. It cannot be overlooked that the play world of children has become more narrow and impoverished. Today, instead of revealing their wonderful play world to us, children give us descriptions of computer game contents. The children no longer know anything substantial about war and terror, but in most cases reproduce only stereotyped and trivial statements. This is not to say that computer games are the reason for this. The author cannot ascertain that, but is only stating a fact.

The author is increasingly doubtful whether children still are able to transform into play images made by adults, which are equipped with adult voices and adult language (Lury, 2002), and which are sold to them on a merciless market (Kline, 1998; Wegener-Spöhring, 2001).

The results of this study are in line with those reported in international media research that give rise to a concern about the globally increasing mediated consumption of violence by children. The U.S. Surgeon General recently has confirmed that the media remain a significant factor in fostering aggressive and antisocial behavior in children (*Youth Violence*, 2001). Similarly, the Canadian Standing Committee on Communications, Culture, and Television Violence found that excessive consumption of violent media is a significant risk factor contributing to children's aggressive attitudes and behavior (Bird, 1993; Gosselin, Guise, Paquette, & Laplante, 1997). Furthermore, media researcher Groebel (1998) found signs of a global, media-transported aggressive culture in his 1997 worldwide study for UNESCO. Media researcher Lukesch (2002) pointed out related interconnections for Germany. Other German authors have put these results in perspective, claiming that there is only a weak correlation between the consumption of media violence and future aggressiveness, which then, however, can have a strong significance for some populations (Charlton, Borska, Mayer, Haaf, & Klein, 1996; Kunczik & Zipfel, 2002). German research always lays special emphasis on the active role of the individual in media usage who co-designs his or her socialization through personalized and experience-related inter-pretations (Theunert, 1996, p. 201; Früh, 1995, p. 172). Theunert (1996) said that media research must "classify and recapitulate the subjective proc-esses of reception and active involvement and creation which take place in the new screen worlds" (p. 23), and Früh (1995) treated the effective violent potential as an "interpreted normative offer of violence" (p. 172). This agrees with play as the place where children interpret their world inde-pendently and transform it experimentally.

This chapter aims to present the results of the 1985 and 2002 studies from a comparative perspective. Elsewhere, the author unfolds some peda-gogical consequences from the viewpoint of activating and critical peda-gogics of media and play. One point must suffice here: Play requires our protection. It has yet not been fully subjugated by the media, at least not in Germany. Play ideas and playlike irreality have been found, yet the balance that controls aggressiveness has become disturbed. This should make us think.

REFERENCES

Bird, B. (Chair). (1993). *Television Violence: Fraying Our Social Fabric*. Report of the Standing Com-mittee on Communications and Culture. Ottawa: House of Commons, 1993.

Bohnsack, R. (1993). *Rekonstruktive Sozialforschung* [Reconstructive social research]. Opladen: Westdeutscher Verlag.

Charlton, M., Borsca, M., Mayer, G., Haaf, B., & Klein, G. (1996). *Zugänge zur Mediengewalt* [Access to media violence]. Villingen-Schwenningen: Neckar-Verlag.

Früh, W. (1995). Die Rezeption von Fernsehgewalt [The reception of TV violence]. *Media Perspektiven, 4*, 172–185.

Gosselin, A., Guise, J. D., Paquette, G., & Laplante, B. (1997). Violence on Canadian Television and some of its cognitive effects. *Canadian Journal of Communication, 22*, 143–160.

Groebel, J. (1998). *The Unesco Global Study on Media Violence*. Report presented to the Director General of Unesco. Paris: UNESCO.

Heckhausen, H. (1973). Entwurf einer Psychologie des Spielens [Outline of a psychology of play]. In C. F. Graumann & H. Heckhausen (Eds.), *Pädagogische psychologie: Reader I* [Pedagogical psychology] (pp. 154–174). Frankfurt/Main: Fischer.

Huizinga, J. (1938/1986). *Homo ludens: A study in the play element of culture*. London: Beacon Press.

Kline, S. (1998). Toys, socialization, and the commodification of play. In S. Strasser, C. McGovern, & M. Judt (Eds.), *Getting and spending: American and European consumer society in the twenti- eth century* (pp. 339–357). New York: Cambridge University Press.

Kunczik, M., & Zipfel, A. (2002). Wirkungsforschung I: Ein Bericht zur Forschungslage [Impact re- search I: A research report]. In T. Hausmanninger & T. Bohrmann (Eds.), *Mediale Gewalt: Interdisziplinäre und ethische Perspektiven* [Mediated violence: Interdisciplinary and ethical perspectives] (pp. 149–159). Munich: Fink.

Lukesch, H. (2002). Contribution to Press Conference of State Minister Stewens on 17 May 2002 at the Bavarian State Ministry of Work and Social Order. Accessed October 4, 2002 at www.stmas.bayern.de/familie/pk020517b_t.htm.

Lury, K. (2002). *"Seen but not heard? The young child's voice in toys and media."* Paper given at the ITRA-Congress: Toys, Games, and Media, London, 2002.

Müller, T. (2002). *Kriegsspielzeug in der Lebenswelt von Grundschulkindern: Eine qualitative empirische Studie im Raum Köln/Bonn: Die Bedeutung des geschlechtsspezifischen Aspektes. Examensarbeit zur 1. Staatsprüfung für das Lehramt an Primarstufen* [War toys in the world of fourth graders: A qualitative empirical study in the Cologne/Bonn Area: The gender- specific aspects. Primary Schools Teachers' Certificate Thesis]. Cologne.

Scheuerl, H. (1975). Spiel: Ein menschliches grundverhalten? [Play: A human constant?]. In id. (Ed.), *Theorien des Spiels* [Theories of play] (pp. 189–207). Weinheim/Basel: Beltz.

Sutton-Smith, B. (1978). *Die Dialektik des Spiels* [The dialectics of play]. Schorndorf: Verlag Karl Hoffmann.

Sutton-Smith, B. (1986). *Toys as culture.* New York, London: Gardner Press.

Sutton-Smith, B. (1997). *The ambiguity of play.* Cambridge, MA/London: Harvard University Press.

Theunert, H. (1996). *Gewalt in den Medien: Gewalt in der Realität* [Violence in the media: Violence in reality] (2nd revised ed.). Munich: Kopaed.

Wegener-Spöhring, G. (1978). *Soziales Lernen im Spiel: Untersuchung seiner Möglichkeiten und Grenzen im Bereich Schule* [Social learning in play: Investigating its possibilities and limits in school contexts]. Unpublished doctoral dissertation, Kiel University, Germany.

Wegener-Spöhring, G. (1985). Faszination an Kriegsspielzeug: Was ist zu tun? Eine empirische Untersuchung in 4. Grundschulklassen [Fascination with war toys: What is to be done? An empirical study in fourth grades]. *Grundschule, 17,* 46–49.

Wegener-Spöhring, G. (1986). Die Bedeutung von "Kriegsspielzeug" in der Lebenswelt von Grundschulkindern [The significance of "war toys" in the world of primary school children]. *Zeitschrift für Paedagogik, 32,* 797–810.

Wegener-Spöhring, G. (1989a). War toys and aggressive games. *Play and Culture, 2,* 35–47.

Wegener-Spöhring, G. (1989b). Die balancierte Aggressivität: Beobachtung und Interpretation von Freispielszenen in Kindergärten [Balanced aggressiveness: Observation and interpreta- tion of free play periods in kindergartens]. *Spielmittel, 2,* 32–39.

Wegener-Spöhring, G. (1989c). Aggressive Spiele bei Kindern: Beobachtung und Interpretation von Freispielszenen [Aggressive games of children: Observation and interpretation of free play periods]. *Bildung und Erziehung, 42,* 103–120.

Wegener-Spöhring, G. (1994). War toys and aggressive games. In J. H. Goldstein (Ed.), *Toys, play and child development* (pp. 85–109). New York/Melbourne: Cambridge University Press.

Wegener-Spöhring, G. (1995). *Aggressivität im kindlichen Spiel: Grundlegung in den Theorien des Spiels und Erforschung ihrer Erscheinungsformen* [Aggressiveness in childplay: Basic notions in the theories of play and investigation of its manifestations]. Weinheim: Deutscher Studien- verlag.

Wegener-Spöhring, G. (2001). *Spielzeug: Spiegel der Welt und Welt des Kindes* [Toys: Mirrors of the world and of the child world], Inaugural Lecture, University of Cologne, 2001.

Youth violence: A report of the Surgeon General 2001. U.S. Department of Health and Human Ser- vices. Accessed November 6, 2003 at www.surgeongeneral.gov/library/youthviolence// youvio06.11.03/report.htm.

4

Toy Culture in Preschool Education and Children's Toy Preferences

Waltraut Hartmann
Gilles Brougère

Preschool children are integrated into educational structures more and more frequently on a larger scale and at younger ages. Although statistics vary by country, attending a preschool class is the norm for a 5-year-old and ever-increasingly common for the average 4-year-old. This phenomenon has trickled down to 3-year-olds, but varies greatly according to country (OECD, 2001), especially with children younger than 3 years. No matter what the term—kindergarten, *école enfantine*, preschool, *école maternelle*—these structures, at least with respect to developed nations, represent essential social environments outside the family circle. They involve dual socialization, which occurs in a public situation not bound by the same sociocultural values found in the family structure.

> Daycare centers are public environments; public institutions, one might say. Meeting people in such environments has its own dynamic, which is quite different from the dynamic in more familial situations. In private life, people's interactions are governed to a large extent by the individuals concerned. (Dencik, Langsted, & Sommer, 1989, p. 14)

Education methods in these structures vary according to local tradition, culture, and societal models (Cochran, 1993; Lamb & Ali, 1992). Some are more scholarly oriented than others, but all take into account the specific needs of a child of this age. This is evident in the time allotted for toys and games, either as the center of educational activity or as a complement to other activities. The result is a material environment geared to promote game playing. A child thus has access to a selection of games and toys in preschool centers, a selection that makes us wonder how it was chosen. With what type of toys does a child come into contact in these centers? Are they similar to or different from those found at home? To what extent do they correspond to a child's voiced preferences? This chapter examines the structure of these play environments, their similarities, their differences, their diversity, and the role of the child in their development.

Compiling data for such a study is too complex. Aside from the differences between education and family environments, such a study must also take into account national and cultural differences as well as those differences encountered across preschool systems worldwide.

Nevertheless, various researchers have conducted surveys on toy culture in different countries. Although the problems encountered and the data compiled are not always comparable, this initial approach has provided the framework for some of the responses to the questions posed. This chapter aspires to provide those first responses and open up topics for reflection, inviting other researchers to contribute to a field of study that merits further investigation.

The study was based on research compiled for Sweden (Almqvist, 1994), France (Brougère, 1993), Austria (Brandstetter, 2003; Trebo, 2000; Wildeis, 2000), Australia (Jenvey & Jenvey, 2002), and Brazil (Kishimoto, 2002). The results of these studies are heterogeneous, although a portion was compiled using a similar model. The Austrian model was inspired by the pioneer Swedish study. The Brazilian investigation was based upon the French study, but with knowledge of the Swedish results. The results from France and Sweden were compared in a separate report (Almqvist & Brougère, 2000). Finally, the Australian version, using a different model, provides additional information.

The basis for this research, underscoring the importance of an often overlooked cultural accessory, consisted of noting the presence or absence of toys and games in preschool settings. The toys and games observed were then classified by category. It is interesting to note the significance of the categories missing from the preschool center but present in the home. The category breakdown, adapted to each country and sometimes created autonomously from other studies, does not allow for easy comparison. However, deciding which toy belongs to what category proves essential to inventory-taking although this can sometimes be considered an artificial exercise. No doubt this limits results to a certain extent, but it is a limit accepted as a necessary and unavoidable tool for such a study. It will be seen, however, that although inventory cannot be compared on an item-for-item basis, it still is possible to obtain adequate results. To this approach then was added country-specific data such as educational applications of the pedagogical model per country, children's comments, and comparisons with the family environment.

The Austrian example that follows allows for comprehension of the general reasoning behind the research and an analysis of the data from which the aforementioned conclusions have been drawn. The findings then are compared with those of another (more succinct) study for a comparison of data that bears on the authors' conclusion.

TOY CULTURE IN PRESCHOOL EDUCATION: CHILDREN'S TOY PREFERENCES IN AUSTRIA AND SOUTH TYROL

The three Austrian samples consisted of 752 kindergarten teachers (Brandstetter, 2003; Trebo, 2000; Wildeis, 2000). Interviews were conducted with 1,773 children ages 4 to 6 years attending kindergarten to record their opinions about toys. The questionnaires for the kindergarten teachers included questions on basic kindergarten conditions, toy culture, and the selection of toys available to their groups. The questionnaire for the kindergarten teachers used by Almqvist (1994) in Sweden was enlarged and adapted by Wildeis in 1999 to the Austrian situation. The Upper Austrian survey used a questionnaire adapted by Brandstetter in 2001. The questionnaire used by Trebo was adapted in 1999 to the situation in South Tyrol and contained questions about 224 different play materials. The questionnaires addressed to the children themselves refer to their favorite toys both at kindergarten and at home, and to the toys they reject and request at kindergarten.

Toy Selection and Financial Resources

All three studies show a similar situation: The financial resources for toy purchases come mainly from the kindergarten providers. The head of the kindergarten and the kindergarten teacher decide what toys to buy. According to them, they take children's wishes into account in two thirds of the cases when buying toys.

Toy Quantities

In Viennese kindergartens, a comparison of 20 toy categories showed that the largest quantity of toys was in the "handicraft material," "water and sand toys," "Montessori School materials," and "miniature living" categories, followed by "phenomenon toys" (soap bubbles, tops, marbles, kaleidoscopes), "puzzles," "doll household" items (doll kitchens, doll garments and doll equipment), "construction toys," and "musical toys."

The lowest quantity of toys was found in the "novelties," "media equipment" (e.g., books, cassette recorders, record players, CD players, TVs, video recorders, computers and computer games, walkmen, slide projectors), "toys to ride on," "dolls and puppets," and "toy animals" categories. It is striking to note that "fictional [action] figures" and "war toys" were hardly mentioned (Fig. 4.1).

The selections of toys available in Vienna and in Upper Austria were similar: Material for promoting fine and gross motor skills and for arts and crafts were highly appreciated. Dolls and doll household items were sufficiently available in both regions.

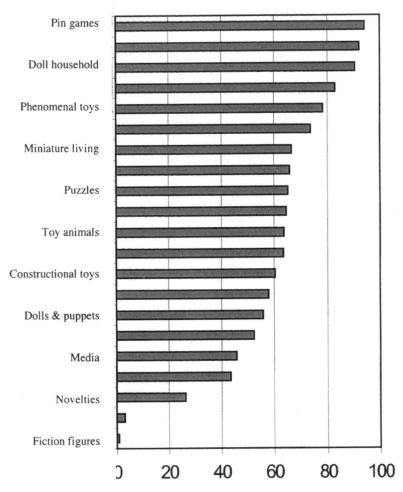

FIG. 4.1. Toys quantities for Upper Austrian kindergartens (Brandstetter, 2003).

In kindergartens in Upper Austria, as in Vienna, there were no toys perceived as promoting aggression. However, there were more water-and-sand toys, puzzles, and phenomenon toys available in Vienna. In Upper Austria, media equipment was mentioned in at least in 46% of the samples, which was more often than in Vienna. There has been little change in toy equipment over the past years.

In South Tyrol, the largest quantity of available toys (71%) was found in the doll household category (e.g., doll kitchens, doll garments, and doll equipment). A similar rate was recorded for the arts and crafts category, which included materials for drawing, painting, cutting and pasting, and modeling clay, as well as materials from nature and reusable materials (70%). Puzzles and "pin games" (e.g., pegboards, stacking toys, string games, beads, marbles, mosaic games, games with magnetic pieces) were equally significant in the equipment of kindergartens, as indicated by the 67% rate of occurrence, putting them ahead of musical toys. In general, the toys provided were largely classical ones (enduring toys). Unstructured materials such as natural materials and reusable materials were equally available.

Toy Preferences and Rejections by the Kindergarten Teachers

Overall, kindergarten teachers were satisfied with the quality and quantity of toys available in their classrooms. These toys were used mainly to promote linguistic, motor, emotional, and social skills to enhance a child's creativity. Toys should be pedagogically meaningful. They should be fun, offering many varieties of play. Safety standards, environmental soundness, and durability are further criteria taken into consideration by kindergarten teachers when they select toys.

War toys and battery-operated, electric, remote-controlled, and mechanical toys were those most often rejected by kindergarten teachers. Action and fiction toys, robots, Barbie and her accessories were mentioned less frequently. Kindergarten teachers did not seem to mind noise-generating toys.

Children's Favorite Toys

Children's Favorite Toys at Home. The selection of favorite toys at home is strongly gender typical. In Vienna, 29% of the girls surveyed mentioned Barbie as their favorite toy at home, whereas the boys preferred toy vehicles (21%). The boys also liked Lego (19%). Dolls and doll furniture were mentioned only by girls (18%), but not by boys.

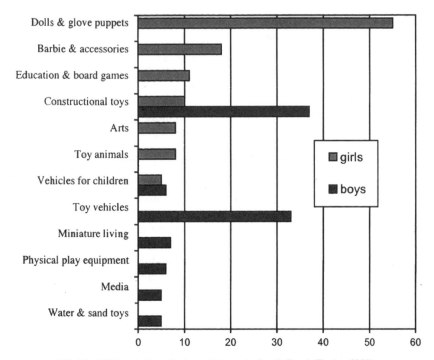

FIG. 4.2. Children's favorite toys at home in South Tyrol (Trebo, 2000).

In Upper Austria, girls preferred dolls and doll household items, board games, educational games, pin games, puzzles, and animal toys. As in Vienna, the boys' favorites were toy vehicles and construction toys (Fig. 4.2).

More than half of the girls in South Tyrol, as compared with 29% of the girls in Vienna, mentioned dolls such as Barbie, Baby Born, and hand puppets as their favorite toys at home. Barbie and her accessories accounted for one third of these replies. The boys preferred construction materials such as Lego, Duplo, Playmobil (South Tyrol 37%, Vienna 19%) as well as toy vehicles (South Tyrol 33%, Vienna 21%) at home. Whereas the boys did not mention dolls at all, at least 10% of the girls stated that they liked construction materials. The pleasure of playing and interest in the toy were the most frequent reasons for toy preference voiced by both boys and girls.

Children's Favorite Toys at Kindergarten. Of the boys surveyed, 21% said Lego is their favorite toy in kindergarten, ahead of other construction materials (19%). Of the girls surveyed, 20% said that all things related to dolls are their favorite toys, ahead of puzzles, drawing and painting, and board games.

At the kindergarten level, the choice of a favorite toy is less gender specific. Girls prefer dolls and board games, but also like construction materi-

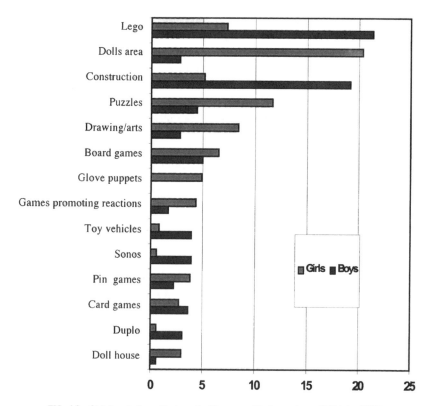

FIG. 4.3. Children's favorite toys in Viennese kindergartens (Wildeis, 2000).

als. Boys favor construction materials, board games, and toy vehicles. However, the reasons behind the children's preferences differ by gender. Girls choose a toy because of the way it looks and feels, and also for its "make-believe" quality. The main reason why they reject certain toys is that these toys require them to play with a boy. Boys, on the other hand, exclude toys that require a long waiting time. Boys often prefer toys because of a specific play function. In Upper Austria as well, girls preferred dolls, whereas boys opted for toy vehicles and construction toys (Fig. 4.3).

In South Tyrolian kindergartens, the girls preferred toys from the doll household category (24%), whereas these were named by only 5% of the boys. The overwhelming majority of boys (70%) favored building and construction materials, as compared with 13% of all the girls. One fourth of the girls mentioned material for arts and crafts such as paint and paper, scissors and glue, and modeling clay, as compared with only 8% of the boys. More of the girls (14%) than boys (5%) mentioned educational and board games as their preferred toys. Whereas 12% of the girls surveyed chose pin games, these were not mentioned at all by the boys.

When asked why they preferred certain toys in kindergarten, the boys (53%) mentioned the play functions and possibilities at a significantly higher rate than the girls (25%). The girls explained their toy preference at a significantly higher rate by the way toys look (appearance) and feel as well as by their "make believe" possibilities during play.

Toys Rejected by the Children at Kindergarten

In Vienna one fourth of the boys surveyed did not like certain puzzles. The girls were not always enthusiastic about puzzles either (16%). Lego and building blocks were rejected by 14% of all the girls.

In South Tyrolian kindergartens, construction materials were rejected much more by girls. Boys, on the other hand, mentioned doll household items, dolls and hand puppets, and arts and crafts materials more frequently.

When asked why they rejected certain toys in kindergarten, differences according to gender also were identified. Girls mentioned quarrels with other children (11%) more often than boys (3%). The boys attributed their rejection of a toy more frequently to a lengthy amount of time and the patience required during play (13%) than the girls (5%).

Kindergarten Children's Requests for Specific Toys

When surveyed about which toys they would request for kindergarten, 26% of the girls in Vienna ranked Barbie in first place, whereas the boys seemed hardly interested in Barbie. However, the boys missed Action Man figures and toy vehicles (8%). The girls (9%) tended to be slightly more satisfied than the boys (6%) with the selection of toys in kindergarten.

In Upper Austria, the girls requested dolls and doll household items. The boys would have liked more toy vehicles and construction toys.

In South Tyrol, 32% of the girls requested dolls, and 83% of the requests were for Barbie. They also mentioned board games (14%). First and foremost, the boys requested specific toy vehicles such as fire engines, ambulances, and tractors (40%), ahead of construction materials (11%). Computers and computer games were requested by 8% of the boys and 7% of the girls.

Analysis of the Austrian Results

The results of the three surveys on toy culture and children's toy preferences in kindergarten are comparable with the Swedish findings compiled by Almqvist (1994). There exists a multitude and variety of toys in Austrian kindergartens: doll household items, water and sand toys, miniature living items, arts and crafts, picture puzzles and pin games, musical toys, construction toys, and Montessori School play material.

An important complement to this structured play material is the nonstructured material brought in from nature: stones and pebbles, woods, shells, waste and packaging material such as rags, boxes, tins, and the like. These are used mainly for arts and crafts projects, as building and construction materials, and as materials for picture puzzles in Austria and in South Tyrol.

As in the Swedish child-care institutions, war toys, action figures, and novelties are unwanted in Austrian kindergartens. Kindergarten teachers reject war toys for ethical reasons because they are thought to induce aggression and violence. Also, children are not allowed to bring weapons and war toys into the classroom. In South Tyrol especially, kindergarten teachers refuse to purchase mechanical, electronic, and remote-controlled toys and deny the children the right to bring such toys from home.

Froebel's influence on toy culture in kindergartens across Sweden, Austria, and South Tyrol is still visible today, in both rural and urban kindergartens. There are few differences in toy equipment between urban and rural kindergartens, except that there are more toys to ride on (e.g., bicycles and scooters) in urban areas, offering the children the possibility to test gross motor activities. Children in rural areas have more opportunities to play outside in meadows and woods.

In Austria, a greater variety of doll equipment is available than in South Tyrol. This mainly consists of baby dolls, miniature dolls, and glove puppets. Battery-powered dolls, makeup doll heads, and Barbies are rarely found. Half of all kindergartens have dolls with sexual attributes. Nonwhite dolls are rare. These findings are corroborated by a study the Charlotte Bühler Institute (1995) conducted, in which kindergarten teachers ranked "understanding technology," "sex education," and "critical confrontation with societal values" last in a list of educational objectives. It seems that the kindergarten teachers consider sex education a task to be dealt with by the family. The lack of interest displayed by female kindergarten teachers in understanding technical relationships apparently results from gender-specific socialization and has been documented in a large number of studies (Almqvist, 1997; Araujo Pessanha, 1996; Faulstich-Wieland, 1986; Halliday, McNaughton, & Glynn, 1985; Hartmann, Mühlegger, & Hanifl, 1997, 1998; Horstkemper, 1991; Jenvey & Kurts, 1996; Macha, 1991).

Although multicultural education is gaining in importance, partly because a large number of refugees and immigrants have emigrated to Austria, this is not reflected clearly in doll equipment.

Media equipment, limited mostly to its traditional forms (picture books, story books, and lexical dictionaries), holds a firm place in kindergarten education. Of the electronic media, only the tape recorder has made its way into the classroom. Other media such as TV-sets, video recorders, slide projectors, computers, and electronic games are rarely available. The exception is the kindergartens in Upper Austria, in which there is a larger range of media equipment.

Puzzles and pin games, considered traditional kindergarten toy equipment, enjoy little popularity with either boys or girls. "Because I don't like it" and "because it is too difficult" were some of the reasons used to explain their distaste of these traditional toys. The time is ripe to reflect on the importance of maintaining these games for today's classroom. Having to sit still and apply precise motor skills corresponds to a more traditional, bourgeois role, one expected especially of the women of yesteryear, who spent their days sewing, embroidering, and knitting.

As such, play and media education in the classroom are at odds with family education. Girls play with Barbie as their favorite toy, and boys with toy vehicles in the home.

Kindergarten toy equipment matches a child's home selection especially in two areas: construction material (e.g., Lego) for boys, and dolls and doll accessories for girls. When asked why, boys mentioned the play function, whereas girls stated the pleasure and interest of play.

TOY CULTURE IN PRESCHOOL EDUCATION
IN FRANCE

The situation in France is similar in some respects to that in Sweden and Austria, although toys play a lesser role in the French preschool system, which is geared toward a more structured educational program, consisting of activities adapted to the age of the student (Brougère, 1995, 2002). Despite the little time allotted for games, toys are available in *l'école maternelle*, but the toys vary greatly according to age group. The quantity of toys available to the 2- to 4-year-olds is greater than that for the 5- to 6-year-olds. Almost all of the younger children (99%) have access to baby dolls, as compared with only 66% of the older group. The stuffed animal, with its strong emotional ties, suffers the greatest drop, from 92% to 33%.

In classes of students younger than 5 years, the activities most represented are those centered around family life: cooking, parent role-playing, and personal hygiene. Tasks concerning other daily activities such as going to the post office or shopping are represented less. Consequently, *l'école maternelle* takes precedence over more traditional toys.

As with dolls, it seems that children also play less with cars as they get older. Toy evolution, or the disappearance of a particular toy, seems to follow an age curve. Some nursery school teachers interviewed wondered whether a 4-year-old child is not too old for a doll. Furthermore, in the past few years, symbolic real-world and other imaginary (role-play) games have practically disappeared from the preschool classes of the eldest students. This phenomenon is even more in evidence when the toys are unrealistic. Science fiction toys are rare in preschool. They are found in 6% of the classes at an average of two per classroom. Not only do toy catalogs for schools not offer sci-fi products, but teachers' also show a reticence for fantasy world objects in contrast to real-world ones.

Adult human character representations, dominant at home, exist in small quantities at *l'école maternelle*. Only 11% of classrooms have Barbie-type dolls, as compared with 89% for baby dolls, yielding an average of 1.7 per class for Barbie-type dolls versus 5.1 for the baby dolls. Undeniably, the Barbie-type doll ordinarily is not found in a classroom setting. Action figures are even less available. Only 3% of classrooms have fictional or comic book characters, and only 4% have soldiers, which fall under two restrictions: violence and doll figures.

Figures compiled for symbolic toys show a penchant for realistic and child-sized objects in the French classroom. This observation can be interpreted in several ways. These toys represent past traditions, before toys were adapted to modern times. School toys have moved toward distinguishing themselves as different from those found in the home, with classroom toys remaining faithful to the past and the home versions, influenced by marketing campaigns, evolving toward new forms. But is the school's supply not just a toy collection amassed by adults who have unrestricted power over purchases, despite their claim that they take the child's tastes into account? In addition, stock renewal is slow. Finally, the educational environment itself puts the child in a situation whereby he or she embraces a game that copies the adult world. These miniature versions of the real world however are not used by teachers to stimulate a child's imagination. Hand puppets are more often designated for this task.

A quick look at the rest of the toy inventory allows us to grasp the logic behind school toy purchases in general. The types of toys most in evidence belong to another category, that of assembly toys and especially puzzles (99%). These average 18 per class, representing a preschool-wide standard for every age group. Assembly toys usually are found in the younger classes (96%). Construction materials in various shapes and sizes are also prevalent.

Of course, learning toys, used for math, language, sensory, and memory, are abundant. Quantities of these toys increase with the age of the child, except for toys based on color and shape, geared to younger students. Board games are in lesser supply (less than 50%) and found mostly in the older classes. Finally, schools usually are equipped with motor vehicle toys, which besides their function as toys, are used also for physical education.

The toy inventory in French preschools can thus be sorted by its strong points, with symbolic toys representing real-world objects for the younger groups, learning toys for the upper age groups, puzzles and motor vehicle toys for all ages. It also can be sorted by its weaknesses, with action figures, fictional characters, and board games especially for the youngest.

The preceding overview reflects a nationwide toy norm for French preschools. As a result, the game is limited by its toy selection and characterized by its educational dimension, largely because of the numerous toys designed strictly for educational purposes. Are these toys or merely educational materials? Several objects are not aimed at play activity *stricto sensu*, even if they appear to belong to toy categories. In essence, useful play platforms are implemented using guidelines and objectives set forth by teachers.

However, this philosophy privileges the imitation of daily life, and as such, child role-playing in the classroom setting. Other dimensions of contemporary child culture are absent from preschool, for example, fictional character representations or Barbie-type dolls. Despite the availability of a free play time, the schism between school and family environments is more than apparent, even though the presence of certain objects such as baby dolls and stuffed animals similar to both environments link the two together.

Cross-Comparison and Analysis

The educational universe and culture of the home differ from those at school in France, as they do in Sweden or Austria. More fragmented statistics compiled for Australia show much the same trend, although the kinds of classroom toys preferred by Australian kids differ from those chosen by their northern European counterparts (Jenvey & Jenvey, 2002). In France, this trend is tied to specifics in the environment itself rather than the toy selection available at school (Brougère, 1995). First, this environment is created by adults, education professionals who do not follow the same criteria when equipping their classrooms as they do with their own kids at home. Children have little say in this environment, although teachers claim to take their opinions into consideration. It is the teacher who, in the end, controls the purchase of one toy over another. There is no discussion with the students over the choice of an item, only over its use. Under these circumstances, it is evident that the school setting offers a child other toys not necessarily representative of those on his or her wish list.

The Austrian situation shows that kindergarten policy regarding toy equipment and play education tries to counterbalance the effects of commercial child culture (Heidtmann, 1995). Thus, multimedia action figures, commercial multimedia systems, prestigious brand names, collectibles, and audiovisual equipment are not part of kindergarten toy culture. Does protecting the child from the mass-marketed consumer world at school while allowing this world into the home contribute to the child's adjustment difficulties, or does it offer a source of enrichment between the two environments? Research does not yet allow us to answer this question, but it does open the topic for debate.

The findings consolidated by the different surveys highlight the importance of an educationally oriented world of play. This pertains to a support system that promotes educational activities in the preschool classroom. However, the success of such a support system may result in control of the entire toy inventory and a ban on toys designated merely for fun.

Recent French studies (Bouisson-Dewolf, 2001) show that non-toy items, similar to those used later on in elementary schools (writing, drawing, and activities that take place in two-dimensional spaces), have begun to take precedence. In fact, these items compete less with the toys at home, and coupled with the proper support, enable the child to integrate an environment oriented more toward work than play. But this only partially explains toy choice. Can it be explained other than by routine and traditions deeply rooted in the preschool system? There is a certain image of education, defined by a series of pedagogical habits or values, that leads to favoring the baby doll over the older Barbie-type doll, as if habit and the long-time existence of certain toys at school suffice to justify their educational worth. Following this logic, educational toys are those usually found at school. In addition, kindergarten teachers, who are mostly women, have a strong impact on toy selection, mainly promoting the toy interests of girls. The generous availability of dolls and doll accessories reflect the toy wishes of girls, but not those of boys. The boys' requests correspond to those often rejected by kindergarten teachers: action figures for Vienna and mechanical, remote-controlled toys for South Tyrol.

Sutton-Smith (1988) pointed out that female kindergarten teachers who at the time had little personal experience with toys that trigger aggression, forbade rough and tumble play. The boys then reacted to this restriction by reverting to aggressive fantasy games.

The kindergarten environment is shaped by commercial and economic issues. On the one hand, toy stock is renewed more infrequently than that of the home. On the other hand, preschool toy manufacturers and their distributors have reason to maintain the status quo. The apparent lack of marketing actually is just a different type of marketing (MacNaughton & Hughes, 1995). There exist specialized toy makers who present their products as obvious and necessary to the classroom. They distinguish their toys from the mass-marketed versions by stressing solid construction, adaptability to a group situation, and educational interest as their advantages. It is beneficial for teachers to have salespeople cater to their needs, creating products not found in toy stores. Thus, a strong alliance develops between the educator and the specialized toy manufacturer in defining "legitimate" educational products. The manufacturers place the teachers in the role of consultant, using their ideas in the development of their products.

In Brazil, where funding is lower and recycling is an important cultural factor, the disparity between toys at school and those at home is less evident. However, as Kishimoto (2002) showed, the existence of a certain toy does not necessarily guarantee its use.

It is not surprising that toy culture differs between the school and the home. Contrary to what happens in the family unit, a child rarely is given an opportunity to take part in toy purchases at school. Outside the school environment, it can be seen how well toys have become an area in which the child becomes a decision maker and toy consumer, influenced by manufacturers who target the child in their marketing campaigns. In school, the reverse is true: The relationship is between the adults and the manufacturers. The situation is set up so that a child has no say, at least at this level, in toy choices and purchases.

The experience is twofold. Two social areas lead to different situations and experiences, both in their level of action and in their relation with the environment. It is as if the toy's function in preschool is to guide the child into the real world, using teaching techniques. At home, the toy serves for a flight from the real world to an imaginary one (Cross, 1997). On the one hand, a toy is chosen by adults to lead a child progressively toward the working world. On the other hand, a toy is chosen by adults and increasingly by children themselves for immediate pleasure, as well as for the enjoyment more or less shared by parents and children alike. Another reason for choosing a toy or a series of toys for play at home is the fact that children (and sometimes parents too) feel the pressure to buy short-lived toy novelties because of advertising campaigns. The situations are different, hence the objects as well.

Toy selection is defined by the general liaison between the various people involved. In a system comprising several different relationships, there exist different objects and their diverse signification. Nothing is indispensable in this difference, nor is it absolutely objective in its definition of appropriate preschool toys. However, it is a complex social procedure, heavily rooted in the past and driven by the collaborators who implement this toy system. There are no television commercials or other media messages directed at the student in this preschool system. The adult maintains complete control over all decisions. Not surprising, this system resembles that which existed before changes brought about by factors such as television. This does not mean that the preschool system is a guardian of tradition. Although its toy selection base certainly is founded in the past, contemporary aspects are present in the choice of materials and distribution networks.

It can therefore be inferred that a certain toy culture exists at preschool. A toy is not a stable object, identical in all places wherever it is found. It varies materially and functionally in the way it is designed, produced, and distributed. A toy varies also in what it represents, in the values attributed to it, and finally in the way children are given access to the toy, the space reserved for its use, and the rules and regulations associated with it. Toys and play activities vary according to their context inside the preschool system. Of course, the context itself varies according to the age of the child, culture, country, tradition, educational references, and theories (Brougère & Rayna, 1999; Rayna & Brougère, 2000). Above and beyond these differences, the preschool system's constraints have an undeniable effect on the similarities of play materials despite the diversity of education. These similarities are attributable to the role of the all-powerful adult decision makers, to the pedagogical investment of every kind (whatever its form), and to the presence of an international market consisting of companies that distribute their products geared to preschools worldwide.

REFERENCES

Almqvist, B. (1994). *Approaching the culture of toys in Swedish child care: A literature survey and a toy inventory*. Uppsala: Norstedts Tryckeri AB.

Almqvist, B. (1997). The role of toys in children's gender socialisation. In G. Brougère (Ed.), *Toys and playthings: The fields of research*. Proceedings of the International Toy Seminar, Angoulême, France, November, 1997. Université Paris Nord and Centre Universitaire de la Charente, pp. 92–98.

Almqvist, B. (2002). *Toy culture in preschool education: The Swedish case*. ITRA World Congress: Toys, Games, and Media. London: University of London, Institute of Education.

Almqvist, B., & Brougère, G. (2000). Matériel ludique et cultures pédagogiques dans le préscolaire: Les exemples de la Suède et de la France. In S. Rayna & G. Brougère (Eds.), *Traditions et innovations dans l'éducation préscolaire* (pp. 465–485). Paris: INRP.

Araujo Pessanha, A. M. (1996). *Comparative play behaviour of boys and girls in their toy choices*. Paper presented at the International Toy Research Conference, Nordic Centre for Research on Toys and Educational Media, Halmstad.

Bouisson-Dewolf, E. (2001). *Des objets et des enfants: Culture de l'école maternelle et composante matérielle des activités*. Thèse de doctorat (doctoral thesis), Université Paris 13.

Brandstetter, R. (2003). *Spielzeugkultur und Spielzeugpräferenzen in Oberösterreichischen Kindergärten als Beitrag zur Qualitätsfestellung und Qualitätsentwicklung*. Paper presented at Department of Development Psychology, University of Vienna, Austria.

Brougère, G. (1993). La signification d'un environnement ludique: L'école maternelle à travers son matériel ludique. In *Premier congrès d'actualité de la recherche en éducation et formation* (pp. 314–319). AECSE. Paris: CNAM.

Brougère, G. (1995). *Jeu et éducation*. Paris: L'Harmattan.

Brougère, G. (2002). L'exception française: L'école maternelle face à la diversité des formes préscolaires. *Les dossiers des sciences de l'education* (n°7, pp. 9–19).

Brougère G., & Rayna, S. (Eds.). (1999). *Culture, childhood, and preschool education*. Paris: UNESCO.

Charlotte Bühler-Institut. (1995). *Bildungsziele und Funktionen des Kindergartens aus der Sicht der Kindergärtnerinnen.* Vienna: Charlotte Bühler-Institut.

Cochran, M. (Ed.). (1993). *International handbook of child care policies and programs.* Westport, CT: Greenwood Press.

Cross, G. (1997). *Kids' stuff: Toys and the changing world of American childhood.* Cambridge, MA: Harvard University Press.

Dencik, L., Langsted, O., & Sommer, D. (1989). Modern childhood in the Nordic countries: Material, social, and cultural aspects. In B. Elgaard, O. Langsted, & D. Sommer (Eds.), *Research on socialization of young children in Nordic countries.* Aarhus, Denmark: Aarhus University Press.

Faulstich-Wieland, H. (1986). Neue Technologien: Eine Chance für Jungen und Mädchen? *Die Deutsche Schule, 4,* 437–445.

Halliday, J., McNaughton, S., & Glynn, T. (1985). Influencing children's choice of play activities at kindergarten through teacher participation. *New Zealand Journal of Educational Studies, 20,* 48–58.

Hartmann, W. (2002). *Toy culture in preschool education and children's toy preferences: Common features and differences in Europe and across the world.* ITRA World Congress: Toys, Games and Media. London: University of London, Institute of Education.

Hartmann, W., Mühlegger, G., & Hanifl, L. (1997). *Bericht der wissenschaftlichen Untersuchung zum Projekt "Erziehung zur Gleichheit" Projektjahr 1996/97 d. Frauenministeriums Luxemburg im Rahmen d. 4. mittelfristigen Aktionsprogramms der EU für die Chancengleichheit von Frauen und Mädchen.* Unpublished research report, Charlotte Bühler Institute, Vienna.

Hartmann, W., Mühlegger, G., & Hanifl, L. (1998). *Bericht der wissenschaftlichen Untersuchung zum Projekt "Erziehung zur Gleichheit" Projektjahr 1997/98 d. Frauenministeriums Luxemburg im Rahmen d. 4. mittelfristigen Aktionsprogramms der EU für die Chancengleichheit von Frauen und Mädchen.* Unpublished research report, Vienna.

Hartmann, W., Stoll, M., Chisté, N., & Hajszan, M. (2001). *Bildungsqualität im Kindergarten* (Quality of education in the kindergarten). *Transaktionale Prozesse, Methoden, Modelle.* Vienna: öbv &hpt.

Heidtmann, H. (1995). Von Bullerbü bis Beverly Hills: Kinderkultur heute. In U. Bischof (Ed.), *Konfliktfeld Fernsehen-Lesen: Kindermedien zwischen Kunstanspruch und Kommerz* (pp. 53–72). Vienna: Österreichischer Kunst- und Kulturverlag.

Horstkemper, M. (1991). "Mädchen-sein": "Junge-sein" im Schulunterricht: Zum Zusammenhang von Geschlechterrolle und Affinität zu Technik während der Pubertät. *Frauenforschung, 4,* 30–39.

Jenvey, V., & Jenvey, H. (2002). *Toy culture in Australian preschools and Australian children's toy preferences.* ITRA World Congress: Toys, Games and Media. London: University of London, Institute of Education.

Jenvey, V. B., & Kurts, B. A. (1996). *The toy preferences of Australian children 1989–1995: Age, sex, and sociocultural variables.* Paper presented at the International Toy Research Conference, Nordic Centre for Research on Toys and Educational Media, Halmstad.

Kishimoto, T. M. (2002). *Toys and the public policy for child education in Brazil.* ITRA World Congress. Toys, Games and Media. London: University of London, Institute of Education.

Lamb, M. E., & Sternberg, K. (Eds.). (1992). *Child care in context: Cross-cultural perspectives.* Hillsdale, NJ: Lawrence Erlbaum Associates.

Macha, H. (1991). Das Verhältnis von Jungen und Mädchen im Vorschulalter zur Technik: Weichenstellungen in Familie und Kindergarten. *Frauenforschung, 4,* 22–29.

MacNaughton, G., & Hughes, P. (1995). Take the money and run? Toys, consumerism, and capitalism in early childhood conference. In L. D. Soto (Ed.), *The politics of early childhood education.* New York: Peter Lang.

OECD. (2001). *Starting strong.* Early Childhood Education and Care. Paris: OECD.

Rayna, S., & Brougère, G. (Eds.). (2000). *Traditions et innovations dans l'éducation préscolaire.* Paris: INRP.

Sutton-Smith, B. (1988). War toys and childhood aggression. *Play and Culture, 1*, 57–69.

Trebo, A. (2000). *Spielzeugausstattung, Spielzeugverwendung, und Spielzeugpräferenzen in den deutschsprachigen Kindergärten Südtirols*. Unpublished thesis, Vienna.

Wildeis, N. (2000). *Spielzeugkultur und Spielzeugpräferenzen in Wiener Kindergärten*. Unpublished thesis, University of Vienna, Vienna.

5

Kitty Litter: Japanese Cute at Home and Abroad

Christine R. Yano

A visitor to Japan may easily be struck by the ubiquity of cute decorative elements in the dense urban landscapes of Tokyo, Osaka, and beyond. Here is a little cartoon badger asking you to press a button to open a door. There is a lavender bulldozer clearing the remains of a recently demolished building. Over there is an older woman sitting primly in a commuter train with a shopping bag at her feet decorated with that endearing American comic strip beagle Snoopy. If one were able to look into the contents of her purse, one may easily find American cartoon characters Tom and Jerry decorating her checkbook, and possibly a keychain with a rubber caricature of a sumo wrestler. Sitting side by side in the same train might be a mother and daughter pair, both of whom sport some kind of Hello Kitty paraphernalia—a small pink backpack for the young girl, a more subdued brown wallet decorated with Kitty's mouthless face for the mother.

Cute is seemingly everywhere in Japan, in small and large doses. As Mark Schilling (1997) writes, "Japan . . . is the Country of Cute" (p. 221), and as one American adult observer put it, "No one does cute as well as the Japanese." Furthermore, in 1992, the young women's magazine *CREA* dubbed *kawaii* (cute) "the most widely used, widely loved, habitual word in modern living Japanese" (*CREA*, November 1992, p. 58, quoted in Kinsella, 1995).

This chapter examines the phenomenon of Japanese *kawaii* primarily in its home base through the products distributed by one of its largest purveyors, the company Sanrio. Specifically, the focus is on the marketing and consumption of Sanrio's flagship character Hello Kitty, an infantilized, mouthless cat who epitomizes Japanese cute. Developed in 1974, Hello Kitty has graced countless items from erasers to computers, chopsticks to toasters, keychains to motor scooters. In a market that typically has been characterized by separation into age-graded niches, Sanrio has managed to surpass its own little girl's niche and extend its sales to increasingly older groups of females. This chapter explores the process by which this has been accomplished. How has Hello Kitty been made attractive, both for children and young adult females in Japan? How has consumer desire been extended from one age-graded niche to another? Furthermore, with the expansion of marketing to the United States (1976), Europe (1980), and Asia (1990), Sanrio has been attracting a slew of global consumers. As an addendum to the main body of this chapter that focuses on Japan, the author briefly addresses this global spread, analyzing some of the marketing strategies that have made this possible, as well as some of the rich, contradictory, complicit, and subversive consumer meanings given to Hello Kitty by her global consumers.

The findings in this chapter are based on a wide variety of sources: interviews at Sanrio headquarters in Tokyo and South San Francisco (international division) from 2000 to the present; interviews with sales personnel; interviews with consumers, including through fan-based Web sites; surveys and interviews conducted in 2003 with Japanese young adults on the concept of *kawaii*; the Sanrio company Web site; media reports; analysis of Sanrio's quarterly Japanese publication *Kitty Goods Collection*; and "Kitty sightings," that is, stories told to the author by Kitty fans and others worldwide.

THE CONCEPT OF *KAWAII* IN JAPAN: VISUAL, RELATIONAL, AND SEXUAL DIMENSIONS

The phenomenon of Hello Kitty must first be understood in relation to the concept of *kawaii* in Japan, as well as that of "cute" in Euro-America. The emergence of the term *kawaii* from its predecessors *kawayushi* and *kawayui* parallels the early 20th-century emergence of the *shoujo* (premarital female, typically age 10 to 14 years) as a significant, threatening public figure because of her very instability (Robertson, 1998, pp. 156–157).

According to Robertson (1998, p. 157), the category of *shoujo* was created in the early 20th century to pinpoint "potentially disruptive girls and women between puberty and marriage." The attitude toward *shoujo* in the 1920s and 1930s was highly ambivalent, because she was seen as a site of danger, a "barometer of decadent, un-Japanese social transformations." By the 1970s, however, the concept of *shoujo* had been transformed into a benign image, that of consumer.

With the rapid ascendancy of Japan as an international economic giant, and with Japanese females as primary domestic consumers, the *shoujo* became a trendsetter (Kinsella, 1995). Furthermore, according to culture critic Tsuka Eiji, *shoujo* can be extended to represent nothing short of Japanese people in general in their patterns of vast feminized, middle-class consumption (Robertson, 1998, pp. 158–159). *Kawaii* emerges in this period linked to a consumerist version of *shoujo* within conditions of affluence that persist amid deep economic recession since the 1990s. Masubuchi (1994) attributed the evolution of the *shoujo* image in *manga* (comics), from the misery-laden girl of the 1950s and mid-1960s to the happy heroine of the late 1960s and 1970s, to increasing prosperity in Japan (pp. 68–77). In other words, with widespread affluence and increasing consumer power, *shoujo* and *kawaii* became increasingly linked. Physically, *shoujo* in *manga* for girls became more *kawaii*, that is, more infantilized, increasingly depicted by smooth, rounded facial features, ever larger eyes, and prepubescent body. At the same time, *shoujo* in *manga* for men juxtaposed an adult body with large breasts with a young girl's face (Masubuchi, 1994, pp. 80–81).

Kawaii may be defined along a spectrum of interrelated dimensions: physical, relational/emotional, and sexual. McVeigh (2000) provided the following typology of cutenesses, although he did not elaborate on each category: baby, very young, young, maternal, teen, adult, sexy, pornography, child pornography, authority, and corporate (p. 135). Physically, the key element of *kawaii* rests in miniaturization. Several Japanese the author interviewed listed babies, young animals, and generally small things as the epitome of *kawaii*. An object can be made *kawaii* simply by shrinking it in size. Hello Kitty herself is small ("the weight of three apples" according to the story and profile provided by the company Web site), likes "small, cute things such as candy, stars, goldfish," and appears on small objects such as coin purses (her first appearance), pencils, and tiny erasers. Small objects, in fact, have become Sanrio's hallmark and figure importantly in marketing.

Masubuchi (1994) defined seven elements of *kawaii* as follows: (a) smallness, (b) naiveté and innocence, (c) youth (especially the very young), (d) *amae* (dependency), (e) roundness, (f) pastel colors, and (g) animal-like qualities. In the interviews the author conducted, most of the respondents named *kawaii* objects on the basis of their physical appearance, independent of but parallel with Masubuchi's list. Indeed, Sanrio characters, especially Hello Kitty, exhibit all these aspects. The domestication of nature lies at the core of this version of cute, in which many characters are animals or quasi-animals who must be cared for and trained. (The 1990s Japanese craze, *Tamagotchi*, the virtual pocket pet that had to be nurtured, fed, and generally cared for, dovetails exactly with these aspects of *kawaii*.) The popularity of Sanrio dovetails with the general *kawaii* craze for animals in Japan during the 1980s. The point of Sanrio "animals," however, is that they are not lifelike, but highly stylized—primarily infantilized with an outsized head and a small area of facial features. Kinsella (1995) defined *kawaii* as "essentially . . . childlike; it celebrates sweet, adorable, innocent, pure, simple, genuine, gentle, vulnerable, weak, and inexperienced social behaviour and physical appearances" (p. 220).

Kawaii also suggests positioning within interpersonal relationships through the verb *kawaigaru* (to give loving care). To be *kawaii* is to elicit a response from beholders that asks for that care. Concomitantly, invoking a *kawaii* response establishes oneself as a caregiver. According to several of the author's interviewees, an object or figure may be ugly and *kawaii*—For example, E.T.—so long as the figure invokes its own unthreatening vulnerability, sometimes by virtue of its very lack of comeliness. *Kawaii* may be thought of within an *amae* (dependency) relationship as an expression of helplessness (Lebra, 1984). The limits to *kawaii* lie, however, in the nature of that dependency: Exceeding the boundaries of helplessness is explicitly not *kawaii*. Therefore, the Japanese media celebrities of the 1990s, centenarian twin sisters Kin-san and Gin-san, were *kawaii* while they were spry and healthy, but bedridden elders, disabled persons, and other truly dependent persons are not.

The concept of *kawaii* thus reflects fundamental relationalities of the helpless and helper, the kept and the keeper, the dependent and the dependable. According to Lori Merish (1996),

> The cute always in some sense designates a commodity in search of its mother, and is constructed to generate maternal desire; the consumer (or potential consumer) of the cute is expected . . . to pretend she or he is the cute's mother. Valuing cuteness entails the ritualized performance of maternal feeling. (p. 186)

However, the relation between the cute and the observer becomes more complicated because not only does the observer want to mother the cute, but the observer also wants to become the cute. Merish (1996) continued:

> Appreciating the cute . . . entails a structure of identification, wanting to be like the cute—or more exactly, wanting the cute to be just like the self. Appreciating cuteness expresses the double logic of identification, its fundamental inseparability from desire. . . . The aesthetics of cuteness thus generates an emotional response in accord with what Mary Ann Doane has described as a commercial structure of "feminine" consumer empathy, a structure that blurs identification and commodity desire. Putting a feminine twist on Walter Benjamin's formulations, Doane sees a convergence between the intimate, emotional address of commodities and certain . . . empathetic structures of feeling . . . that assimilate consumption into the logic of adoption. (pp. 186–187)

One thus desires cute things such as Hello Kitty in multiple ways—simultaneously wanting to care for it, own it, and become it.

Kawaii has its sexual dimensions as well, even if these do not necessarily play an overt part in Sanrio's marketing. The author argues that the merging concepts of *kawaii* and *shoujo* as depicted in girl's comics and sexualized in men's comics in Japan have now become part of that country's female subculture, in which Sanrio also participates. For example, the Japanese late-teen and early-twenties magazine *Cutie for Independent Girls*, which began publication in 1986, shows *kawaii* as explicitly sexualized consumer culture. The May 1998 issue featured a wide-eyed female model with rosy cheeks and braids on the cover and in a six-page photo spread in poses of bondage and other sadomasochistic sexual scenes. Here is *kawaii* embedded within a host of alarming sexual practices: *rorikon* (Lolita complex) fetishism of older Japanese men for prepubescent females, night clubs with hostesses wearing school girl uniforms, and *enjo ksai* (teenage prostitution). The scenes depicted in *Cutie* would not be so startling, perhaps, if they were published in men's magazines, but here they present images to girls—"independent girls," no less—and these images represent nothing but females as passive victims awaiting their rape. The rest of the magazine, as is the case with many magazines in Japan, presents a paean to consumerism, with information on clothes and accessories that complete the *kawaii* look, stores where one may purchase these items, and brief interviews with "star consumers." Even if this cover and photo spread were meant as a joke, that joke can be viewed only as disturbingly complicit with female subjugation, at both sexual and consumer levels. This is rape as *kawaii* consumer chic.

Another magazine, *Cawaii!* [sic] (1999), which began publication in 1996, presents articles and consumer guides for young females in their late teens to twenties. The four females depicted on the September 1999 cover are deeply tanned, with bleached hair, heavily mascara-laden rounded eyes encircled with pale eye shadow, broad smiles, and sky-high platform shoes. Their physical representation completely subverts a more traditional standard of Japanese female beauty that includes fair skin, black hair, almond-shaped eyes, small closed mouth, and proportionately shorter legs kept modestly covered by a floor-length kimono. This physical *kawaii* subversion of traditional norms continues within its pages. A five-page photo spread features three models posing in Barbie-doll fashion before an orange background of a repeating mantra in English, "I am a Barbie girl," as part of the then-current Barbie craze in Japan (p. 15). According to one Japanese woman in her twenties with whom the author spoke, one of the highest compliments that could be given a young woman in Japan at that time (summer 1999) was either to be called *baabii* [Barbie] or to be told she looked just like Barbie.

The road from Hello Kitty to Barbie may seem questionably distant. The author contends, however, that the two ends of the spectrum are discursively linked through *shoujo*. The premarital female, like Barbie (according to the magazine), is both sexy and cute. This is how her school uniform (including her white "loose socks"—knee-high baggy socks that have become a sexualized icon of teenage girls in Japan), taken out of the school yard and into nightclubs, becomes a symbol for teenage prostitution. Although not suggesting that Sanrio necessarily promotes or even takes part in this overtly sexualized extension of *kawaii*, the author does argue that the line between innocence and sexuality, between childhood and adulthood is not so neatly drawn in Japan. In other words, sexuality is part of childhood, part of *asobi* (play), part of nature. A concept such as *kawaii*, then, links the physical, relational, and sexual by association. The *kawaii* means of reaching out through dependency goes hand in hand with interpersonal appeal, as well as with sexual desire. *Kawaii* by way of *shoujo* is not presexual or asexual, but always carries the potential for sexuality, even when not overtly sexualized.

MARKETING *KAWAII* TO ADULTS

Sanrio's extension of its market into adult goods in Japan began in the late 1980s, when demographers predicted a shrinking youth population in Japan (Yamazaki, 1999; quoted in McVeigh, 2000). What began as small items that a child could carry to school extended to household items and goods specifically promoted to young "office ladies" (so-called OL or secretaries), and eventually to housewives. The product endorsements by key media celebrities such as teen idol singer Kahara Tomomi boosted sales tremendously among young female adults. Sales of Sanrio items more than doubled among OL and housewives between 1995 and 1998 (Masuda, 1998; quoted in McVeigh, 2000).

This extension of the Sanrio market shows how the concept of *kawaii* has been broadened to include young female adults. If *kawaii* may apply to young female adults, as well as to children, then *kawaii* products can serve both groups equally well. This is not to say that both groups consume Hello Kitty with the same kinds of meanings, only that both may share products. Indeed, when one goes to a Sanrio store, the majority of products span a range of ages, from children to adults: stationery, eating implements, towels, personal artifacts (e.g., handkerchiefs, coin purses, bags). There are relatively few items strictly for children, and relatively more items primarily for adults: snowboards, rice cookers, waffle irons, and exercise equipment.

One critical way by which Sanrio has extended its market is by promoting itself as a facilitator of interpersonal relations, which are important in

Japan at any age. In contrast to Sharon Kinsella's (1995) assessment of cute style as "antisocial" (p. 251), Sanrio markets itself as eminently social. The company's Web site states its goal:

> [To] provide the means to enrich interpersonal communication. . . . Sanrio provides a vehicle for the young and young-at-heart to express their feelings to friends and family—each Sanrio product brings a message of friendship and happiness. Giving someone a cute Hello Kitty letter set doesn't just say "let's stay in touch"—it gives them a means to do so. (p. 251)

The target market, according to the Web site, is those "young and young at heart" who value "interpersonal communication." Who, then, could be exempt? Moreover, the emphasis on language-based interaction draws upon female culture in contemporary Japan.

Sanrio's Web site continues: "Gift-giving is at the heart of our business; we see every customer as the giver of a gift—even if it's a special something for herself." This emphasis on gift exchange as the primary form of sociality makes consumer culture central to interpersonal relationships. Sanrio therefore carries gifts at a wide range of prices, for occasions big and small, with the greater emphasis on the small, the everyday. This makes gift buying a constant activity. If, as its Web site says, a Sanrio gift is "more than just a gift; it's an expression of love and friendship," then gift-buying, like love and friendship, are neverending. One is always made to shop and shop always. Buying Hello Kitty means buying into a lifestyle of sociality, maintained specifically by consuming.

DOING *KAWAII*, BEING *KAWAII*

The Sanrio magazine/catalogue, *Kitty Goods Collection*, gears itself almost exclusively to female adults, not children. Here is the OL life, as it merges into housewife life. As marketed by Sanrio, *kawaii* does not negate adult responsibilities (Kinsella, 1995, p. 251), but embeds these responsibilities within a particular style. These responsibilities include the workplace, with specific Sanrio items geared to the office. For example, the winter 1998 issue of the *Kitty Goods Collection* (1998, vol. 3) features "OL Collection!" with text as follows:

> Even for OL, these days of recession are harsh. For this reason, one must have the power to fully recharge one's batteries with the cheerfulness of Kitty goods. We introduce you to items which will transform the top of your desk. (p. 18)

The article pictures mouse pad, clip holder, floppy disk holder, pencil holder, stapler, memo pad, and hole puncher, all in Kitty pink. It is not enough, then, that OLs (also dubbed "office flowers") "decorate" the office by their presence. Now they also must decorate their desks to uplift office morale, including their own, amid economic gloom.

Adult responsibilities also include reproducing a new generation of Kitty fans. According to Sanrio marketing, one may become a better mother through Hello Kitty consumption. According to the company's Web site, the 1998 "Kitty Babies Series" of characters "was created in response to a strong request by young mothers who have been loyal fans of Hello Kitty since her debut" (p. 18). The 1998 spring issue features a new "baby (*akachan*) series" of bassinet items from bottles to crib sheets. The 2000 issue provides information on "Sanrio ABC Kurabu," a program for mothers to teach preschoolers English, "naturally" by way of videotapes and books (*Kitty Goods Collection*, 2000, vol. 11, back cover). Several photo spreads include mother–daughter teams of consumers. One 27-year-old mother confesses, "Before saying 'Mama' or 'Papa,' my [2-year-old] daughter said 'Kiti-chan.' " She continues, "Even though I myself was a Kitty fan from way back, I did not really start to collect these Kitty goods until my daughter was born" (2000, vol. 3, p. 95). Having a child (especially a daughter), then, allows her to indulge more fully than previously in Kitty consumption. According to the magazine, then, one may fulfill societal obligations as a female adult specifically through Hello Kitty consumption, whether in the office one decorates or in the home one populates. At Kitty-led mother's hand, a child learns to participate in society as an expert consumer.

Hello Kitty, however, is not only about the work of adult life. It is also about leisure and selfhood. The July 2000 (vol. 11) issue of *Kitty Goods Collection* presents *Kiti no happii sukejuuru* (Kitty's happy schedule), giving consumers 20 ideas for spending one's leisure time in "doing Kitty," divided into 30-min, 60-min, half-day, and full-day "courses" (*Kitty Goods Collection*, 2000, vol. 11, pp. 9–33), which include activities such as flower arranging, crafts, manicures, and decorating. The first thing to note about these activities is that they are done alone. According to this, leisure time provides the opportunity to focus on oneself, by oneself, luxuriating within *honne* (one's true feelings) to a schedule packed tightly with *tatemae* (public face).

Second, most of the suggested activities are not complex or expensive (e.g., taking a trip to Pyuurorando, Sanrio's theme park outside Tokyo), but relatively simple and inexpensive (e.g., making a scrapbook of one's trip to Pyuurorando). This makes leisure accessible, do-able, and affordable.

Third, the image of Hello Kitty looms ubiquitous, as might be expected in such a promotional publication. Most activities involve consuming Hello Kitty goods. Other activities focus on recreating Hello Kitty in various forms (wax, soap, food) or transforming the ordinary into Kitty-based *kawaii* (dishes, refrigerators, cars).

These activities all center on a return, specifically by way of Hello Kitty goods and images, to a particular construction of childhood—one filled with picnics, days at the beach, amusement parks, pets, and naps. This is life as, according to the magazine, *nonbiri* (carefree, idle). Hello Kitty, then, becomes both a means to the *nonbiri* and a symbolic recreation of an idealized childhood revisited in adult lives, squeezed into a tight schedule. The magazine suggests that one may snatch a return to childhood, catch-as-catch-can, to the days of *nonbiri*, whether one has 30 or 60 minutes, a half or a full day—or even, by implication, the moment it takes to glance at the figure of Hello Kitty. The sight of Kitty itself provides a flashback.

The magazine reinforces this notion of Hello Kitty as a site of collective memories in its interviews with fans and consumers. For example, a 1998 article entitled "My Treasure; Nostalgic Goods throughout Japan" solicits photos of goods from readers, along with childhood memories associated with them (*Kitty Goods Collection*, 1998, vol. 2, pp. 58–60). Respondents, all female, range in age from 15 to 32 years. The article pictures Kitty goods from the past from large to small, from overnight bags to hair clips, as prompts for memory. The article presents most memories anonymously, without name, gender, or age, but with reference to particular pictured items. They include the following:

"I remember taking this Kitty bag to the pool every summer."

"When I was in elementary school, I would put my clothes on this Kitty hook everyday."

"When I received these Kitty index cards from my friend, I was so happy."

The memories invoke special occasions, as well as everyday life, with the focus on the goods rather than the individuals.

A few selected recollections focus more on the individual, with a photo of the consumer and her personal narratives. Some of these narratives talk of Hello Kitty spanning generations. One 15-year-old Kitty fan recalls the pleasure of uncovering her mother's own childhood Hello Kitty collection. Another 28-year-old woman predicts, "Soon I will be having children of my own, and I want to collect Kitty goods together with them." Yet another 32-year-old woman nostalgically recalls childhood memories of Kitty, and suggests that these memories give her peace in her adult life: "As I look at Kitty, I think nostalgically of playing with my friends when I was a child. . . . Even now, my feelings from childhood still remain, and I find peace in my heart [*hotto kokoro ga nagomu*] through my love for Kitty" (*Kitty Goods Collection*, 1998, vol. 2, pp. 58–59). Kitty for her becomes a companion who straddles different phases of her life. With these Kitty-led recollections placed in the public forum of a magazine, these personal reminiscences become memories of the collective *shoujo*, reconstituted to connect generations as well as periods of one's life.

Hello Kitty, in this way, becomes a form of selfhood (Clammer, 1997, p. 68) retrieved from the past through goods, connecting friend to friend, for a few, even gaining celebrity as *kitiraa* (slang for diehard Kitty fans). Doing Kitty in these ways proffers a "Kitty habitus," a patterned self accrued to the body by repetition over time. Kitty becomes a verb—doing Kitty—and thus a practice by which one may act within and upon the world through consumption. These recommended Kitty doings offer a Kitty "sensaround" world: One sees Kitty everywhere. One eats Kitty (*okonomiyaki*, sandwiches), drinks Kitty (herbal tea), feels Kitty (sand sculpture), wears Kitty (whether painted on one's nails or donned as one's pajamas), and even smells Kitty (aromatherapy). Most important, one feels Kitty reaching out in small ways through "social communication" goods and gifts. In doing Kitty, one performs a Kitty self, enacting *kawaii* from morning to night, inside and out, in public and private.

Sanrio's marketing of Hello Kitty to adults in Japan thus draws upon the related concepts of *shoujo* and *kawaii*, with their connections to emotion, nurturance, nature, and nostalgia. Hello Kitty enacts not a return so much as a performance of identities rooted in childhood. According to the marketing literature, one becomes a better adult through Hello Kitty, finding inner peace, establishing and affirming social ties, decorating one's desk at the office, and teaching one's children. *Kawaii* thus becomes not a negation of responsibility, but a means to fulfilling the multiple responsibilities of adulthood. Hello Kitty connects people—mother to daughter, friend to friend, generation to generation. The fact that this concurs with Sanrio's goals of profit making does not diminish the efficacy of Hello Kitty, who by this time has become itself a companion rather than a product.

Furthermore, *kawaii* surpasses itself as a temporary stage in one's life. It becomes an activity and a consumer option, which construct a thoroughgoing lifestyle. One does *kawaii* primarily through buying *kawaii*, surrounding oneself with things *kawaii* whether in work or play, office or home. One consumes *kawaii* bodily, and also as part of one's very physical self. These practices create a *kawaii* self, which is both performative and constitutive, rooted in the past. Doing *kawaii* in these many ways offers gendered selves for sale, stitching together collective memories across time and space as an unbroken chain. Kawaii suggests ways by which adults become *shoujo* and *shoujo*, become adults.

LOCALIZING *KAWAII* FOR THE GLOBAL MARKETPLACE

What happens, however, when *kawaii* hits the global stage? What kinds of marketing strategies make it work? How do consumers react? What kinds of meanings do global consumers give Hello Kitty? And to what extent does this *kawaii* imaging affect the image of Japan in global marketing?

According to Kazuo Tohmatsu, manager of the General Affairs Department of Sanrio Co., Ltd. (the parent company in Tokyo, Japan), Sanrio designs and markets its global products differently for the American market than for the Asian market: Asian exports are nearly identical to what is sold in Japan, but American Sanrio goods have only a 20% overlap with Japan. The other 80% of goods are designed specifically for the American market (personal communication, May 5, 2002). In other words, Sanrio perceives the need for an approach in the Euro-American market different from that in the Asian market.

As a company, Sanrio's strategy tends to rely on local input to determine best what will sell in regional markets. For example, the author was able to witness the product selection process at Sanrio, Inc., the marketer and distributor of goods to the Americas during May 2002. This process takes place several times a year as the product catalogs arrive from the Tokyo office. At the selection process the author witnessed Bill Hensley, Marketing Director of Sanrio, Inc., call several female employees into a conference room, where they paged through the latest catalog. Each staff member commented on the items that she thought Sanrio should carry in the Americas. Many of these comments were based on previous sales, but other comments were far more personal, including what the employees themselves would like to purchase. Although Hensley determined the quantities they would order, the selection of the items themselves came primarily from the female employees.

Furthermore, employees at Sanrio, Inc. have been invited to submit new character ideas to the parent company in a design competition. The winner gets to see his or her design realized and promoted as a new character in Sanrio's lineup. Sanrio thus relies on local subsidiaries for new product ideas as well as feedback from regional markets. The localization process is built into design development, marketing, promotion, and consumer research.

According to Hensley, Sanrio does not conduct "aggressive advertising." Instead, it focuses on word-of-mouth and publicity, especially publicity generated by celebrity interest stories. To that end, it conducts a "celebrity outreach" program:

> We put our primary emphasis in our publicity, getting the new product story out to magazines, newspapers across the country, television stations where we can, leveraging when we have, say, celebrity interest in a line or in Hello Kitty in particular, leveraging that story because the news media is celebrity obsessed. So if we can say that yes, Mariah Carey [pop singer] is a big Hello Kitty fan, and it's not just us saying it, because she's not a paid spokesperson for us, but, here's the proof, because she's on MTV showing her Hello Kitty t-shirt, because she's photographed in *People* and *Us* [American popular magazines] carrying her Hello Kitty boombox, so we kind of spin that back, and

then that story feeds on itself. We cover celebrity outreach, and we do send products to—every quarter it's 50 or 70 different celebrities generally. Sometimes there is a repeat group that we've identified as friends, that we give stuff to. But it's kind of like prospecting . . . [We contract] with the same organization that represents us for TV and film placements. So they have access to how to get products to the celebrities. (Hensley, personal communication, June 19, 2002)

Besides celebrity outreach, product placement has become an important part of Sanrio, Inc.'s strategy. Like many companies in the United States, Sanrio contracts with a firm that negotiates the appearance of their goods in media productions, including TV shows and movies such as *Friends, Everybody Loves Raymond,* and *Seventh Heaven,* in which Sanrio is even part of the scripted dialogue. Hensley also considers it a coup that comedian Mike Meyers requested a Sanrio store as part of a backdrop for a Tokyo street scene in his 2002 *Austin Powers in Goldmember* movie.

This kind of media and celebrity exposure creates a familiarity with Hello Kitty for American consumers that is part of the company's "out-of-store marketing," in the words of Hensley. "In-store marketing," by contrast, focuses on generating a positive customer experience, primarily through the company philosophy cryptically expressed as "Small Gift, Big Smile." This motto refers to the following: the small gifts a customer may purchase at Sanrio that can evoke a big smile in the purchaser as well as in the recipient of the gift, the small trinkets that Sanrio gives away free to its customers, and the gifts that visitors to Sanrio's corporate headquarters may receive as part of a company philosophy of hospitality. Sanrio trains its sales personnel through a video emphasizing the five steps toward "Big Smiles":

1. *Approach.* 30-second rule! Greet every customer entering the store within 30 seconds.
2. *Ask.* "Have you been to our store before? Can I show you how to read our prices?"
3. *Present.* Show new items if she has been in the store before, or other items based on her needs.
4. *Sell.* "You will love that. Let me take them to the register for you."
5. *Encourage.* Remind her that the store gets new items every month. "Come back soon!" (Sanrio Co., Ltd., 2002)

These kinds of sales techniques may be common to many companies, but Sanrio pays particularly close attention to the personal interaction that they see as their trademark. In this way, Sanrio takes a Japanese level of service to a global scale.

But how does a global company such as Sanrio negotiate its own identity as a Japanese company in an international setting? What and how much of products' identity as specifically Japanese matters in marketing? According to Sanrio, Inc. Executive Vice President Gastaldi:

> It's very important to me that we don't lose the Japanesey-ness, if you will, of our product line.... The detail, the cuteness, the use of colors, the things that make it very special, make it unique, make it Sanrio, make it Japanese, that fine attention to detail, the designs, I don't want to lose that. We are a Japanese company. That is our roots. We are very special in that sense. And yes, we are certainly moving in the direction of globalization of our markets. But it's very important that we don't lose a sense of our roots.... We don't want to lose that. (personal communication, June 19, 2002)

Sanrio works constantly to define that "Japanesey-ness," although it clearly is a moving target.

Dan Peters, senior promotions designer in the marketing department of Sanrio Inc., concurs that the Japanese identity of Sanrio products, including Hello Kitty and a sense of kawaii, are important elements in the promotions that he designs.

> Part of what I find to be of great appeal of Sanrio is the Japanese quality of it. So I ... don't like to Disney-fy everything into this kind of cookie-cutter American culture type of—this is what's acceptable, this is what Warner Brothers does, whatever. I love the fact that Sanrio is different. And so, I could very easily edit things and smooth them out into [Disney's] Sleeping Beauty type, you know, kind of like descriptions. But I love the quirkiness [of the Japanese products]. You know, that comes with dealing with Sanrio. And Japanese culture. And I think that's part of our appeal. At least to me it is. (personal communication, June 30, 2002)

Although Peters cannot put his finger on exactly what "Japaneseness" means in relation to Sanrio products, the quirky element of which he speaks is a defining part of *kawaii* that makes it somewhat different from the English "cute." The notion of cute is more straightforward and predictable. *Kawaii*, on the other hand, seems to represent an almost dreamlike state involving small leaps of logic, which makes it more childlike, vulnerable, and durable than the notion of "cute."

But what do global consumers make of this bricolage and subversion? To what extent are many of them buying "Japan" when they purchase Hello Kitty? Many casual buyers do not necessarily know that Hello Kitty is Japanese. They see this cat as simply a cute figure with a vast number of products to buy. More serious fans and collectors, however, are all well aware that Hello Kitty is Japanese.

One 20-year-old female fan from Dallas, Texas, says she knows that Hello Kitty is from Japan by the Japanese writing on the tags and the fact that the Sanrio theme park is located in Japan. Her avid interest in Hello Kitty stems from childhood, so that Hello Kitty "[keeps] my youth alive and [puts] a smile on my face." She is a true collector, and "hope[s] to one day move to Japan to find the Hello Kitty items that I can't find here in the States. I see Hello Kitty [as] being particularly Japanese (despite her birthplace, London, England)."

One 26-year-old businesswoman in France confesses to being a cat lover who began her Kitty collection at the age of 8 years when her parents brought back a number of Kitty goods from Japan. Since then, she has bought a few things in Paris where they recently have been considered fashionable, but really she expanded her collection when she traveled to Vietnam: "These last 2 weeks we have been on holiday in Vietnam!! And over there, WWWOUAAAAHH, I could not stop buying Hello Kitty stuff; we could find some everywhere and so cheap!!!"

One avid middle-aged female collector in Minneapolis links Hello Kitty to her own subjectivity, tying together her love of cats and her interest in Asia. She was first introduced to Hello Kitty through cat shows in the Midwest, where many cat fanciers displayed their Japanese *maneki-neko* (begging cat) figurines. When she saw a Hello Kitty doll there, she immediately connected it to the other *maneki-neko*. Since then, she and her husband have searched toy stores throughout the United States for more Hello Kitty goods, displaying her collection in a shrine-like setting that she changes seasonally. She also has become interested in Japan through her fondness of Hello Kitty.

Sanrio's largest group of customers in the United States is Asian Americans. One 30-year-old Japanese American female fan from California says that she and her other friends (mostly Japanese Americans) were big buyers of Hello Kitty in elementary and middle schools. In fact, the nickname for one of her friends was "Hello Kitty," because her head, like Kitty's, was big and round. She and several others the author spoke with talk about gaining a sense of Asian American identity through Hello Kitty, buying goods in Chinatown or Japan town shops, showing their goods to other primarily Asian American friends, and even now, as adults, looking back nostalgically on the days when Hello Kitty was "their" character, sold only in "their" stores rather than the mainstream department stores where it can be found today.

The second largest group of Kitty devotees in the United States is Hispanics. According to Peter Gastaldi, executive vice president of Sanrio, Inc., what Hispanics and Asians share are "family values, children at the center of the family, buying things for the children, things that will make children happy" (personal communication, June 13, 2002). But are Hispanics "buying Japan"? Gastaldi says,

> No, they're buying cute. In the case of Hispanics, I don't think that the fact that it's from Japan really has a whole lot to do with it. It's cute, it's colorful, it's child-oriented, it's whimsical. It's a gift, it's something for the child, and the child is family values—the child is the center of the family. (personal communication)

Another group of Kitty customers is the gay male clientele, at least in San Francisco and Honolulu, where the author interviewed store employees. According to Mark Servito, assistant manager of Sanrio's main San Francisco store at San Francisco Center, the gay clientele is primarily White and shops in pairs. These customers often buy Sanrio items as performative elements: not plush toys or stationery, but items of public display such as oversized shoulder bags. "They find it hilarious, but interesting" (Servito, personal communication, June 20, 2002).

Hello Kitty, of course, does not come without its detractors. It is notable when these critiques also become critiques of being Asian and female, as Hello Kitty is thus identified. One 25-year-old female nursing student in Hawaii distances herself from Asia by critiquing Japanese females and Hello Kitty both as "too cutesy." She says, "They're too cute! Pink and cute—that should only be for babies. I can envision little Japanese girls going 'Hee! Hee! Hee!' " Denise Uyehara, a radical feminist Asian American performance artist, uses Hello Kitty in her productions "Sex Kitty" and "Beyond Sex Kitty" as a symbol of hypersexualized Asian female stereotypes. These and other consumers map their own versions of "Japan" and themselves onto the flat space of Kitty.

CONCLUDING THOUGHTS: IN THE WAKE OF *KAWAII*

What, then, are we to make of this onslaught of *kawaii*, both in Japan and abroad—what the author calls "pink globalization"? Is this a form of neo-feminism or antifeminist backlash or both? What does the extension of *kawaii* from children to young adult females in Japan suggest about societal trends? Are these trends applicable to global markets in which Hello Kitty has been successful?

As Sanrio, Inc.'s Gastaldi proclaims, "Hello Kitty is bringing . . . cuteness to the world." That cuteness/*kawaii*, however, takes on different meanings and interpretations in each of its local habitats. According to Parkes, "Everyone has a different *kawaii*." Parkes' words do not ring quite true. Everyone agrees that a figure such as Hello Kitty is *kawaii*. What differs is the set of meanings and attitudes given to *kawaii* itself, from complicit acceptance to ironic distancing to outright contempt. In Japan, the attitude toward *kawaii* probably is most benign. Consumers either accept a figure such as Hello Kitty wholeheartedly or reject her outright. If one may become a better mother or secretary through consuming *kawaii* things, then even the most central societal institutions of family and company sanction buying objects such as Hello Kitty.

Furthermore, as *kawaii* figures work hand in hand with governments and businesses large and small in their widespread use of cute characters to convey official messages, to humanize top-down directives, and to feminize public and private spaces, then a commercial icon such as Hello Kitty can be interpreted as merely another in a panoply of appealing figures, painting the canvas of the nation pink. It matters little to consumers and fans that the canvas may mask gender-based inequities or structural barriers to a wider range of individual choice and opportunities. What matters more is that on an individual level as well as a group level of consumers, Hello Kitty makes the world that much more benign, comfortable, and pleasant. *Kawaii* is not a negation of responsibility so much as the spinning of those responsibilities back into what looks like child's play.

The *kawaii* world of Hello Kitty, however, becomes more complex in its various global habitats, where cultural assumptions both overlap and diverge from the original Japanese context. Some of these habitats accept *kawaii* uncritically as the domain of childhood and females. Others take an ironic stance concerning *kawaii*, pushing the limits of performative cuteness. It is dangerous, therefore, to put a global spin on the spread of *kawaii* when assumptions, meanings, and interpretations differ. What binds these disparate users and uses, however, is Hello Kitty herself. Through this mouthless cat, consumers may see a sisterhood of *kawaii* not as engagement with specific meaning so much as engagement with each other through a common object. This holds true despite the strangeness of the bedfellows. "Pink globalization" may thus represent an unruly bundling of neo- and antifeminisms, led by a Japanese product, but taken to a number of competing and sometimes contradictory directions by local consumers.

REFERENCES

Cawaii! (1999, September). Tokyo: *Cawaii!*

Clammer, J. (1997). *Contemporary urban Japan: A sociology of consumption*. Oxford: Blackwell.

Cutie for independent girls. (1998, June 22). Tokyo: Author.

Kinsella, S. (1995). Cuties in Japan. In L. Skov & B. Moeran (Eds.), *Women, media, and consumption in Japan* (pp. 220–221). Honolulu: University of Hawaii Press.

Kitty goods collection. (Vol. 1–3). (1998). Tokyo: Sanrio.

Kitty goods collection. (Vol. 11). (2000). Tokyo: Sanrio.

Lebra, T. (1984). *Patterns of Japanese behavior.* Honolulu: University of Hawaii Press.

Masubuchi, S. (1994). *Kawaii shōkōgun* [Kawaii syndrome]. Tokyo: NHK Publishing.

McVeigh, B. (2000). *Wearing ideology: State, schooling, and self-presentation in Japan.* Oxford: Berg.

McVeigh, B. (2000). How Hello Kitty commodifies the cute, cool and camp: "Consumutopia" versus "control" in Japan. *Journal of Material Culture, 5,* 225–245.

Merish, L. (1996). Cuteness and commodity aesthetics: Tom Thumb and Shirley Temple. In R. G. Thomson (Ed.), *Freakery: Cultural spectacles of the extraordinary body* (pp. 105–203). New York: New York University Press.

Robertson, J. (1998). *Takarazuka: Sexual politics and popular culture in modern Japan.* Berkeley: University of California Press.

Sanrio. Available online at http://sanrioworld.ne.jp/

Schilling, M. (1997). *The encyclopedia of Japanese pop culture.* New York: Weatherhill.

Treat, J. W. (1996). Yoshimoto Banana writes home: *Shōjo* culture and the nostalgic subject. In J. Treat (Ed.), *Contemporary Japan and popular culture* (pp. 275–308). Honolulu: University of Hawaii Press.

Yano, C. R. (2000). Dream girl: imagining the girl-next-door within the heart/soul of Japan. *U.S.-Japan Women's Journal (English Supplement), 19,* 122–141.

6

From *Pokémon* to Potter: Trainee Teachers Explore Children's Media-Related Play, 2000–2003

Elizabeth Grugeon

In March 2000, 70 trainee primary school teachers in their third year of an undergraduate education program at De Montfort University in England were asked to observe and record a 15-min breaktime on a primary school playground as part of a study of children's informal language and culture. This chapter draws on extracts from some of their recording and observation on playgrounds in Bedfordshire, Cambridgeshire, Hertfordshire, Northamptonshire, and Milton Keynes in 2000, and from subsequent students in 2001, 2002, and 2003. The data could be grouped under several headings: jokes, traditional rhymes and games, football, media influences, and narrative fantasy games. Traditional playground games, and girls' play in particular, have been discussed elsewhere (Bishop & Curtis, 2000; Grugeon, 2000; Opie, 1993). The author has chosen to concentrate on the way recent media influences are being absorbed into the language and culture of the playground. As Marsh (2003) suggested,

> Children engage in a semiotic world in which texts in different modes are conceptually linked. They do not see a neat dichotomy between print and televisual texts as they move seamlessly from one mode to another in their quest for meaning-making. . . . They use visual, literate, oral, and corporeal modes of communication in a range of multimodal practices. (p. 43)

Over a period of 4 years, approximately 275 teacher trainees have observed more than 4,000 min of playground activity in more than 60 primary schools. The aim of the project was to encourage teacher trainees to become aware of children's interest in popular culture and, as professionals, to consider the relation of these interests to school literacy and culture. A growing archive of material now exists that allows researchers to track some of the ongoing changes in children's everyday play activities. This material partly feeds into the current debate about using children's interests in popular media and consumer texts to enhance learning and motivation in the primary classroom (Bromley, 2002; Dyson, 2001; Lambirth, 2003; Marsh & Millard, 2000). It also provides a means of updating well-established forms of "mass observation" of children's popular folklore, of the kind most widely identified with the work of the Opies in Britain (Opie & Opie, 1959).

The first thing the trainees observed were gender differences: Girls often played games that involved verbal interaction in small, cohesive groups, whereas boys tended to spend more time with games involving running and chasing: football, Power Rangers, and stylized fighting routines. The trainees were surprised to discover how much language was involved in these very active games and made interesting observations about the prevalence of football, overwhelmingly the most popular game for boys on the playground. It shall be seen that these gender differences also were apparent in the children's uses of media and popular culture in their play.

2000: THE *POKÉMON* PHENOMENON

From the start, the trainees found that popular culture was exerting a powerful influence on children's play. They noted ways that this emerges in role-play games when television "brings new words into the language" (Keaney & Lucas, 1994, p. 43). Spring 2000 was the height of the Pokémon controversy in U.K. schools. All the trainees encountered disgruntled groups of children who were no longer allowed to bring their *Pokémon* cards to school. Jane, a trainee in a junior school on the outskirts of a large town, asked two year 4 boys about *Pokémon*. They told her, "We wanted to play *Pokémon*, but we're not allowed the cards anymore, so we have to pretend," explaining how they managed to play *Pokémon* games without cards:

Child A: "Well, there's the cartoon you can watch; there are the cards, . . . but we're not allowed any more."

Jane: "Tell me more about the cards then."

Child B: "You collect them and play games with them. You try and beat each other with the powers on the card. On the cards are different *Pokémon*, like Picachu, Beedrill and Bulbasaur. If they have

> more power than the other *Pokémon*, they take away the power and can kill them if they want."
>
> Jane: "So what are you playing in the playground then?"
> Child A: "Our *Pokémon* game. He's a Squirtle and he can squirt water; I'm a Beedrill and I can drill through things."
> Child B: "What about the ball?"
> Child A: "Oh yeah, the Power Ball. You can throw it at people and make them slow down so you can use your powers on them."
> (Jane, March, 2000)

Many trainees recorded similar instances of children absorbing and adapting the *Pokémon* characters and stories into their fantasy play. This involved a confident use of the language of the *Pokémon* universe. The game was intended for children 10 years of age and older, but was massively popular with much younger children in the United Kingdom. In a village school, Sarah-Jane recorded two boys during "wet play" playing with *Pokémon* cards. Although M was 5 years old and T was 6, they were adept at using the terminology, although not sure of the rules. The following conversation is an extract from a much longer transcript:

> M: "Choose which *Pokémon* you want to fight against my Magikarp."
> T: "Mmm ... [*flicking through his cards*] Tangela. Nothing can beat Tangela. He's got loads of health" [*pointing at the hit points indicated by an HP on the card*].
> M: "Yeah, but choose one that's as good as mine this time. ... Now, which one is your best?"
> T: "Tangela. He can beat anyone."
> (Sarah-Jane, March, 2000)

Sarah-Jane comments, "This card game involves 'a complicated system of trumps, hit points, attacks and retreats' " (Neumark, 2000). It is clear from the transcript that neither boy was sure how to play the game correctly, so they had developed their own rules. On the playground, they played a chasing game based on *Pokémon*, in which they took on a role and acted out a narrative based on confrontation between the characters. As Moyles (1994) suggested, "Outside the school building lies an area in which the writ of adults plays a less decisive part."

Clare, with 5- to 7-year-old children in a large village school, felt that this influx of cartoon-related products was not a bad thing. Through watching television, often alongside their play, children were developing specific skills (Simatos & Spencer, 1992, p. 115).

There was one child who was obviously very knowledgeable about *Pokémon* and how the battles were decided. This meant that he appeared to take on the role of adjudicator with many of the children approaching him to clear up disputes they had over who had won the battle and arguments about "fair swaps." He is a child who is quiet in the classroom, often refraining from raising his hand because he lacks confidence in his own ability. When I questioned him about the role he appeared to undertake in the playground, he told me that people came to ask him because, "I've got the most *Pokémon*s and I understand them best." This showed me that when dealing with a subject he is confident with, he is more than able to express himself clearly to others. (Clare, March, 2000)

Clare also recorded girls participating in *Pokémon* games, "either with each other or with boys," and she reflected, "I think this may be to do with the fact that *Pokémon* games are played statically and do not involve a high level of aggression or competitiveness."

The *Pokémon* games that the trainees were recording at this time reflected the latest media craze, but there was much evidence of children drawing on other media material. In a small village school, Claire observed six 5- to 6-year-olds, four boys and two girls, playing a game of what she thought was the traditional chasing game "It":

Claire: "What do you call this game?"

Child A: "Croc."

Claire: "Who taught you to play this game?"

Child A: "I don't know. I've got Croc on my PlayStation."
             (Claire, March, 2000)

On a multiethnic urban infant school playground, Sharon found that

WWF [World Wrestling Federation] was a particularly popular game, during which a child's head was held in an arm lock, or there was an attempt to pull the child to the ground. Other favorites were *Power Rangers*. It was apparent that the boys were attempting to imitate the macho images they have seen on the screen. (March, 2000)

Schools on the whole disapproved of wrestling and fighting games, but many students observed that children knew the difference between play fights and the real thing, and that the former often were quite controlled and stylized performances. In 2000, there was no doubt that *Pokémon* was the most popular game played by children 5 to 11 years of age, and that part of its prestige was a response to overall adult disapproval.

WHAT HAD CHANGED IN 2001?

A year later, trainees continued to report role-play games with evident influence from popular culture. Paula reported that *Pokémon* still was in evidence. She overheard a group of boys choosing roles: "You don't want to be him; he's not got full powers; he's no good; he can't evolve." But they later told her, "*Pokémon* isn't in anymore, Miss Richards."

Linda saw more diverse activities, and there was much evidence of the influence of TV, film, and computer games, such as *Mario*, based on a TV and computer character involving weapons with prescribed effects. Players called out "Thunderbolt," "Green Shell," and "Yellow Star," and other players knew their powers and how to respond. *Star Wars Episode 1: Racer* involved rushing round in "pod racers." There was a weapon, the "flame jet," so powerful that no one was allowed to have it. *Pokémon Blue* was a chasing game played by a mixed group, running in a circle, sitting on the ground, and chanting, "Pokémon, Pokémon, Pokémon Garadoss." *Pokémon* cards, so immensely popular in the previous year, were largely out of fashion, but trading with *Pokémon* Game-Boy games, done by linking machines together, was very popular indeed. Linda was assured that Game Boy machines were allowed in school as long as teachers did not see them! Computer games with which they were familiar, such as alien games (*Quake Tree Arena*), action games (*Indiana Jones*) and cartoon games (*Yoshi*) also were influencing the games that they played.

The most significant new addition, however, was *Harry Potter*. In Milton Keynes, Kate recorded one of the changes that had occurred: "We like to invent new Harry Potter tales and other times we copy the books." At the same time, in a small rural village school, Jenny recorded:

> At the edge of the playground . . . on one wall is an activity center designed to look like the workings of a machine. It has tubes to collect rainwater, which in turn drives cogs and wheels and many components and pistons which can be moved by the children.

Here, a group of four 7- to 8-year-olds (three boys and a girl) were muttering and chanting and performing various tasks with the "machine." On discreet observation, it became clear that the children were playing *Harry Potter*. Their discussions involved "hogwarts," "Hedwig," and "Dumbledore." The children had assumed roles and were inventing tales for the intrepid Harry. At one point, the children formed a huddle and chanted, "He who must not be named will soon be dead; Harry'll get him with the scar on his head." Later, Jenny talked to them:

> They told me about the games that they play; they told me that they pretend Harry's enemy's coming and they must make spells and potions to get rid of him. . . . They used a small blackboard attached to the wall to write spells on.

They told me that no one ever plays Voldemort (Harry's enemy) as "it would be too scary and no one knows what he is like." A child told me that his friend became very worried because he had used the name Voldemort and not the accepted "he who cannot be named."

Heather, in another village lower school, also had encountered Harry Potter:

At the other end of the playground, some eight-and nine-year-old boys were engaged in dramatic play focused on the super hero, Harry Potter. There seems to be no structured dialogue to this game, but using key words and phrases, they give evidence of a repertoire of words from one of their favourite stories. The six boys start to run around the playground accompanied by appropriate sound effects. They seem to have a deep knowledge of the fantasy genre, gained from their reading but also from media texts. Harry Potter is a new phenomenon in children's book publishing, having its own audio cassettes, web sites, computer games and forthcoming film. After a few minutes, four of the boys throw themselves onto the ground. I am intrigued to understand this development . . . I discover that they are role playing the characters of Harry, Hermione, Ron Weesley, and the twins, George and Fred. The setting is Hogwarts and they are playing a game of quidditch, played on a broomstick, the aim of which is to look for the 'Golden Snitch'. This involves a special manoeuvre known as Ronski Feint which involved the protagonist or seeker diving towards the ground pretending they have seen it . . . the skill of the leading seeker is, just prior to diving into the ground, to swoop skywards in flight, tricking the other seekers into crashing into the ground . . .

Heather felt that "the narratives brought into school from home, through literary texts, TV, film, CD-ROM, computer games, or the Internet must not be devalued or rejected by the class teacher."

The observations in 2001 also drew attention to other relatively new phenomena. In an urban lower school, Louise focused on the way children were using collectible soft toys in their play:

The evidence in the playground is that boys up to 8 share this addiction, bringing their favorite ones to school and involving them in their games. Sam, aged 8, was delighted to show me his new dragon, Puff, and read out the rhyming description on its tag. . . .

She also noticed that

many children were involved in games based on *Pokémon, Bouncing Bone Heads*, and *Beanie Babies*. . . . They were not necessarily playing with the objects, but using them as a stimulus to develop very involved drama based games requiring discussion, collaboration, negotiating, and listening.

She watched three 6-year-old girls:

> One had Mystic, the unicorn *Beanie Baby*, and for most of the game, it hung out of her coat pocket while the following activity was carried out. All three girls leapt out of the school door and wove their way around the playground flapping their arms. I later found out that these were their wings. They finally met up in a grassy area of the playground well away from the school buildings. They gathered leaves, twigs, and grass from the nature area and arranged them in little piles.

In conversation with Louise, the girls described how they were making little nests. This was clearly an intertextual reference to *The Lion, the Witch and the Wardrobe* because they told Louise, "Our teacher read us the bit about the fawn who lived in the forest." Louise thought it also referred to *Bambi*— they were all familiar with the Disney video. As they played, she overheard their discussion: "Unicorns don't lay eggs; they have babies." However, they agreed to eggs and collected food for the expectant unicorn. These collectible little toys come with their own texts printed on their labels:

Mystic

DOB 21/5/94

Once upon a time so far away,
A unicorn was born one day in May;
Keep Mystic with you, she's a prize;
You'll see the magic in her blue eyes!

Louise quoted an article she had read: "The manufacturers of bean bag–type soft toys will stop at no permutation of cuteness to part parents from their money and confirm little girls in their addiction to collectable soft toys" (Neumark, 2000, p. 63).

Meanwhile, Frances, in a lower school in a small town, found that the children's preferred games included cat and mouse, *Digimon, Football Heads*, and toys, although she was unable to see these in action because "these games were encouraging unacceptable behavior and were banned." However, she noted, "Children are changing the names and rules slightly and playing them out of earshot. *Pokémon* cards and *Football Heads* are now hiding in coat pockets." She was the first to mention another new craze, *Power Pods*—miniature dolls of famous footballers in a personalized club kit with oversize heads in hollow chocolate balls (similar to *Kinder Eggs*). The children sang the song from the TV ads: "Football crazy, chocolate mad, Grab a Power Pod and play football with the lads." It was sung constantly. Girls changed it to "netball crazy." Frances felt that TV had promoted *Power Pods* to cater to boys' interests. Boys played with these and also role-played the characters. She observed a boy after scoring, shouting like a commentator: "And Beckham scores a fantastic goal for Man United." Later, she saw him doing the same thing with his toy. She also observed the girls playing *Powerpuff* girls, a TV program for girls similar to *Power Rangers*, albeit rather more tongue-in-cheek. The characters are Buttercup, Bubbles, and Blossom, who fight monster villains, each a different color and with different powers.

Keeley produced five transcripts of conversations with boys and girls from each year group:

> I found that casual conversations were the most effective way of gaining insight into the children's world. . . . I was impressed by the speed at which the children can get into role, shift register, and take on the phrasing and vocabulary of a range of speakers in their play.

In addition to finding out about traditional games and rhymes, Keeley found media links and computer influences. She said, "The Web site that a child told me about, *Neotel*, shows a link between old and new crazes and the ever-developing maturity and detail of children's interests and activities." She agreed that "children will continue to be emotionally engaged with popular culture outside school," concluding that "we need to achieve a balance between recognizing children's pleasure in this culture whilst at the same time providing them with the tools to deconstruct its ideology" (Marsh, 1999, p. 157).

Meanwhile, another trainee provided evidence of a new craze emerging: mobile phones and text messages. Phones were banned but practice in texting went on in exercise books and notes passed between the children, such as "cuL8er," "ru up4it?" "n-eway," "up2u." Creating this kind of private communication proved irresistible. Here again, banning by teachers continued to provide an incentive for many games.

As in 2000, WWF wrestling continued to form a popular resource for children's play. Jan observed children playing at wrestling, taking on characters from WWF: the Rock, Stonecold Steve, Triple H. Two children wrestled, and one was the commentator and referee: "Well, the Rock's holding Stone Cold Steve down with a hard arm. SCS isn', he's just laying 1..2..3." He counts him out. (They played this only while teachers were out of sight). Jan commented:

> Wrestling is a show of high hyped drama and action. . . . When I researched into wrestling I found that it was not just about fighting. Wrestlers take on a character and normally have a name that matches their style like "Bossman." He comes dressed in a shirt and bosses everyone around. The "Undertaker," dressed in black, looks very solemn and scary. He usually has funeral music playing as he enters the ring. "William Regal" wears a suit and drinks cups of

tea surrounded by the British flag. . . . When I looked at the names of all the wrestlers, many of them played with words and spellings. "Justin Credible," "Sgt. Slaughter," "K Kwik." Some names referred to famous people or film stars: "The Godfather," "Billy Gun."

In contrast, Michelle observed very young children in a reception class (age, 4 years+) playing *Powerpuff Girls*, shooting with laser beam eyes. She noticed gender preferences for TV series children enjoyed playing. Girls played games based on *Pingu*, *Hollyoaks*, *Pokémon*, and *Digimon*, whereas boys played games related to films they had seen on the *Cartoon Network* (*Ed, Ed and Eddie*), rude and funny, and recreated scenarios from computer games (e.g., a game called *Link and Sonic* based on *Sonic the Hedgehog*, which involved the character Sonic and his friend Link). The aim of the game was to kill invisible people that only they could see, and this was achieved by jumping onto them. Link had a special sword that protected him. Girls did not join in these games.

The passion for *Pokémon* had not diminished. Trainees were finding it all over the area. Anna, working in an urban junior school, observed that

> children of all years and both genders seemed to enjoy the *Pokémon* craze, ar-
> ranging to swap cards, pretending to be characters and singing the theme
> tune. . . . I observed a group of year 4 boys and girls playing together. They
> were taking it in turns to choose weapons with which to destroy each other.
> They talked about firepower, wind power, and water power. They all seemed
> to know exactly whose turn it was and how badly injured they were, accord-
> ing to what they had been attacked with. *Pokémon* cards are banned! But this
> showed how they can still bring their favorite subjects into school.

In the same school, 9-year-old boys were playing *Gladiators* with clear rules, whereas the younger children took small toys to the playground. Many of these were related to computer games and TV such as Metanic Robots, *Pokémon* characters, Powerpuff Girls, and Dinosaurs.

On a large urban playground, Paula felt that

> the playground can be described as a multilayered text. The children must
> develop an accommodating idiolect to become involved in the text. In the
> playground, children learn to slip in and out of ways of talking . . . as they play
> different games. The language of tag is different from the language of football,
> clapping rhymes, and make believe. . . . The games themselves are rich and di-
> verse texts.

She also noticed their intertextuality:

> Take for example, the band Steps and their song *5678*, which is a current fa-
> vorite with year 4 girls (aged 8–9). With its repetition, word play, rhythm, non-

sense language, intertextuality, reference to boyfriends and its dance routine, it could be a clapping song.

Overall, the trainees were noting similar media influences and commenting on the extent to which these emerged in the children's narrative games and how these games reflected the "media discourse with which children interact daily" (Marsh & Millard, 2000, p. 5).

2001–2002: CONTINUITY AND CHANGE

In 2001, the newcomer on the playground was Harry Potter. There had been three sightings in different schools. The books were coming out thick and fast, accompanied by very successful marketing and media hype. But the release of the film at the end of the year meant a big change. In 2000 *Pokémon* was undoubtedly the favorite game. There were sightings in almost every school and much banning of the merchandise, cards, stickers, and models. In 2001, there seemed to be not so much a tailing off, although *Pokémon* was evidently less trendy, as a diversification with the arrival of the similar Digimon and more diverse merchandise: card games, stickers, and collectibles relating to different films and computer games. For the girls, the major attraction was evidently the TV program *Popstars* and the creation of the band *Hearsay*, while *Beanie Babies* and other small collectibles also were very popular and appearing regularly on playgrounds. In March 2002, WWF and *Pokémon* still were two of the most reported games. However, they were outnumbered by games related to both the Harry Potter film and the books that both boys and girls were playing. These were recorded in 19 schools. Another change was the number of girls playing games related to the TV *Pop Idol* program, recorded in nine schools. The Disney film *Monsters Inc.* and various Playstation games also had a significant impact.

In all these ways, the children's playground games continued to reflect different media promotions and merchandise. However, children are not simply responding to these texts or events in a passive way. A look at what the students have recorded shows the extent to which children from 4 to 11 years of age creatively absorb this material into their play culture, exploring themes and issues that they make their own through imaginative narratives. A look at what the children say and do shows the extent to which these games, far from deadening their imagination, feed and extend possibilities for new narratives.

In March 2002, Clare interviewed three 8-year-old boys:

Child 1:   "Well, we get our ideas from Card Captors and *Pokémon*. . . . Me and Jacob had the idea of using transporters—like little machines, walking transfers."

Child 2:   "Transport us in the worlds . . ."

Child 1:   ". . . bringing the future into the world of dragons and back into the present—into our normal world . . ."

Child 3:   ". . . and magical world."

Clare: "What is it called?"

All: "Dragon Cards."

Listening to them, Clare realized that these "cards" were entirely imaginary. She writes: "They go on to describe how they fire arrows through the cards, which unleash the dragons and allow them to battle with them." She feels that they have drawn upon a range of media influences here:

> Card games such as *Pokémon* and *Card Captors* have inspired child 1 to come up with a game that has similarities to those games mentioned, but with his own imaginative input. They have produced imaginary cards of dragons with varying powers. The three children all know what the different cards are and what they do, without having actually to see them. They have given the dragon cards names such as "Ghost Dragon," "Thunder Dragon," and "Ice Dragon." These represent the elements and what the children might class as dangerous things. The idea of magical worlds comes from their different media experiences. The words they use clearly reflect these. Included in their game is a city called "Diagon City," which has been taken from *Harry Potter*. Another of their interests is the TV program, *Dungeons and Dragons*. Their game includes weapons, guardians, and creatures of power.

Interesting, all these are constituent parts of the archetypal myths that have underpinned fantasy fiction from the oral tradition to *Star Wars*.

Clare: "Do you have any accessories, bits you need to play the game?"

Child 1:   "Well, we need the cards."

Child 2:   "The stick that we use to fly on and we use to shoot the animals,

Child 1:   . . . and me and Jacob and John have just started a story . . ."

Child 3:   ". . . the Fairy Dragon."

Child 1:   "No, Ice Dragon—our first ever card is the Fairy Dragon, and our second card . . . is the Ghost Dragon."

Clare: "Do you buy the cards?"

Child 1:   "No, we pretend we have them."

Clare: "Oh, do you make them up?"

All: "Yes."

Child 1:   "We find them—we can't capture the champion levels, which are Ice Dragon, Fire Dragon, or Lightning Dragon, because they are more powerful than any card—so we have made up cards—mine's the Ghost Card."

Child 3:   "Mine's the Demon Card."

Clare: "Do you have those? Do you draw them out or do you pretend you have got them?"

Child 1:   "We pretend we've got them."

As the transcript of this long discussion shows, the imaginative involvement of these three boys in their game is impressive.

Clare: "And you made the whole thing up yourselves?"

Child 3:   "Yep, with a few ideas from other things."

This heightened involvement is illustrated by examples the trainees have collected, and on which they frequently comment. Natasha writes:

> Most prevalent on the playground were "pretend" games. They varied between those that used stories and characters obviously derived from popular media and those that involved more of the children's own imaginative construction. The children were extremely keen and able to describe the narratives of their games. They appeared to be very intense. There were many games based directly on stories or themes taken from the media such as *Harry Potter, Buffy the Vampire Slayer, Blind Date* and *Pop Idol.*

Natasha also observed boys absorbed in playing with James Bond cards:

> These are collected from magazines, and play involves voluntary exchanging and play for cards based upon strength and weapons described in each character's profile. The game leads to discussion about characters, and there is a great deal of competition about who knows more about the cards and also the films. I found that boys would draw designs for computer games based on the cards.

Many of the games required the players to have considerable knowledge to enable them to construct games. Carla saw children playing "a narrative game based on ideas from the Disney and Pixar film *Monsters Inc.* (2002)." She felt that to create this game, the children needed to have a "sound knowledge and understanding of the characters, setting, and plot to make it into their own version." She also noticed that "when playing the game, the children were able to demonstrate clear comparisons between the good and bad monsters through their use of language and actions."

Child B: "You have sharp teeth and claws."

Child C: "Yeah, like Randall. I like being him. He's nasty and cheats and changes color."

Carla, like many others, also witnessed the role-playing of the very popular 2002 TV program, *Pop Idol*:

> I interviewed a group of year 4 girls (ages 8–9 years) who were carrying out a singing contest imitating the structure and content of *Pop Idol*. . . . The girls took on roles of the TV personalities and popstars. They demonstrated a clear understanding of the rules and structure of the game, allowing each contestant to sing a song while the "judges" sensitively listened and gave support.

On another playground, Sonia observed the judges being less supportive:

> Based on the talent-spotting television show, girls reenacted the audition, selection, and rejection process of the contest. As in the show, the judges were portrayed with certain personality traits. On one occasion, I witnessed a "judge" criticizing a "contestant" with a continuous series of derogatory comment. Interestingly, these were all in the form of similes, such as "Your voice sounds like a strangled baboon," and "Your hair is like the straw on a scarecrow's head." As this was expected of the judge in question, the remarks were taken in good part, and contestants were expected to react accordingly by either leaving the "stage" in tears or stomping off.

Sonia noticed how the girls were enjoying playing with language in this way, vying with each other to find alternative ways to describe performances, using terms such as "incredible," "unique," and "outstanding."

2003: HARRY POTTER, IRAQ, AND BEYBLADES

In 2003 a powerful media influence was sweeping the playgrounds that students were visiting: the US/UK invasion of Iraq. Hiding places around the periphery of playgrounds were being described as "bunkers." A group of girls carrying rolled up bundles in their arms told a student, "We are taking our babies to the Anderson shelter. Our husbands have gone to the war." In another school, a group of boys and girls were playing a game that involved falling from airplanes. And, inevitably, jokes were appearing. Mark reports on the influence of the conflict in Iraq and of TV programs in March, 2003: "Why are their no Iraqis in *Star Trek*?" "Because it's set in the future." And Catherine discovered that in 2003 "the new craze is *Beyblades*. Forget *Pokémon, Beyblades* is the new uprising fad." She asked a group of boys how they played it, "and I was bombarded with comments about characters, toys, and lunch boxes." She comments that Barratt, Bromley, and Marsh (2000) believed that it is "this intertextuality that makes these products so exciting." Catherine found that the boys were engrossed by it and knew a lot of information from memory.

> I was particularly impressed by their knowledge of character names as these were so complex. Not only could they name the characters, they also were taking on their roles. Through extensive knowledge of the cartoon program, they became the Beyblades or the boys who own them.

Catherine also noticed a phenomenon that has emerged while the trainees have been observing children's play: The fad of 2000 may have vanished by 2003. As *Ghostbusters* and *Power Rangers* have given way to *Pokémon* and *Harry Potter*, so *Pokémon* is threatened by *Beyblades*. Children evidently are not simply being seduced by consumer capitalism, but have some power to choose and manipulate the content of their play.

Catherine: "What are you playing?"

Boy A: "Beyblades."

Catherine: "How do you play it?"

Boy B: "Have you seen the program on the telly?"

Catherine: "Is it like *Pokémon*?"

Boy A: "It has the same pictures but different people and fighters."

Boy C: "We aren't allowed to bring the toys to school. They are dangerous."

Boy B: "The Beyblades are round and you pull a long thing out and they spin off. You aim at other ones in a battle and see who wins."

Boy C: "The people own the Beyblades and watch them fight . . ."

Boy A: "They have new names, not like *Pokémon*; it is much better."

Boy D: "Yeah, my favorite is Master Dronza; he is really powerful and wins lots. I'm going to be Ray and Master Dronza. Pow! Pow!" [*imitates throwing a Beyblade*].
(Catherine, March, 2003)

CONCLUSION

Interviewing these children is giving Catherine an insight into the way they engage with media texts and make them their own. The point of this small-scale ethnographic research activity was to enable the trainees to experience firsthand the alternative literacies in which children engage outside the classroom, and to consider how this might lead to broader literacy practices in their teaching. The trainees involved in this research project were observing and discussing the multimodal nature of children's experience of media texts, in which "each story exists in a veritable cosmos of texts all revolving around a core fiction" (Mackey, 2002, p. 31). Looking at their pupils' playground culture showed trainees how children deal imaginatively with "a wildly confusing textual world where technological and commercial options press for ... attention" (Mackey, 2002, p. 38) and are able to create versions that are meaningful to themselves.

This research also gave the trainees a chance to explore for themselves the claims being made for the inclusion of popular culture in the primary school curriculum (Mackey, 2002; Marsh, 2003; Millard, 2003). In this respect, it helped them to take part in the wider debate about dominant literacy practices within school, and to consider the existence of multiple literacies and the need to look beyond the focus on print literacy, which dominates their training. Lambirth (2003) suggested that

> working with a unitary model of literacy, as contemporary curricula do, arguably creates a danger that it will inevitably, implicitly ignore other literacy practices that occur in homes, working places, and other social settings away from the school. (p. 11)

Lambirth (2003) has found that teachers generally are wary about the inclusion of popular culture texts in their teaching despite the very strong arguments for more appropriate forms of literacy for the education of children in the 21st century (Kress, 2003; Street, 2002). The evidence that the trainees collected from the children on the playground gave them insight into the pervasive influence of new technologies in their pupils' lives and the extent of their engagement with popular culture. Their analysis of their data will act as a springboard for their own understanding of the extent to which, as newly qualified teachers, they will need to address the "multiliteracies" needed to function in the modern, media-saturated world. They will be ready to consider Millard's (2003) notion of a "transformative pedagogy," which proposes a model of literacy that effectively fuses children's cultural interests with the school requirements. This "literacy of fusion," Millard (2003) argued, "relies heavily on a teacher's attentiveness to the interests and skills brought into the classroom and their [sic] skill in helping children transform what they already know into stuff that will give them agency in a wider world and allow them to become more critical of their own and others' meanings" (p. 7).

The independent research of the trainee teachers has given them a starting point. They have been particularly attentive to children's interests.

Their careful interviews show how creatively children interpret media texts and take ownership of them. Seeing how children subvert media messages and mock the texts they are using has helped the trainees to recognize that children are hardly the passive recipients that adults often fear. The trainees also have become increasingly aware of ways in which teachers are effectively cutting themselves off from significant aspects of children's everyday lives by constantly banning media-based crazes, toys, and games from school playgrounds. By the end of their research they can see that there is a powerful argument for welcoming these. The activities the trainees have observed and recorded are both multimodal and intertextual, ranging across visual, audiovisual, and verbal media forms. They are a reflection of the "integrated marketing" that characterizes children's contemporary media culture. Schools have a task ahead of them if they are to address the multiliteracies needed to function in the modern media-saturated world. The trainees involved in this playground research hopefully are better prepared to take on this challenge.

ACKNOWLEDGMENT

The author thanks all the members of the De Montfort University Year 3 Primary B Ed. Language in Education course, 2000–2003.

REFERENCES

Barratt, K., Bromley, H., & Marsh, J. (2000). Playing with Pokémon. *The Primary English Magazine, 6*(2), 8–12.

Bishop, J., & Curtis, M. (Eds.). (2000). *Play today in the primary school playground: Life, learning, and creativity.* Buckingham: The Open University Press.

Bromley, H. (2002). Meet the Simpsons. *The Primary English Magazine, 7,* 7.

Dyson, A. H. (2001). Where are the childhoods in childhood literacy? An exploration in outer (school) space. *Journal of Early Childhood Literacy, 1,* 1.

Grugeon, E. (2000). Girls' playground language and lore: What sort of texts are these? In E. Bearne & V. Watson (Eds.), *Where texts and children meet* (pp. 98–112). London: Routledge.

Keaney, B., & Lucas, B. (1994). *Looking at language.* Cambridge, England: Cambridge University Press.

Kress, G. (2003). *Literacy in the new media age.* London: Routledge.

Lambirth, A. (2003). They get enough of that at home: Understanding aversion to popular culture in schools. *READING Literacy and Language, 37*(1), 9–13.

Mackey, M. (2002). Extreme literacies and contemporary readers. *English in Education, 36*(2).

Marsh, J. (1999). Teletubby tales: Popular culture and media education. In J. Marsh & E. Hallet (Eds.), *Desirable literacies* (pp. 153–174). London: Sage.

Marsh, J. (2003). Contemporary models of communicative practice: Shaky foundations in the foundation stage? *English in Education, 37*(1).

Marsh, J., & Millard, E. (2000). *Literacy and popular culture: Using children's culture in the classroom.* London: RGP.

Millard, E. (2003). Towards a literacy of fusion: New times, new teaching, and learning? *READING Literacy and Language, 371*), 3–8.

Moyles, J. (Ed.). (1994). *The excellence of play.* Buckingham, England: The Open University Press.

Neumark, V. (2000). *Times Educational Supplement Primary Magazine,* Spring.

Opie, I. (1993). *The people in the playground.* Oxford: Oxford University Press.

Opie, I., & Opie, P. (1959). *The lore and language of schoolchildren.* Oxford: Oxford University Press.

Simatos, A., & Spencer, K. (1992). *Children and media.* Liverpool: Manutius Press.

Street, B. (2002). *Literacy and development.* London: Routledge.

PART

II

CHILDREN AND
DIGITAL MEDIA

7

The Internet Playground

Ellen Seiter

Computers often evoke strong feelings in parents. On the one hand, there is a tangle of generational and class values, and on the other a desire to recruit children's play for vocational training. At first computers appeared to be the ultimate fulfillment of adult desires to see play turned to a purposeful end, to use play for progress and child development—all this without children noticing the beneficial effects. Computers and the exploration of the Internet would make learning fun for children highly motivated by their intrinsic aptitude for computers.

For upper middle-class parents anxious about increasing workplace competition, computers apprentice children to a lucrative, employable future as competent professionals of the digital age. Working-class parents therefore saw in their children's computer use the promise of white-collar employment. Politicians and school reformers placed their bets on computers to save the messy and unpredictable system of public education. New technologies promised to streamline the business of education, virtually teacher-proofing the classroom.

All these attempts to harness children's fascination with computers for instruction epitomized adult efforts to recruit play for progress, for the future. On the other hand, children's interests, habits, and abilities in the online environment became the subject of intense interest by marketers. Hardware and software companies promoted the idea that children, with their instinctive attraction to computers and their admirable lack of technophobia, would be the gateway into homes. Children could convince parents to buy the hardware (and update it frequently so it would be suitable for the latest technical advances in gaming), subscribe to Internet service providers, and buy an extra telephone line or a DSL connection.

However, children circumvented the seriousness of parental plans for computer usage. At computer labs installed at high cost in public schools across the United States, children feign doing homework while playing games, e-mailing one another, cruising the Web, and circumventing the (often highly arbitrary) filtering software. At home, children convert the computer into a toy, thus recruiting it for "the empowerment of play rather than as teaching machines that can replace what parents want their children to learn" (Sutton-Smith, 1997, p. 145). Actually, the computer is much closer to a television set, used by children to peruse popular music, fashion, toys, video games, television celebrities, sports, and gossip.

Children's pursuit of play with and through computers was readily assisted by the host of entrepreneurs who entered the business of selling to children in the 1990s. Firms large and small envisioned grand schemes of reaching parents' pocketbooks through their children. These entrepreneurs probably had a more realistic idea than parents or even school administrators of what children actually would do with computers, that is, play with them.

Nevertheless, the entrepreneurs made many strategic errors, for instance, in predicting that children's impulse spending habits could be recruited for online retailers, and that teens would desert the mall for their computer screens. The vast majority of these firms have gone under. But their commercial ventures helped shift parents' and children's perception of the domestic computer from that of a learning tool to that of an entertainment appliance.

PLAY IN THE COMPUTER LAB

In 1999, the author founded an open computer lab in an urban, working-class elementary school in southern California. For the past 3 years, she has observed children's play on the Web from the lab's 15 i-mac computers with high-speed Internet access.

The author teaches an after-school class 4 to 5 hr each week in which students write, research, and photograph news stories for a community newspaper. Because they do a great deal of our research for stories on the Web, the first idea for writing that comes to the children usually is some aspect of the entertainment industries.[1] Play on computers is the hook that

---

[1]For a discussion of attempts to shift children's attention from entertainment topics to local news reporting, see the author's journal article, Children Reporting On-Line: The Cultural Politics of the Computer Lab, *Television and New Media*, (2004, May).

draws children to the free class. Nearly 150 students ages 8 to 11 years have attended since the program began. The school is under fire with the superintendent as a so-called low-performing school, so the teachers rarely have time for computer class. The principal prefers that they stick to matters "directly related to academic achievement"—that is, improved scores on standardized tests (Seiter, forthcoming).

Fewer than 10% of the children in the after-school class have functioning computers at home, and even fewer have Internet access. Many of the parents make sacrifices to ensure that their child is available for the class each week. Unfamiliar with computers themselves, and repeatedly refusing any invitations to enter the lab or get a demonstration of the equipment, they are nonetheless very anxious that their children know the technology. The author designed the course with the intention of extending children's understanding of software beyond game playing to more sophisticated tools of expression such as digital imaging, layout, and word processing. It also was an effort to bridge the digital divide by bringing some resources of the university into communities in which few children consider college to be even a remote possibility.

At least half of the class time is spent by the children enjoying open access to the Internet through a T-1 (high-speed) line. To the surprise of most of the students, open play and exploration is encouraged, and students enjoy free, unlimited use of a laser printer. Five generalizations can be made about the nature of these children's play with computers, based on observations, interviews, and daily fieldnotes collected between 1999 and 2002:

1. Browsing the Web is the consistent activity of choice over using installed software on the computer, which included games such as Bugdom, and other CD-ROM games. About 20% of the students preferred to work in KidPix, a versatile, well-designed art program.

2. Television holds the tightest connection to the Internet in the children's minds. This is reflected in their favorite sites, which largely correspond to television channels (Disney, Fox Kids, Kids WB, Nick, and MTV) or to programs (Rug Rats, Charmed, Digimon, Dragonball Z, X-Men, and Worldwide Wrestling Federation).

3. Children locate new Web sites through word of mouth rather than search engines, portals, or banners. Despite the fact that few of the children had online access outside the class, they frequently heard about new Web sites or newly available features of familiar Web sites. Their information sharing about Web sites appeared to be highly efficient. They often knew about Web sites such as neopets.com (discussed later) before the author had heard about them in the press. Often, children entered the class with a destination in mind, and once a couple of children visited a new site and found it fun or interesting, news of it spread through the class within minutes.

4. All the favorite sites were those with video and audio streaming as well as the capability of handling large amounts of traffic. Students often succeeded in downloading a variety of plug-ins—with no formal instruction of any kind but lots of peer tutoring—to view and hear video clips. Videos of favorite wrestlers screaming threats or come-ons have been perennial favorites, as have music videos of female pop stars, especially Jennifer Lopez, Christina Aguilera, Aaliyah, and Destiny's Child. Some of the students' most expert manipulations of the technology were manifest in these activities, which they learned from one another.

5. Game playing was the preferred activity of younger students. Older students, or those who had attended for more than 1 year, gravitated toward fan activities. Printing out pictures of favorite singers, actors, or wrestlers—to be used for bedroom displays—was the most avidly and excitedly pursued activity. The computer seemed to function as a transitional object, moving children from playing with toys and games (e.g., collecting Digimon cards or Barbie images) to pursuing media-based fan activities. For children such as these, with very little disposable income, the Internet provided the equivalent of teen magazines and fan club materials that were intensely sought after and prized.

In this chapter, the author considers two popular web activities that constitute forms of children's play: one pursued at the lab and one unavailable to children without an e-mail address, such as those in the author's class. What can these examples tell us about likely future efforts to make money from children's use of the Web? How will the digital divide affect children's access to preferred forms of play online? The first example in this chapter is neopets.com, a popular and profitable role-playing game, which stood out as the exception to the rule of TV-driven Web materials (no television cartoon exists for the concept, although Viacom has contracted to make video games featuring the characters). The author first heard about the neopets Web site in June of 2000 (the site was commercially launched in February 2000), when the children in her class picked it up as a favorite site. The second example is Instant Messaging, the peer-to-peer chat software that is wildly popular among teens, and spreading rapidly to younger children—those with an Internet connection at home and fixed e-mail addresses.

NEOPETS

Whereas entrepreneurs have despaired of capturing the children's market on the Web, and hundreds of Web sites have gone under since the mid-1990s, the business press repeatedly praises neopets.com as a model for future efforts. Neopets constitutes one of the most successful—and one of the "stickiest"—Web sites yet designed. According to recent accounts, 30% of

U.S. tweens (8- to 12-year-olds) rank neopets.com as their top site, followed by Warnerbros.com and Cartoonnetwork.com. In Canada it is the number one destination for male teens, who spend an average of 576 minutes each month on the site, and it is the second favorite site for girls after MSN Messenger (Dennis, 2002).

In June 2002, the community of neopets owners was estimated at 32 million. Among its members, 39% are 12 years of age or younger, 40% are 13 to 17 years of age, and 21% are older than 18 years (Winding, 2002).

The geography of neopets.com is dense and complex. The site is scaffolded like a video game, in which the investment of many hours of play is rewarded by qualitatively different levels of access to the game. As an online environment, neopets includes such proven favorite activities on the Web as gambling, simulation games, and competition against anonymous online gamers. A staff of 30 game designers updates and monitors the content each day.

Neopets is a role-playing game, in which players own creatures that are part *Tamagotchi* and part *Pokémon*. They also are highly reminiscent of *My Little Pony* and its many imitators (Seiter, 1993). Each pet has a cute name and body (owing much to anime, although the original material was designed by British college students), and comes with a variable set of traits, which range from their fighting abilities to their health and personality.

Neopets closely modeled *Pokémon's* strategies for cross-gender appeal. Neopets players may gravitate toward caretaking and adoption or abandonment and neglect; assume pleasing, friendly behaviors or mean and nasty ones; and accumulate points through combat or shopping.

When players log on to neopets, they navigate a series of worlds embedded in the game where they can gain points to expand their collection of pets, buy food or services for their pets, or engage in combat with other pets. The worlds resemble a Tolkien story crossed with a theme park: The Lost Desert, Tyrannia, Faerieland, Terror Mountain, Mystery Island, Virtupets Space Station, or Haunted Woods. In each world there are stores and games. The stores stock food and accessories that can be acquired through purchase with neopoints, or can be bid for, as in an e-Bay auction. Players themselves host the stores, and much of the fascination in the game has to do with trading assets player to player. Neopets players can establish their own online store offering accessories and treats for their neopets. These take the form of pet pets, toys and games for their pets, or even books to read to them. At this much deeper level of play, product placement occurs. For example, neopet owners can acquire Capri Sun drinks to feed their pets, or Hot Wheels cars or Diva Starz dolls for their play.

Neopets offers games in the form of puzzles, action, or a category termed "Luck/Chance." The aspect of neopets closest to *Pokémon*—the old-fashioned way of winning points in video games—is participation in battle sites, in which a neopet is placed in competition against a single combatant, and the player, choosing from a store of weapons, moves, or skills, attempts to win the game. For players uninterested in combat and those lacking the lore and strategy to succeed in battle, points can be earned by viewing advertising, and this usually allows the player to gain many more points than could be had playing a game. The simplest approach is to visit Web sites for Cartoon Network, for recently released films, or for various retail items and services, such as comparison shopping portals. For example, a visit to the Spy Kids theater (produced by Cartoon Network's parent company) may gain a player 250 points. But a visit to a comparison shopping Web site, in which the required task is to get prices for three different electronic devices (digital cameras, MP3 players, and DVD players) can earn a player 1,650 points.

As a business enterprise, neopets is selling information about the children and young adults who are its fans instead of selling a media product itself. The more information a user surrenders, the better she or he is positioned to play the game, to publish fan drawings, stories, or poems, and to gain neopoints.

More lucrative exercises require divulging more data. Neopets.com rewards those who disclose personal information (address, zip code, telephone number, e-mail address) and consumer preferences (answers to polls; choices of name, color, and style; desirable sweepstakes prizes). Surveys offered on a regular basis collect information about age, gender, location, use of the Internet, and frequency of candy consumption. In one recent survey worth 800 points, kids were asked to name their favorite lollipops, select from a list of brands those they had heard of, and then describe "how they would feel" about having a new kind of Starburst lollipop on neopets. At the end of the survey, the participants are thanked "for helping make neopets a better place."

Another way of gaining neopoints is through gambling or games identified as "Luck/Chance." All kinds of games of chance have been adapted for Neopia: poker, blackjack, kino, bingo, roulette, slots, and lottery. Neopets, like hundreds of other Web promotions, introduces children to the pleasures of gambling long before they would be legally able to enter a Las Vegas casino. Yet when they go to Las Vegas, they are likely to visit gaming palaces owned by Nintendo, hotels owned by the parent or partner companies of Cartoon Network, and casinos operated by the same conglomerates that dominate the children's media industry. Eased restrictions on gambling in the United States have produced one of the largest growth sectors of the U.S. entertainment industry. Their presence is very visible on the Web. Pop-up banners for card play and casino games appear on the children's screens every time they search the Web in the author's computer lab. To see neopets' development of this type of game playing on its site is to watch the recruitment of the next generation of gamblers—one of the "killer apps" of the Internet—as much as it is to see kids recruited for watching cartoons on TV.

Neopets strives to add the same compulsion to play that has characterized video games, causing such a concern for adults. As in *Pokémon* gold and silver versions, neopets undergoes changes while a player is logged off, including sickening from neglect and becoming obstinate about following commands in battle. New materials and new games are posted daily, and players soon recognize that playing at less popular times of the day will be rewarded with greater ease in gaining points, or better access to specially prized areas in the Web site. Thus, neopets rewards daily, obsessive play in a myriad of ways.

Meanwhile, *Advertising Age* commissioned neopets to carry out a study of the Internet compared with television and impressions of advertising. Neopets also has trademarked the concept of "immersive advertising." It boasts Kraft foods, Nabisco, Proctor and Gamble, Disney, Universal, and Warner Brothers as its clients, and calls itself the "leading online global youth network." For its clients, neopets offers extensive tracking of brand awareness and adoption of its virtual premiums through pre- and post-campaign market research. A pleased Mattel executive remarked: "It's usually impossible to measure the exact effect of online initiatives but [these] data show you exactly how your brand is doing" (Winding, 2002). In its capacity as a market researcher, neopets projects that young people spend 12.1 hr on the Internet per week as compared with 7.5 hours watching television, that the Internet is preferred as a more engaging and less passive experience than television, but that it prefers advertising messages on television. Green, the CEO of neopets, also has now signed Viacom to begin producing neopets videogames and books (PR Newswire, 2002).

Neopets has been attacked by Ralph Nader's Commercial Alert for offensive tactics, but it is on the offensive in response to critics, citing its techniques as better than banner advertising (which no one will pay for anyway), and claiming that advertising represents "less than 1% of the site's content." As the CEO claims,

> Look at Saturday Morning television; the show lasts for 22 minutes, and 8 minutes of that is commercials. Our appeal is that there is so much content and it's all free—but we stay in business because of our advertisers.

The press release quotes one fan's response to criticisms of immersive advertising: "This is better than blatant and ugly banner advertising!" (Weintraub, 2001).

Neopets was the favorite Web site of many students in the author's computer class. The children most interested in neopets were girls who also had Internet access at home and were spurred on in their efforts to gain prestigious pets or possessions in the virtual environment by the accomplishments of a 19-year-old sibling. This sister, now moved away from home, was a source of great pride. The siblings showed off their sister's neopets store and worked hard (because navigating neopets can be time consuming as players wait to gain access to high-trafficked areas in the site) to display her certificates and artwork on the site.

This intense personal connection to neopets was highly motivating for the children. Looking at the site, the author is stunned at the embedded advertising and the commercial audacity evident in some of the schemes for gaining points. When the children in the author's class look at the site, they primarily see opportunities for victory, fame, and fortune in a fan community. After some reflection on why her reactions were so different from those of her students, the author realized that she should ask the children straight out why they thought neopets.com existed. To her surprise, the students almost universally agreed that neopets was just the cool idea of a lone individual who wanted others to share in the fun. Each child in the class had the same answer, more or less: Neopets was there because somebody somewhere had made up something neat, had a good idea and put it on the web for our enjoyment. Their image of the creator was that of a private hobbyist. Their high level of involvement helped to dull their awareness of the commercialism. As one ratings analyst said, in praising the site, "As a user, you're creating part of the content, and so you feel a personal, emotional connection to it" (Weintraub, 2001).

As part of the author's research, she has polled about 150 elementary school students about advertising on neopets.com. She has done so with children from affluent and poor backgrounds, in informal and in school settings. She sends children to the Web site and challenges them to be the first to find any advertising.

At the inner-city site where the author teaches, the students unanimously concluded at first that there was no advertising on neopets. These children are alert to all aspects of television advertising, and cynical about the motives of TV advertisers. At the next class meeting, the author explicitly identified sponsorship and product placement as things she considered to be advertising. Several children then became very engaged in the exercise of locating ads, printing out dozens of pages with product mentions buried deep within the games.

At the affluent, suburban elementary school, the children immediately identified the flashing banners as examples of advertising. They found no other examples, however, even after searching for 15 minutes.

Both groups of children answered "no" to the question "does it cost money to produce neopets?" All the children envisioned the creator of neopets as a lone individual whose costs did not exceed that of the personal computer used to make the Web site.

INSTANT MESSAGING

Instant Messaging is a software program that allows the user to "invite friends and family to a personal chat and keep track of them online." Originally Instant Messaging was a feature available only to America Online (AOL) subscribers. Then AOL decided to release the software, although not the open source code, to anyone with an Internet connection, including non-AOL subscribers. Between 1999 and 2002, children and teens elaborated Instant Messaging into many forms clearly recognizable as play that go far beyond simple conversation. These include disguise and impersonation, hide-and-go-seek (switching screen names to elude others), and practical jokes, as well as the more typical playground behaviors of posturing, teasing, and gossiping. Instant Messaging also is a group activity, both in real space—as children team up together in front of a computer screen to send messages to others—and in cyberspace, where dozens of chats are handled simultaneously by adept users (whose typing skills are prodigious).

Instant Messaging is much more than simple e-mailing because of the nuances and possibilities for game playing realized through simultaneous one-on-one conversations with large groups. As practiced most expertly by teenage girls, Instant Messaging is reminiscent of a world run more like a theater than like everyday life:

> Children play the parts of stage managers, directors, and actors all at the same time, moving freely about the parts as they get ready to put together their own shows for themselves, and even if the show never gets off the ground, all of these activities are known to them as their play or their games. (Sutton-Smith, 1997, p. 152)

This description is taken from Brian Sutton-Smith's (1997) account of fantasy play, but it touches upon the core of Instant Messaging. Youth engaged in it have established an autonomous culture of play, in which special languages and forms of expression, elaborate protocols of turn-taking, initiation and termination, dares, pranks, and masquerading under assumed identities are regular features. The special appeal stems in part from the ability to say things young people feel too inhibited to say in face-to-face conversation while the youth appear casual and spontaneous as they do so. Further excitement is added by the ability to see everyone on one's buddy list who currently is online. As Ostrom (2001) pointed out, "You just can't pick up the phone and see who's talking." According to Clifford (2001), 40% of teen users report using Instant Messaging to say something they do not want to say in person.

Instant Messaging seems to be functioning in a way that both facilitates interaction between boys and girls and disrupts cliques. Popular girls and nerdy boys find themselves in conversation much more often than is typical at school. Profiling—the linking of personal web pages to "buddy lists"—allows others to eavesdrop on the thoughts, tastes, inside jokes, proclivities, favorite quotes, and gossip of others, often providing an easy entrée into conversation.

Instant Messaging has speedily closed the "digital gender gap" that was the subject of such concern in the 1990s (Cassells & Jenkins, 1999). It has proved to be far more successful than the numerous forays into "pink software" by entrepreneurial feminists[2] and special interest sites targeting girls. If boys often were driven by their interest in video gaming to seek out the Web, girls remained a recalcitrant market for computer games, not because they do not enjoy playing games, but because they do not wish to spend their money on them, preferring instead to invest in music, makeup, clothes, and magazines.

As much as online gaming is now seen as the most potentially profitable Internet enterprise, it involves only a fraction of the youth involved in Instant Messaging. In summer 2001, the Pew Internet and American Life Project reported that 70% of teenagers with Internet access use Instant Messaging. Moreover, 70% of the teens who use it do so several times a week. The users of Instant Messaging now number more than 115 million (Barken, 2002).

Instant Messaging is extremely popular with teens, particularly those who spend the most hours online, and with girls. There is something hopeful about the runaway success of Instant Messaging, because it represents millions of children flocking to the Web for an activity that truly is interactive and noncommercial. To date, the only incursion of advertising into this realm has been the presence of a single banner ad on the top of the buddy list. Unlike neopets.com, which requires children to pay for their fun either by learning about brands or answering questions about their preferences, the Instant Messaging environment has been "free." However, its users also are a more attractive demographic segment than normal Web browsers, and hence of interest to marketers. They tend to be those with home Internet connections, speedier connections, and more regularly updated hardware and software.

Instant Messaging is a middle-class phenomenon. It requires a computer at home and an online connection from home because the computer's address is registered with the provider. Originally, a service just for AOL sub-

---

[2]For a discussion of the business strategies and the politics behind the girls' games movement, see Justine Cassells and Henry Jenkins (Eds.), *From Barbie to Mortal Kombat: Gender and Computer Games*. Cambridge, MA: MIT Press, 1999.

scribers, it currently is available through AOL/Instant Messenger to anyone who downloads the software.

The children at the author's computer lab are blocked from this kind of participation in online leisure activities by a variety of factors. Their parents do not qualify for a credit card; they do not have a working computer at home with sufficient speed to handle the latest software; or installment plan buying of computers is not available to their parents (Regional Technology Alliance, 2001). Because AIM requires the registration of a specific computer in a fixed location, doesn't work from public or classroom computers, which regularly post signs "no e-mail," "no chat," "no games." Working-class girls do not have a community of friends who also are online from home. Computer usage of this kind exists within the physical and social dimensions of family life, and these circumstances are dramatically different between working-class girls and their middle-class peers.

In 1999, AOL extended the "free ride" of Instant Messaging to nonsubscribers, knowing that building its base, collecting millions of e-mail addresses, and gaining dominance for its brand of software would prove to be valuable at a later date. Marketers are watching the Instant Messaging phenomenon very closely, envisioning ways to introduce advertising and product mentions into personal conversations. Icons are offered free to users so they can decorate their message boxes with an animation from the latest (Warner Brothers) movie release. To date, the most successful attempt to incorporate advertising is infiniteprofiles.com, a site that provides additional space for personalized web pages, but flashes pop-up ads over the profile when it is looked up. Instant Messaging includes a feature that allows individuals to include more text on a separate page. Typically, these features are used by kids and teens to write "inside jokes," to quote song lyrics, or to record diary-type entries (the "away messages" function in a similar fashion). Subsidiary Web sites now offer extended space for these profiles, which many kids update on a daily basis. Once on the subsidiary site, pop-up ads proliferate.

Other attempts to commercialize AIM include providing commercial "buddies" or add-on software that allows buddies to observe which Web sites their friends currently are visiting. Pilots for commercial buddies have included the band Radiohead and the brand Eddie Bauer. The idea is that the personal joking responses of a computer-generated buddy would be humorous enough to be considered an inoffensive intrusion, and that they must be actively downloaded by the participants. The CEO of the venture, Active Buddy, claims to be sensitive to the personal nature of Instant Messaging. Although in "the forefront of the expansion of Instant Messaging from a private to a commercial space," the CEO wants "to protect the space and keep it consumer friendly," saying "it has to be totally 100% opt in" (Guernsey, 2001). "Fatbubble" is one example of such add-on surveillance software. "Friends can then discuss or ridicule the sites their peers are visiting or share Web addresses or otherwise make social the solitary activity of Web surfing" (Zippern, 2001). Similar to handheld devices using GPS technology to map the whereabouts of mobile customers or friends, these applications constitute a sort of high-tech stalking. As television scholar Mark Andrejevic (2003) has argued, in reality television programs and the culture of the Internet, tolerance—even enthusiastic embrace—of surveillance is a strong current in contemporary popular culture. Instant Messaging does increase everyone's tolerance for surveillance. When one is on, who one might be talking to, and where one is surfing the Web are no longer secret information.

Unlike education researchers, who are pressured to quantify results of children's engagement with computers, play researchers can take solace in the forms of activity children seek out on the Web, properly recognizing these as more social, more subterranean, and less goal oriented than adults might like them to be. Partly because of developmental psychology's dominance as a model, childhood experts insist on seeing play as a kind of linear progress, as a prelude to real work. But play theorists have made a point of elaborating the ways that children's activities do not really measure up to simple models of imitation. In their provocative book, *Theorizing Childhood*, Allison James, Chris Jenks and Alan Prout (1998) have commented that "while it is clear that play provides the opportunity for children to rehearse future adult roles, ... how this occurs is less well explained." Thus, although children's play might be regarded as one context within which children learn about future adult social roles, it may be through novel or innovative forms that this knowledge is acquired. Neopets and Instant Messaging represent new forms of play with technology that appear to be deeply gratifying to children, yet also leave them newly vulnerable to commercial exploitation.

CONCLUSION: NICE PLAY IF YOU CAN AFFORD IT

How will the shakedown in the Internet economy affect children's access to the Internet and its possibilities for play? As computer usage moves increasingly to a model in which the Internet is used to serve up the necessary software and databases on an as-needed basis, families with children may find that the Internet connection from the home is a more important enabling feature than the type of hardware one owns. For the working-class children who attend the author's computer lab, possession of a high-speed Internet line from home is virtually an impossible dream. Even if Internet appliances replace computers and reduce the initial costs of purchase, contracts with phone companies for DSL lines or cable companies for high-speed cable service are priced far beyond the means of these families (and there is no intention of wiring their neighborhoods for cable services because of the low-income demographics). The parents of these children can only intermittently afford to keep a single telephone landline in use, or to pay the TV cable bill. The obstacles are threefold, involving tight household budgets, difficulty negotiating with the utility providers when English is a second language, and a high rate of transience. The latter is commonplace as these families move between apartments to beat the bill collectors, or need to move in with friends or relatives during a period of unemployment or debt.

In the United States, computer access for poor children and children of color through public facilities such as the author's lab is rapidly dwindling, a phenomenon now referred to as "digital red-lining" (Tomsho, 2002). President George Bush, after drastically cutting the budget for community technology centers, issued a series of proclamations that the digital divide was nothing but a myth, despite the fact that Internet connections in wealthy schools outnumber those in high-poverty schools by a ratio of two to one (*Low-income students*, 2001). The Bush administration abandoned the Clinton–Gore position on new technologies. The Federal Communications Commission chair, Michael Powell, compared the digital divide to "a Mercedes divide": "I'd like to have one, I can't afford one" (Bridis, 2001). By 2002, the state of California suffered staggering deficits, a result of the sky-rocketing prices for energy charged by Enron and its subsidiaries before scandal and bankruptcy broke out. The 2003 California deficit exceeded the annual payroll of the entire state employee system. Obviously, school funding and technology access initiatives will be decimated as a result. The bust of the Internet economy means that philanthropic efforts to bridge the digital divide have evaporated. Thus, the Internet playground soon will be exclusively available to those who can pay for private access.

In other words, working-class children have little chance of enjoying computer and Internet access that is residential and high speed, the kind that facilitates music downloading, online gaming, or Instant Messaging. And while these activities seem like nothing more than play, we know that they are vital to social inclusion. This is what is more important about children's computer use than simply learning keyboarding or how to save and delete files. As education researcher Mark Warschauer (2003) pointed out: "What is at stake is not access to ICT [Information Communication Technology] in the narrow sense of having a computer on the premises, but rather in a much wider sense of being able to use ICT for personally or socially meaningful ends" (p. 65). Instant Messaging undoubtedly strengthens social and community bonds among some groups of children, but it more forcefully excludes them than other social institutions have done.

The benefits gained from children's play with computers are indirect. It is true that children learn basic computer skills extremely rapidly, sometimes after only a couple of hours. Computers are highly motivating to children, which is why boys who actively resist ever playing the part of the good student and who would never have gotten off their skateboards long enough to return to school after hours if it were not for Internet access, nevertheless attended the author's lab faithfully, some of them for several years.

Working-class children have as much right to play on computers as middle-class children. The teachers at the author's school complain bitterly that parents buy their children video game consoles when they do not have a computer or many books at home. The logic here is that there is no need for fun and play if you are poor and if you are performing poorly at school. This is a point to which play researchers in particular need to be especially sensitive as budget cutbacks relegate children at low-performing schools to a relentless, mind-numbing back-to-basics curriculum, without computers. When children get their hands on computers, they generally turn out to be very good at using them, because their openness to play with the machines allows them to learn much that eludes adults. Web sites such as neopets, like video games, only less costly, reward tinkering, strategizing, obsessive play, and absorption.

Ignorance about the commercial nature of the Web among children is rampant, not in the sense that they do not understand advertising or product placement, but in that they cannot see how monitoring and profiling data mining can be a business in and of itself. The most intense marketing activities on the Web occur at this more abstract level, making the activities associated with television (host-selling, deceptive advertising, product placement, and sweepstakes and premiums) seem quite straightforward. In the case of "free" sites such as neopets and Barbie.com, which are easily accessible through public access sites, children need to understand the full ramifications of brand awareness, retail markups for branded items, and the mercenary uses of fan enthusiasm (Clark, 2003). We need to think of new ways to teach children about the Internet and the information economy. Clearly, neopets has successfully offered children a range of activities and a level of complexity they find compelling, and probably has done much to attract girls to the pleasures of role-playing and simulation games. But neopets is not free, and adults have a responsibility to help children understand this fact.

Children with the luxury of the high-end residential setup need to be aware of how much information they are leaving behind about themselves, whether through music downloading systems, which monitor all web traffic through cookies planted on consumer's hard drives, or through customized web pages. The author has learned to make a point of regularly asking children in her class what is abbreviated in "dot com." To date, not a single child has known the answer. Several children responded that "com" stands for "community," a completely understandable mistake, if a dismaying one, given the hype about the nature of human relationships on the Web. If we call on children's sense of fair play as citizens, we may raise a generation who not only are very, very good at computers—having learned much that eludes adults through their play with them—but also can imagine and even demand uses for the Web beyond making money.

Considering computers as toys helps us focus on a theoretical gap in our understanding of the relation between play and adult roles. Computers remind us that play, in Brian Sutton-Smith's (1997) terms, is about transformation as much as it is about imitation and repetition (pp. 136–137). Despite adult attempts to domesticate, devalue, or disempower children's use of computers, play turns out to be a very good way of getting very good at computers. It is nice play if you can afford it.

REFERENCES

Andrejevic, M. (2003). *Reality TV: The work of being watched.* Lanham, MD: Rowand and Littlefield.

Barken, L. (2002, June). *Instant messaging risks and rewards.* e-Business Advisor.

Bridis, T. (2001, February 15). Bush staff wants to slash programs set up to close digital divide. *Wall Street Journal,* Online.

Cassells, J., & Jenkins, H. (1999). *From Barbie to Mortal Kombat: Gender and computer games.* Cambridge, MA: MIT Press.

Clark, L. S. (2003). Challenges of social good in the world of Grand Theft Auto and Barbie at the Community Technology Center. *New Media & Society, 5,* 69–85.

Clifford, J. (2001, August 25). Quick cliques. *San Diego Union Tribune.*

Dennis, G. (2002, May 6). Internet: Missed opps beyond the banner. *Strategy,* p. 14.

Guernsey, L. (2001, June 28). Message to marketers: RU4Real? *New York Times,* p. G1.

James, A., Jenks, C., & Prout, A. (1998). *Theorizing childhood.* Cambridge, England: Polity.

Low-income students are less likely to have Internet access, report finds. (2001, May 10). *Wall Street Journal,* Online.

Ostrom, M. A. (2001, November 13). The IM era. *San Diego Union Tribune,* Computer Link, p. 6.

PR Newswire. (2002, March 18). Although Television Still Reigns Supreme in Advertising Effectiveness Internet Tapped as Favorite Media by American Youth, Finds Neo Pets.

Regional Technology Alliance. (2001). *Beyond access: Bridging the digital divide.* San Diego, CA: Regional Technology Alliance.

Seiter, E. (1993). *Sold separately: Parents and children in consumer culture.* New Brunswick, NJ: Rutgers University Press.

Seiter, E. (in press). Children reporting online: The cultural politics of the computer lab. *Television and New Media.*

Sutton-Smith, B. (1994). Does play prepare the future? In J. H. Goldstein (Ed.), *Toys, play, and child development* (pp. 130–146). New York: Cambridge University Press.

Sutton-Smith, B. (1997). *The ambiguity of play.* Cambridge, MA: Harvard University Press.

Tomsho, R. (2002, July 5). Children's access to technology still affected by income and race. *Wall Street Journal*, Online.

Warschauer, M. (2003). *Rethinking the digital divide*. Cambridge, MA: MIT Press.

Weintraub, A. (2001, December). Real profits from an imaginary world. *Business Week*, p. 12. Online.

Winding, E. (2002, June 10). Immersed in child's play. *Financial Times (London)*, p. 17.

Zippern, A. (2001, May 14). After Instant Messaging comes instant kibitzing. *New York Times C4 14.*

8

The Internet and Adolescents: The Present and Future of the Information Society

Magdalena Albero-Andrés

In recent years, various studies examining the way children use the new means of communication have expressed concern for the possible effects that these tools might have on their development (Buckingham, 1999; Livingstone, 2001; Sefton-Green, 1999). In common with earlier studies of television, many of these reports contrast the percentage of use for these new technologies with those of more established systems (Johnson-Smaragdi, D'Haenens, Krotz, & Hasebrink, 1998; Livingstone, 1998; Van der Voort et al., 1998), discuss the ways that children might be protected from the violence present on the Internet and in computer games (Magrid, 1998; Oswell, 1999), and analyze how schools might use these new technologies to help teachers and pupils in the teaching–learning process (Albero-Andrés, 2001; Buckingham, 1998). In analyzing the way that children and adolescents use the Internet, there is also a tendency to see this technology as an ideal vehicle for developing skills of reasoning, creativity, and communication (Castells, 2001; Tapscott, 1998). In general, however, the research takes a rather superficial look at what is a particularly complex issue. Technological determinism is still, it would seem, the dominant paradigm in many of these perspectives, and this impedes the raising of questions that might help us understand how children are integrating the new technologies of communication into their daily lives, which elements are shaping this integration, and what implications this might have in the design of objectives and functions for schools in today's society.

This chapter reports the results of an exploratory study that examined how adolescents use the Internet. It seeks to contribute to the debate on the possible social, emotional, and symbolic uses of the Internet by analyzing a group of adolescents (ages 12 to 17 years) living in and around the city of Barcelona. The study aimed to examine how their family, group culture, school, and previous experience with other means of communication determined the way that they used the Internet. Furthermore, it also investigated the way that their schools are using the Internet to determine the extent to which the schools' proposals for the use of this technology match their students' interests, motivations, and needs when they go online. This study was founded on the principle that culture is a product of our daily lives, and therefore establishes the analysis of communication within the needs, wishes, conflicts, failures, and successes of the common man and woman as they seek to give meaning to their lives.

As with all exploratory studies, the aim of this research was to undertake an initial analysis of the way that adolescents integrate the Internet into their daily lives. The aim was not, therefore, to obtain results that might be generalized across the community, nor to test any specific hypothesis, but rather to obtain reliable information that might guide future research. Such an approach would seem to justify the use of qualitative research methods. With this decision made, the subjects were chosen at random, with the sole proviso that they had been Internet users at least 1 year. In the selection of the subjects, it was considered that only 45.7% of Catalan homes have a computer, and of these, only 27.1% are connected to the Internet (*Estadístiques de la Societat de la Informació,* Catalunya, 2001). This means that some of the adolescents who participated in the study used the Internet in cyber cafes or at a friend's house. A total of 80 adolescents, ages 12 to 17 years, were selected from 20 schools in and around Barcelona to participate in the study. The differences in their socioeconomic backgrounds were not taken into consideration for this study, and the factors of age and gender were similarly ignored. The principal aim was to discover the significance attached by the adolescents—as a group that shares similar motivations, communicative needs, and prior experience with other technologies of communication—to the Internet in their daily lives.

The 80 adolescents were first interviewed individually to determine the frequency with which they used the Internet, their reasons for going online, the activities they carried out, what they liked doing and why. In a second interview, the subject was questioned in the company of his or her friends to learn more about the group's motivations and to identify any possible differences with those of the individual. Two observation sessions also were conducted: one with the subject on his own while online and the other with the subject and his friends while surfing the net together. An interview also was conducted with the parents of each subject in the study. The aim of this interview was to determine the value attached by the family to the Internet, to discover how much the parents knew about this technology, and to find out whether they controlled their children's access to the Web and why. Finally, two teachers from each of the schools of the subjects were interviewed. The interview with the teachers sought to learn whether there was a specific plan for introducing the Internet into the school, the amount of training the teachers had received in the new technologies of communication, and their attitude toward the use of the Internet in the school. The study was conducted between January and December, 2001.

USES OF THE INTERNET FOR COMMUNICATING, PLAYING GAMES, AND LEARNING

The first part of the study sought to identify the reasons why this group of adolescents used the Internet. The aim was not only to determine the extent to which going online formed part of their daily routine, but also to observe when, how, and with whom they used the Internet as a means of communication, whether these conversations differed from those held face-to-face, and what types of expression were used in these conversations. The study also sought to discover how adolescents used the Internet when playing games and looking for information about their hobbies or other interests. In this part of the study, it also was hoped that data could be obtained concerning the way that adolescents used the Internet when searching for information to use in their studies at school, the way in which they went about learning the different functions of the Internet, and the difficulties they encountered.

Uses and gratifications theory, which often has served as the basis for determining why a particular means of communication is used, has not been as widely applied in the study of new communication technologies, or more specifically in the study of Internet use. The few studies to date that have examined reasons for using the Internet have focused on adult users (Feruson & Perse, 2000; Papacharissi & Rubin, 2000; Perse & Dunn, 1998). Although a number of studies have sought to explain the use for the new means of communication among children and adolescents (Livingstone, 2002; Sefton-Green, 1998; Stern, 1999; Suess et al., 1998), little is known about how adolescents communicate with each other, play games, and look for information on the Internet. Some studies suggest that it is in fact today's children and adolescents who are defining the uses for the new technologies of communication (Montgomery, 2000). Other studies, however, show that adolescents spend more time online than adults do, and that they use e-mail and the messenger more frequently than adults (Kraut, Mukhopadhyay, Szczypula, Kiesler, & Scherlis, 1999; NOP Research Group, 2000a, 2000b).

Other studies have taken into consideration the characteristics of adolescence and how these might affect the use of the Internet (Roberts, 2000). Social identity and interactions with the peer group acquire greater importance during adolescence, and this is reflected in the way the young use the Internet (Durkin, 1997). According to some studies, there seems to be an inclination among adolescents to use the Internet for social interaction, particularly in their friendships, in identifying with certain groups and their values, and in the development of their own individual identity (Montgomery, 2001; Suess, Garitaonandia, Juaristi, Koikkalainen, & Oleaga, 1998). The results from these previous studies of the Internet and adolescent users were taken as the starting point for this study in considering how to further understanding concerning the uses and meanings that adolescents—bound within their own sociocultural context—attribute to the Internet.

Communication

Judging by the interviews and observations undertaken with the adolescent participants in this study, it seems clear that the Internet is an important tool of communication, but solely for communicating with friends. This finding differs from that reported by Tapscott (1998). The children and adolescents in Tapscott's (1998) study also were found to use the Internet on a fairly regular basis to communicate with persons they did not know. It might be the case that because adolescent Australians, Britons, Canadians, Americans, and South Africans share the same language, this desire to communicate with strangers is somewhat easier to fulfill. However, it is more than likely that this is not the only reason. If it were, then why is it that young Spanish speakers in different countries do not communicate with each other more regularly via the Internet? One of the reasons might be related to the large differences between the cultures of English- and Spanish-speaking countries. The latter are characterized by the greater importance attached to the group, the use of public spaces, and participation in leisure activities outside the home.

Among the adolescents in this study, entering chat rooms and using the messenger were found to be regular evening activities. It seems that the Internet has, to some extent, replaced the long telephone conversations between friends that used to be so frequent in adolescence. The adolescents use the network to continue conversations begun during the day at school, to make plans for the weekend, or to resolve conflicts that might have arisen in a face-to-face conversation. In other words, the Internet seems to have brought about a switch in the vehicle of communication for adolescents when they are at home, but it seems not to have modified their need to communicate with each other nor to have changed the most typical topics of conversation during this period of life. Neither has there been any change in the adolescents stated preferences. If given a choice, they still prefer to meet up with their friends, as Livingstone and Bovil (2002) suggested. The subjects observed appeared to have no problems communicating via Internet. Some claimed that they feel they can say things to their friends when using the network that they would not dare to say in a face-to-face conversation.

In parallel with this use of the Internet to communicate with friends, communication with strangers via the network also was reported in the youngest group of adolescents (ages 12 to 14 years), only to be curtailed later on. Tapscott (1998) reported a similar pattern of use with age. Interestingly, entering a chat room and talking with strangers generally is something they do when going online in a group. In most cases, adolescent participation in chat rooms is treated as a game, and they enjoy creating different characters for themselves. Lying about their age, gender, and physical appearance is part and parcel of the game, and they are fully aware that the other participants in the chat room are doing the same. For this reason, the friendships initiated in a chat room do not last. Chat room users do not appear to have any interest in meeting each other, even if they live in the same city. They report acting with caution when entering a chat room, and they do not give real personal details. The subjects observed enter chat rooms only where the language spoken is Catalan or Spanish, and they do not participate in international chat rooms. The reason for this lack of interest lies perhaps in the language of communication. In most international chat rooms, English is used, but this still is a language that Spanish adolescents do not dominate. Although English is introduced in schools for children ages 7 or 8 years old, the current education system does not appear to dedicate sufficient time or resources to ensure optimum conditions for the teaching of foreign languages. The result is that young people still have serious difficulties understanding written English, and considerably more difficulty expressing themselves in this language. This difficulty understanding English also might affect their use of the Internet and hinder their search for information.

The observation of the way that adolescents express themselves when communicating via the Internet shows that the use of abbreviations is widespread. They typically omit the vowels that are not needed to understand a word, and use capital letters to indicate when they are shouting. There is a clear parallel here between the texts written on the Internet and those used in mobile telephone messages. The language that has developed out of the need to compress words sent by mobile phones (that is, using as few characters as possible) has been transferred to the Internet. Although the same limitations on space do not exist, conducting a conversation in real time calls for speed in the writing of the message. The language used in messages on the network and mobile phones is markedly informal, not that far removed from the language used in those scribbled notes that used to be thrown from one side of the classroom to another in previous generations. However, the use of abbreviations did not begin with mobile phones or the Internet, but rather when the young pupil reached secondary school and needed to be able to take rapid, efficient notes in class. Thus, with the advent of the new systems of communication, abbreviations started to be used in a different context, but before this, they had been used systematically in private texts—notes taken in class, diaries, and messages to friends. Furthermore, the adolescent knows perfectly well when and where to use this type of expression and does not produce these informal texts in examinations, for example.

One aspect that this study that the researchers wished to examine from the outset was how young people use the Internet to express their interests, how they make these interests known to other people, and just how common a practice this was. It was thought that analyzing the web pages they designed themselves might be a good way to gain insights into these questions. However, a surprisingly small number of subjects were prepared to create their own web page. The few that had already done so did little more than add a few links to their favorite football or basketball teams, or hang a few photographs of themselves and their friends. What is more, most pages were quickly abandoned when the subjects were faced with the difficulties of having to update them. When the subjects of the study were asked why they did not create their own web pages, the usual response was that they did not know how. The adolescents seemed unwilling to spend time learning how to do this themselves, and only a few expressed the wish that their schools would teach them how to create web pages. This finding is significant because it seems to call into question the possibilities for creativity that are automatically associated with the Internet (Castells, 2001; Tapscott, 1998). The simple existence of the Internet does not appear sufficient to generate this creative spark. There seems to be something within the family, school, social, and cultural contexts of these adolescents that makes them see themselves as passive recipients and not as creators. It is in these contexts that changes are needed to ensure that young people come to view the Internet as a potentially creative tool.

Playing Games

The use of the Internet as a source of entertainment is restricted basically to chat rooms, which adolescents usually enter together in groups. When playing by themselves, many adolescents observed prefer to use a TV games console or to play games on CD-ROMs. In the case of CD-ROMs, adolescents tend to use the Web to download information that allows them to extend the range of strategies and so upgrade the game. The subjects participating in the study did not appear particularly willing to get involved in games on the Internet, giving as their main reasons the difficulties involved in opening the particular Web sites and using the search engines. A further factor was that the TV games console was seen as the place for playing. These consoles, present in many Spanish homes, are the solution adopted by numerous families when faced with the vast amount of memory needed to play computer games. This requirement can cause the need to change the family's computer equipment more frequently.

In general, the adolescents tend not to identify with the characters in the games, but when this did occur, it usually was boys older than 15 years who seemed to identify with the leading character, who more often than not is aggressive, individualistic, and not prone to showing his feelings. Some of these games encourage the development of certain skills, such as conflict resolution, and reward practical intelligence in that they allow the player to advance to higher levels in the game. Similarly, they promote powers of concentration and the observation of small details. However, most of those participating in this study stated a preference for the simpler online games, but only when they had nothing better to do. They appeared not to be interested in games of logic or investigation, or those that made demands on their intellect. This seems to suggest that for these adolescents the computer was associated solely with entertainment. This association of the computer with recreational activities means that these adolescents were somewhat reluctant to use it for activities involving intellectual effort, something they generally identify with schoolwork.

Another type of network entertainment is to be found on the web pages the subjects visit. Thus, in addition to the pages that refer to their hobbies (typically, sports and music, in the case of the boys, music and fashion in the case of the girls), many visit pages in which humor plays a part, such as quefuerte.com (lurid pictures, scathing humor), paisdelocos.com (humor, varied content), and elterrat.com (the home page of the Catalan producer "El Terrat," where it is possible to leave a message or participate in various activities, including a chat room and a forum). The number of pages they visit in which humor features prominently is an interesting characteristic of their use of the Internet (chat rooms, web pages). Among children, humor is one of the main attractions for watching television (Albero-Andrés, 1996), and it seems to retain its importance into adolescence and with the Internet. This is hardly surprising because humor acts as a fundamental element in human development. Humor is a sign of intelligence, evidencing an individual's higher capacity to generate subtle distinctions when interpreting his or her environment. It occurs in no other species than man. Humor can help us understand certain situations, overcome our fears, and take the tension out of moments of conflict. Humor and imagination are fundamental elements that combine with our reasoning in the process of understanding our world and our search for a place in it. It is therefore not surprising that the search for situations of humor is frequent in adolescence, and that it helps in many cases to overcome the constant mood swings that typify this period of life.

Learning

The use that the adolescents in this study were found to make of the Internet as a source of information is quite distinct from that described in studies by Tapscott (1998) and O'Brien (2001), who reported that adolescents used the Internet to develop their intellectual curiosity and their capacities for research and reasoning. The results obtained in this study seemed to indicate that adolescents use the Internet to find information related to their formal education only when they have to complete a project or essay assigned by a teacher. In general, when required to undertake a project that involves some research, they surf the Internet and simply print out the information they find. The projects they hand in usually are long, well written, and well illustrated, but they do not attempt to appraise, organize, or expand on the information. Often, the students do no more than print out the information, not even bothering to read it first. What we find therefore is a practice similar to that used by students consulting an encyclopedia, with the aggravating circumstance that at least in the latter case the student used to read the section before copying it.

The participants in this study do not visit educational web pages. Most find these pages boring and of no interest. These pages seem to be lacking in imagination and show little sense of humor, two elements that might awaken the curiosity of the adolescent. Similarly, the sites offer little evidence that they understand and value the adolescents' world and the problems they have at this age. One of these problems, indeed one that youngsters have to face in formal education, is the constant flow of information out of context that has to be learned. Unfortunately, many web pages, although designed with the best intentions, demonstrate the same mentality, the same underlying principles, and the same content as those used in the writing of school textbooks. For this reason, educational portals do not as a rule incorporate the elements needed to encourage interaction between the user and the information, which might enable students to develop their research skills and creativity. The strengthening of these skills is possible, but only if the full potential of the Internet is tapped.

On the whole, the adolescents studied did not show any curiosity for seeking new information, and when they opened up a web page they were much more interested in its design features—its colors and how to move around—than in the content. Indeed, most of the subjects recognized that they were not interested in looking for information on the network to widen their knowledge (other than that related to their hobbies). They considered that what the teacher tells them has priority, and is itself enough, and they do no more than read their class notes when studying for their examinations. Why should this be the case? Might it be that they are now too old to inquire why something should be the way it is, as younger children do? Are they perhaps too young to pose new questions? Or does the educational system not give sufficient value to initiative of this type?

Searching for information concerning current affairs or the society in which they live does not motivate these adolescents to use the Internet. Such issues do not seem to awaken their interest. No more than a minority demonstrated any curiosity for the controversial issues of the day (e.g., human cloning or the right to abort). Some of the adolescents commented that they sometimes try to clarify their doubts concerning sexuality on the Internet. They often look at the digital versions of the newspapers to find out the latest sports news, but they do not as yet appear to have defined very clearly just what their social interests are. These findings are in stark contrast to those reported in other studies. O'Brien (2001), for example, claimed that young people use the network to channel their social concerns. However, reports in Catalonia describe an increase in the participation of young people in non-governmental organizations and other social organizations (*Observatori de la Joventut en Catalunya*), but the difference seems to be that such activities are carried out in situations of face-to-face communication, which is unlike going online.

THE INTERNET AND THE FAMILY

If one starts from the premise that the consumption of communication technologies is learned at home (Silverstone, 1992; Turrow & Nir, 2000), then one needs to know how the families use the Internet, what symbolic value they attach to this technology, what place it occupies with respect to other technologies of communication, and how all these elements may influence the value attached to it by adolescents. The study conducted by Pasquier, Buzzi, D'Haenens, and Sjöberg (1999) among Flemish, French, and Italian and Swedish children and adolescents shows how the use of communication technologies strengthens existing family habits with regard to freedom of use and restrictions on access to the technologies of communication. The results from this study also show the preponderance of male and young users in the family. Similarly, it was found that the use of these technologies was not as interactional as that of other media, such as the television.

This concern to understand the nature of Internet use among children and their families is evident in other studies. Caron and Caronia (2001) asked how families use the mass media in their daily lives and concluded that the uses and functions assigned to each are changing, at times because of the changing dynamics that the technologies introduce into family life. Similarly, Toni Downes (1999) examined the reasons why families use the Internet and discovered a contrast between the educational value attached to the technology by the parents and the value attributed to it by the children, who saw it as a means of entertainment. The same study reported the need for parents to control their children's access to the Internet to protect them, while seeing their children as experts in this field.

According to the comments recorded by the parents of the adolescents in this study, the way that they use the Internet, their reasons for using it, their concerns regarding how their children use it, their expectations, and their preferences for the different means of communication to which the family has access are largely similar. With few exceptions, it can be seen that use of the Internet does not form part of these parents' daily routine. Most do not express any curiosity or interest for this type of technology, and in contrast to their children, is something many associate with work, not with their hobbies or their typical leisure activities. However, the parents in some cases do use the Internet for banking, planning holidays, obtaining information before buying a new car, or looking for information on matters affecting the family, such as medical information.

Very few parents have taught their children how to use the Internet. In general, the fathers expressed a certain degree of interest in learning how to use it, whereas the mothers were a little more reluctant. All mentioned lack of time as one of their reasons for knowing so little about the Internet. Indeed, self-teaching how to use this tool means that one must have a considerable amount of time available for sitting in front of the computer. The demands of work and domestic duties on most of those interviewed mean that they are free to do so only after 11 or 12 o'clock at night, a time when they would rather sit down and relax than engage in an activity that requires a considerable amount of concentration. This lack of time perhaps explains why mothers are less interested than fathers. In most cases, the men do less housework on returning from work, and therefore have more time to spend online if they so wish.

The importance of having time to use the Internet may account for the use of this tool by the adolescents' grandparents. In some of the families interviewed, the grandparents were the expert users who enjoyed browsing the Web. They reported seeing it as a way of carrying out their hobbies, maintaining their correspondence with family and friends, and even teaching their grandchildren. All were self-taught, and none had found any great difficulties learning to navigate. The existence of an increasing number of Internet users in this age group means there is a need to reconsider the traditional belief that it is easier for a younger person to learn to use a computer. These data seem to show that individuals in developed societies experience stages in life—childhood, adolescence and old age—in which they have more time for their interests. If these lead them to learn how to navigate on the Internet, they will do so with ease. In the adult stage of life, however, work and family responsibilities leave individuals little time for learning how to channel their interests via new media such as the Internet. Only during periods of personal crisis may the situation be different. For example, recent divorcees quite commonly learn how to use the Internet to meet new people in a chat room. In contrast to adolescents, many adults who find themselves facing a personal change in their lives are interested in making new friends. In general, these adults have few qualms about meeting someone with whom they have enjoyed chatting on the Web.

Most of the families that participated in this study had obtained an Internet connection over the past 3 years, always at the request of their children. Almost all paid a flat rate, and quite a large number of these families had chosen to install an ADSL line. The Internet had been introduced into the homes after the TV games console, and typically had coincided with the renewal of computer equipment. In some cases, the arrival of the first computer and being connected to the Internet occurred simultaneously. In general, the parents were convinced that the Internet was a particularly useful tool for their children's studies. The Internet, therefore, was introduced into the home to help with homework, but not as a vehicle of entertainment such as the television set or the games console. Thus, it seems that the symbolic value attached to the Internet by the family is predominantly work related. The Internet gives access to more knowledge, thus improving the children's future employment opportunities. It seems highly likely, however, that this assessment will change in the coming years if the Internet as a source of entertainment continues to gain ground over its educational uses among the young.

Parents' concerns regarding their children and the Internet are centered largely on the number of hours they spend online. Many noted that their children spend most of their time on the Internet engaged in activities of entertainment and feared that this might begin to interfere with their other leisure activities, which the parents considered to be healthier, such as going out with their friends or taking part in sports activities. Moreover, although most of the parents were unaware of just what their children actually did on the Internet, in general, they expressed full confidence that their children did not access information that might be harmful to them. Those parents who did express a concern regarding the content of the Web sites to which their children might have access worried more about violent content than pornography. Similarly, some parents expressed concern that their children might initiate conversations with strangers, or that they might reveal personal details of their own or their family. When parents found that the Internet had not had a negative effect on their eldest child, they appeared to be less worried about the use of the Internet by the younger child or children in the family.

The parents considered chat rooms to be a waste of time, and those who had not yet obtained an ADSL connection complained that their telephone line is blocked for many hours during the day. Although some parents confessed that they have had to take the computer keyboard to work to stop their children from going online when left on their own, they all looked more positively on the fact that their children were using the Internet rather than watching the television.

The parents' opinions regarding the positive and negative features of the Internet did not differ from those generally expressed on the issue. Thus, although they were worried by the violence to which their children might have access, they also were satisfied by the great possibilities the Internet offers in terms of obtaining information. Because they are not particularly adept users themselves, few parents see the difficulties their children have in making the most of the Internet as a source of information. The parents interviewed believed that the Internet can help their children to learn. For many, the need to use the written word carries with it positive feelings for computers and the possibilities they offer, something that cannot be said for the media based exclusively on the image, such as television or game consoles. Parents, as a rule, are unaware of how their children work with the Internet at school, and only a few of those interviewed expressed any interest in finding out about the possibilities offered by the Internet so they could help their children.

THE INTERNET AND SCHOOLS

With the appearance of the mass media and the interest that this aroused, together with a certain amount of concern for the speed with which they established themselves as a ubiquitous form of entertainment, expectations were expressed in academic and government circles that the media might be given an educational orientation. In general, it was hoped that television—as indeed it is hoped that computers—would help teachers in their work, alleviating the problems of students with lack of interest and poor performance in many schools. Thus, the idea gradually took hold that the technologies of communication, when used to entertain the masses, offered information that was disorganized, violent, useless, and prejudicial, but that these same technologies offered information for education that was organized, informative, useful, and necessary for improvement of skills at school, enabling students to complete their studies and face their professional and personal future with certain guarantees of success. However, whereas the technologies of communication as instruments of entertainment have prospered, to the extent that this is virtually their sole function, the use of these media for educational purposes has met with one failure after another, with only an occasional success story.

Much has been said about the introduction of media in the classrooms, and the discourse is repeated with each advance in communication technology. However, as Pappert (1995) pointed out, school has been unable to integrate the technologies of communication, and thus has chosen simply to abandon them, as in the case of television, or has tried to convert them into just one more subject to be studied, as is occurring with computers. In general, the concept of progress associated with the Internet means that attempts are made to introduce computers into the school without first conducting the necessary studies to determine how to get the best out of them (Bruckman, 1999).

According to Healy (1998) there is a significant gap between the campaigns that seek to promote the educational value of the computer and the uses to which they are put in both the school and the home. The failure to understand the significance that children and adolescents attach to computers leads in most cases to the production of educational products based on the memorization and repetition of contents; audiovisual texts that adopt the same approach; the development, duration, and objectives as written texts; and web pages that do not awaken the interest of the students. Valentine and Holloway (1999) maintained that the vision governments have of the new communication technologies is overly deterministic, with the result that they separate technology from the context of social practice. After a study conducted in three British schools of varying characteristics, Valentine and Holloway (1999) claimed that there is a general failure to consider the importance of time and place, the way the technologies of communication are promoted, and the meaning attached to them by their various users. The results of their study clearly show that each school, according to its characteristics and pupils, holds a different view of the role such technologies should play. This, in turn, influences the way that teachers understand communication technologies and how they use them in their teaching. This is most obviously manifest by the place where the computers are installed in the school, the way they are used in the classroom, and the access the children have to them outside class hours.

Sefton-Green, Buckingham, and Tobin (1998), Buckingham (1998), and Castells (2002), after an examination of the educational implications of the communication technologies, drew the conclusion that the changes needed to ensure the effective use of communication technologies in education will involve a radical transformation in the current organizational principles of our schools. Faced with this situation, we need to ask what factors within the cultural, social, and economic context conspire to ensure that schools do not use communication technologies well. Where do the myths regarding the use of computers by young people originate, and why do they per- sist? Why are more teachers not questioning the way they teach with these resources? Why is a dialog not established with young people to gain a better understanding of the way they perceive the Internet? Why has there been a failure to consider the challenge posed by technologies of communi- cation with regard to the time, place, and the authority in the form of teach- ing and learning currently practiced in our schools?

This study cannot answer these questions, but many of its findings can help clarify what is going on in our schools, why this situation has arisen, and the steps that should be taken in beginning to find a solution. Perhaps the place to begin seeking to understand the gap between the expectations regarding the introduction of the Internet into schools and the real possibil- ities of its use is by ascertaining the number of computers and connections to the Internet per student in Spanish schools. According to Eurobarómetro 2001, in Spain there are currently 12.4 students for each computer and 25.3 students for every computer connected to the Internet. The statistics place Spain well below Sweden, which tops the table in Europe, with 4.1 and 4.8, respectively, and also below the mean values for Europe, which stand at 8.6 and 14.9. But other important factors must be considered in the search to understand the way that the Internet is being integrated within the schools. The results from the interviews with the teachers who participated in this study seem to demonstrate this.

According to an initial finding of some importance, most of the teachers agree that in the schools where they work, there are no established guide- lines or principles that might help them to use the Internet in their respec- tive subjects. The data obtained for this study seem to show that in most of the schools, working with the Internet in class is simply another task that teachers must take on from an already very long list of responsibilities. In general, this means that their work with the Internet is limited to giving the students a list of Web sites to consult, in the same way that they might pro- vide them with a reading list on a given subject.

At the time these interviews were conducted with the teachers, the Cata- lan Government (Generalitat de Catalunya) had just launched Edu365.com, an award-winning and pioneering project in Europe that sought the involve- ment of families, teachers, children, and adolescents in the systematic and continuous use of the Internet for educational purposes, both inside and outside the school. Schools were given the task of collecting the inscription forms for the program that the children and their families had received at home. When asked their opinion about Edu365.com, many of the teachers said they did not have much information about it. Indeed, the majority had not visited the program's portal, and few had discussed the possibilities of- fered by the program with their students. What was the reason for this lack of interest in what, in principle, appears to have been an ideal initiative?

One possible reason for this rejection may lie in the fact that schools have other priorities, more pressing needs and problems that dictate the day-to-day teaching activity. The shortage of materials and teaching staff, the maintenance of classroom discipline, and the effort to teach all the subjects on the syllabus are perceived as the most important priorities.

In most schools visited for this study the Internet was hardly used, but it also is true that some did participate in educational projects with other schools, thanks generally to the initiative of one or two teachers. These projects typically involved e-mail correspondence with students in other schools. However, more often than not the regular use of the Internet was limited to certain subjects such as computer studies and English. Some schools were participating in the project promoted by the national news-paper, *El País*, whereby they were producing their own virtual newspaper. Thus, despite a number of positive experiences with the Internet, the teachers claimed that, in general, its use in schools is not promoted as a learning tool, and that the students therefore are not taught how to select information, how to assess its value, or how to proceed in their study of a certain topic.

Most of the teachers interviewed had received some form of basic train-ing in the use of communication technologies. A few schools had organized training courses for their own staff. Several teachers commented that by taking these courses they had been sufficiently motivated to continue learn-ing more about these technologies on their own, but this experience was by no means typical. All the teachers that participated in the study agreed that the courses they had taken had trained them to use the technology, but that they had not received information on how to use the Internet in their classes. These teachers also shared the conviction that their students knew more about the Internet than they did. Thus, when a school decides to orga-nize a course for its students, it is found that the course is pitched at too low a level, and that most of the students do not develop their skills for working on the network. Many adolescents—at home, in cyber cafes or at their friends' houses—have already learned the basics of the Internet by themselves.

Most of the teachers interviewed still are somewhat negative in their evaluation of the Internet's usefulness. This has various explanations. First, because virtually no information has been given to the teachers about the Internet as an educational tool, they cannot see how their teaching of their subjects (e.g., mathematics) might benefit. Second, many teachers list the major difficulties they must face (lack of discipline, lack of interest on the part of the students) to complete the teaching of the syllabus, which means they have no time for any additional activity. Third, most teachers have to face obstacles produced by the school infrastructure. This means they must transfer their students to the computer room, which creates a disturbance and reduces the time available for the class. Very few schools have computers in the classroom, and when they do, there usually are not enough for all the students in the class. The teachers also mentioned that they could not ask the students to work on the Internet outside class hours because access to the computers for completing their school work was restricted to the school break times. In some schools, the pupils actually were asked to pay a small amount to use the Internet. Similarly, in the private schools attended by children from the city's better-off families, it also was apparent that despite more computers per student, the use made of the Internet varied little from that in the schools with fewer resources. This seems to indicate that in addition to the limitations of the technical infrastructure, which are particularly evident, there clearly is confusion as to what should be done with a tool that gives access to information that might call into question the principles underlying the transmission of knowledge in the education system today.

The negative attitudes and feelings of wariness observed in some teachers are more a reflection of their limited understanding of the Internet's actual possibilities and their lack of support for working with this technology than an outright rejection of everything associated with the network. Thus, many teachers recognize that the Internet can serve as a hook to attract the attention of their students, but also that the motivation of the students regarding the use of this tool lies in its relative newness. This opinion might indeed be right if the Internet is used, as it has been largely to date, as a textbook. The age of the teachers at times seems to correlate with their acceptance or rejection of the Internet. Thus, older teachers see fewer possibilities for the use of the Internet, whereas younger teachers express greater hopes of being able to put it to greater use in the future. However, this attitude does not reflect the degree of adaptability to the use of communication technologies in relation to age, but rather the influence of the number of years spent teaching a subject in a certain manner. Introducing change is always difficult, particularly if the change requires the introduction of certain mechanisms that are not available.

FINAL REFLECTIONS

Perhaps a main finding of this study is that although the number of homes with an Internet link still is considerably lower than that in other European countries, the young people with access to the network, be it in or out of their own homes, have incorporated its use to their daily activities. In this process of discovering, understanding, and mastering some of the Internet functions, they are largely self-taught, although the skills they have acquired in handling the network represent no more than a small part of the possibilities offered by this tool. The potential of the Internet as a means of accessing knowledge is not the reason why these adolescents are assiduous in their use of the network. Actually, adolescents see the Internet as another vehicle through which to channel their interests as a peer group and as individuals. Thus, it can be seen that participation in chat rooms and use of the messenger have replaced the telephone when adolescents chat with friends from their homes. However, online communication has by no means replaced face-to-face communication.

Observation of adolescents when online has shown two major limitations. First, their poor knowledge of English hinders their ability to gain access to information and also their ability to use search engines. Second, they appear to show no interest in the educational possibilities of the Internet. They continue to rely on television for their information on current affairs, but the majority react to this information passively and feel no urge to widen their knowledge or to discuss it. The adolescents in this study did not go to the Internet to obtain information, in the same way that they (even the eldest in the group) showed no interest in reading the press. They saw themselves as receivers of information, not as seekers of knowledge. They drew a clear distinction between entertainment and learning, which could be seen in the way they used the network. Thus, the Internet was entertainment when they were chatting with their friends or when they were searching for information related to their hobbies, and it was learning when they had to find information to complete a task set for them at school. However, this latter search was undertaken only when the teacher had asked them to do so. When this happened, the adolescents usually restricted themselves to visiting the Web sites provided by their teachers or to downloading information from the first web page they found that spoke of the topic about which they needed information. In general, the subjects of this study reflected little on the information they found. They did not try to widen their search for data, and they made no attempt to compare their various sources. This once more shows the error in technological determinism, which still apparently holds to the theory that the potential of new technologies will change the way that people behave. People, and the adolescents in this study were no exception, behave in accordance with certain cultural and social patterns that they have received since infancy, and it is these that they apply when integrating new communication technologies into their daily lives. Thus, if mass media have always been used as a source of entertainment, the same will be true of the Internet, and if at school children are asked basically to learn what the teacher tells them, this function will be transferred to the Internet as well.

To expand their current uses of the Internet, adolescents will need to be trained so they can learn different ways of accessing knowledge. A significant factor that needs to be considered is the direct relation between the degree of the parents' cultural grounding and the time they dedicate to their children and their academic performance (Livingstone, 2001; Tapscott, 1998). This relation will become increasingly more evident as families begin using the network. If the necessary measures are not introduced, the Internet will help only increase the current imbalances in access to information and school performance, which are influenced not only by whether one has access to communication technologies at home, but also by the general level of material resources, their accessibility, and the degree of family interest and support. What is required therefore is the creation of specific needs for Internet use that involve families of all socioeconomic levels. These needs will be very difficult to define if the more typical problems that low-income families face are not known. A good policy of support for the family, in its role as generator of cultural interest and resources for the children, would provide adolescents with better training before they go to secondary school, which in many cases would increase motivation and interest while reducing problems of discipline. In these circumstances, teachers could feel more inclined to make the personal effort needed to ensure that they constantly are improving their teaching and introducing innovations in their work. However, increasing the motivation of teachers also requires that their job be given greater social recognition, and that their initial training be improved (what is needed is not just graduates in a subject, but professionals with the necessary skills to teach the subject). In addition, teachers' access to ongoing education must be ensured, and economic incentives encouraging them to provide teaching of excellence must be improved.

The relatively scant interest that the adolescents seem to show for the Internet as a tool for learning come as no surprise when seen in the light of the comments made by the teachers interviewed and the observations made in the schools visited. In these schools, the Internet was neither integrated nor exploited as an educational tool. The reasons for this should not be sought in the teachers' visceral mistrust of new technologies, nor in the insufficient supply of computer resources still to be found in many schools. If as Castells (2001) claimed, knowing how to use the Internet correctly is a social necessity, an essential skill in the near future, what then is required to ensure proper training in the use of the Internet? First, it is necessary to consider the type of orientation that schools and teachers should receive in learning how to use this technology. Teachers need to be helped in finding a balance between fulfilling their teaching role in as attractive a manner as possible and undertaking this role in an educational structure that still is too rigid. And this cannot be achieved if as up until now, computer studies are seen as a subject whose sole purpose is to ensure that the user understands the system's technical functions, or the Internet is seen as just another textbook. The transversal use of computer technology in secondary education and all the possibilities of working with the information that this would open up have yet to be achieved and must be tackled by those who run our educational system. Until this happens, it should come as no surprise that adolescents access the Internet only to be entertained, and that teachers see its introduction into the classroom as just another demand on their time, a demand, furthermore to which they must respond without having been given the necessary basic information, although they show much good will while receiving little or no recognition in return for their efforts. Contrary to what seems to be the case, the Internet does not appear to be changing the principles of adolescent socialization, although it is expanding some of the ways this process is brought about. Neither does it seem to be changing the processes of learning. Young people are integrating the Internet into their daily lives, using the already existing cultural parameters that specify their interests as a group, their relation with communication technologies, and their attitude toward their schooling. The fact that the level of use for this information tool among adolescents is very basic highlights the fact that two levels of access to the Internet exist. On the one hand, the Internet can be used to channel individual and group leisure interests. On the other hand, it can be used to seek information that can be consciously selected and analyzed in a process capable of developing thinking and creativity. Whereas access at this first level occurs unprompted, access at the second does not, nor will it occur unless coherent mechanisms of intervention are developed within the educational system aimed at creating the need for the active search to find information that will enable the young to learn how to transform information into knowledge and knowledge into wisdom.

REFERENCES

Albero-Andrés, M. (1994). Televisión y socialización: Apuntes críticos desde una ecología socio-cognitiva. *Telos, 38*, 14–17.

Albero-Andrés, M. (1996). Televisión y contextos sociales en la infacia: Hábitos televisivos y juego infantil. *Comunicar, 6*, 129–139.

Albero-Andrés, M. (2001). Internet, escuela y vida cotidiana en la infancia, telos (Revista de Estudios Interdisciplinarios Universidad Dr. Rafael Belloso Chacín). *Maracaibo (Venezuela), 3*(1), 9–20.

Bruckman, A. (1999). The day after net day: Approaches to educational use of the Internet. *Convergence, 5*(1), 24–45.

Buckingham, D. (1998). *Teaching popular culture: Beyond radical pedagogy.* London: UCL Press.

Buckingham, S.-G. (1999). Children, young people, and digital technology (special issue). *Convergence, 5*(4), 2. (Editorial).

Caron, A., & Caronia, L. (2001). Active users and active objects: The mutual construction of families and communication technologies. *Convergence, 7*(3), 38–61.

Castells, M. (2001). *The Internet galaxy: Reflections on Internet, business, and society.* Oxford: Oxford University Press.

Castells, M. (2002). *Critical education in the new information age*. London: Rowman and Littlefields.

Catalunya. (2001). *Estadistiques de la societat de la informacio*. Barcelona: Generalitat de Catalunya.

Downes, T. (1999). Children and parents discourse about computers in the home and school. *Convergence, 5*(4), 104–111.

Durkin, K. (1997). *Developmental social psychology: From infancy to old age*. Malden, MA: Blackwell.

Feruson, J., & Perse, S. (2000). The World Wide Web as a functional alternative to television. *Journal of Broadcasting and Electronic Media, 44*, 155–174.

Healy, J. (1998). *Failure to connect: How computers affect our children's minds—for better and worse*. New York: Simon and Schuster.

Johnson-Smaragdi, U., D'Haenens, F., & Hasenbrink, U. (1998). Patterns of old and new media use among young people in Flanders, Germany, and Sweden. *European Journal of Communication, 13*(4), 479–501.

Kraut, R., Mukhopadhyay, T., Szczypula, J., Kiesler, S., & Scherlis, B. (1999). Information and communication: Alternative uses of the Internet in households. *Information Systems Research, 10*, 287–303.

Livingstone, S. (1998). Mediated childhoods: A comparative approach to young people's changing media environment in Europe. *European Journal of Communication, 13*(4), 435–456.

Livingstone, S. (2001). *Children and their changing media environment: A European comparative study*. London: Lawrence Erlbaum Associates.

Livingstone, S., & Bovil, M. (2002). *Young people and new media*. London: Sage.

Magrid, L. J. (1998). *Child safety on the information highway*. Washington, DC: National Center for Missing and Exploited Children.

Montgomery, K. (2001). Youth and digital media: A policy research agenda. *Journal of Adolescent Health, 27*(25), 61–68.

NOP Research Group. (2000a). *Four million kids now online*. Accessed at http:/www.nop.co.uk/survey/internet

NOP Research Group. (2000b). *Mobile phones: The teen's must have*. Accessed at http:/www.nop.co.uk/survey/internet

O'Brien, E. (2001). *From sales pitches to civics lessons: Something for everyone online*. Washington, DC: Center for Media Education.

Oswell, D. (1999). The dark side of cyberspace: Internet content regulation and child protection. *Convergence, 5*(4), 42–61.

Papacharissi, Z., & Rubin, A. M. (2000). Predictors of Internet use. *Journal of Broadcasting and Electronic Media, 44*, 175–196.

Pappert, S. (1995). *La máquina de los niños*. Barcelona: Paidós.

Pasquier, D., Buzzi, C., D'Haevens, & Sjörberg. (1999). Family lifestyles and media use patterns: An analysis of domestic media among Flemish, French, Italian, and Swedish children and teenagers. *European Journal of Communication, 13*(4), 503–519.

Perse, E. M., & Dunn, D. G. (1998). The utility of home computers and media use: Implications of multimedia and connectivity. *Journal of Broadcasting and Electronic Media, 42*, 435–456.

Roberts, D. F. (2000). Media and youth: Access, exposure, and privatization. *Journal of Adolescent Health, 27*(2), 8–14.

Sefton-Green, J. (1998). *Digital diversions: Youth culture in the age of multimedia*. Los Angeles, CA: UCLA Publications Department.

Sefton-Green, J., Buckingham, D., & Tobin, J. (1998). The difference is digital? Digital technology and student media production. *Convergence, 5*(4), 10–19.

Silverstone, R. (1992). *Consuming technologies: Media and information in domestic spaces*. London, New York: Routledge.

Stern, S. (1999). Adolescent girl's expression on Web home pages: Spirited, sombre, and self-conscious sites. *Convergence, 5*(4), 24–41.

Suess, D., Suonien, A., Garitaonandia, C., Juaristi, P., Koikkalainen, R., & Oleaga, J. A. (1998). Media use and the relationship of children and teenagers with their peer groups: A study of Finnish, Spanish, and Swiss cases. *European Journal of Communication, 13*(4), 521–538.

Tapscott, D. (1998). *Growing up digital: The rise of the net generation*. New York: McGraw-Hill.

Turrow, J., & Nir, L. (2000). *The Internet and the family: The view from parents, the view from kids*. Philadelphia: Annenberg Public Policy Center.

Valentine, G., & Holloway, S. (1999). The vision thing: Schools and communication technology. *Convergence, 5*(1), 24–45.

Van der Voort, H. A., Eeentjes, J., Bovil, M., Gaskell, G., Koolstra, C., Livingstone, S., & Marseille, N. (1998). Young people ownership and uses of new and old forms of media in Britain and in The Netherlands. *European Journal of Communication, 13*(4), 457–477.

9

Learners, Spectators, or Gamers? An Investigation of the Impact of Digital Media in the Media-Saturated Household

Stephen Kline

The era of Java Enterprise Computing has arrived. No longer must we be tied to a single master. Today we consider the following to be inalienable and available to all. The right to harness technology to stay, not just one, but several steps ahead of the game. The right to a new computing dynamic with the vision to take you into the future. And not only do you have the right to information technology that works the way you want it to, you have the right to change it at will. It is your due, now is the time to realize significant return on your technological investment. It is not simply about systems, it's about the emancipation of information. Java Enterprise Computing is here and it will set you free. [Stretched across the two-page ad is the text "LIBERTY!"]

TAKING THE HYPE OUT OF HYPERMEDIA

The Java ad is a fine example of the silicon-coated technological hyperbole that captured the public imagination at the gateway of the new millennium. Around the world this theory of mediated (digital) convergence not only has primed the pumps of a roiling speculative economic bubble, but also has forged a new cyberspace ideology whose Janus gods connectivity and interactivity have promised solutions to all our social problems. This chapter exposes the technological determinism that underwrote this ideology and proposes a more critical way of thinking about the impact of the virtual playgrounds it has helped to construct for our children.

The informatics manifesto declared in Java's advertising can be traced to Alvin Toffler's (1981) book *The Third Wave*, which first popularized faith in computers as a progressive force for social change. History, claimed Toffler (1981), teaches that technological invention was the most powerful force for changing the whole of society. The growth of agricultural techniques constituted the first wave, and manufacturing technologies the second, but it was communications technologies that would precipitate the third and most radical wave of social change. According to Toffler (1981), industrial era technologies, such as the mechanized assembly line and mass media, encouraged rigid hierarchies, harsh class divisions, and depersonalized mass cultures. Computers on the other hand, were a protean technology capable of vastly enhancing the intelligence of all media, ultimately ensuring that openness, flexibility, and adaptability were afforded to the humans who used them. Toffler (1981) said:

> The Third Wave of historical change represents a straight-line extension of industrial society, but a radical shift of direction, often a negation, of what went before. It adds up to nothing less than a complete transformation at least as revolutionary in our day as industrial civilization was 300 years ago.

Rather than bend humans to mechanical age rhythms and routines, computers would help make mass society more responsive to the range of human needs and desires. So if the medium was the message, then computers were setting America on the road toward change, flexibility, and adaptation.

The technological hyperbole of computer revolutionaries gradually diffused from the geeky circles of computering copy writers into the mainstream of corporate economics. As William Leiss (1991) noted, their vision of a born again capitalism permeated the public discourses of the 1990s, echoing the progressive rhetoric of the 1920s and 1950s, with the only difference being that human progress now depended on a computerized "demassification" rather than brute mechanical power. Massachusetts Institute of Technology cyber guru Nicholas Negroponte's (1995) *Being Digital* provides a crowning example of the technological hyperbole rhetoric that bubbled into public consciousness. Computering, he claimed, will bring greater democracy and freedom to the world: "Like a force of nature, the digital age cannot be denied or stopped. It has four very powerful qualities that will result in its ultimate triumph: decentralizing, globalizing, harmonizing, and empowering" (p. 229).

As if our future social life were inscribed in silicon, Negroponte (1995) offered a vision of our future reorchestrated by powers of computerized communications technologies that saturate the whole cultural environment:

Your right and left cuff links or earrings may communicate with each other by low orbiting satellites and have more computer power than your present PC. Mass media will be redefined by systems for transmitting and receiving personalized information and entertainment. Schools will change to become more like museums and playgrounds for children to assemble ideas and socialize with other children all over the world. The digital planet will look and feel like the head of a pin. (p. 6)

Guided by their visions of unending profits, computer entrepreneurs such as Sun and Oracle transformed Tofflerian hyperbole into a wired futurism in which the "unlimited potentialities" of networked interactive multimedia would lead us to prosperity and peace. Frances Cairncross (1997) of the *Economist* wrote with conviction about the promise of convergence. She said:

The death of distance will probably be the single most important force shaping society in the first half of the next century. It will alter, in ways that are only dimly imaginable, decisions about where people work and what kind of work they do, concepts of national borders and sovereignty, and patterns of international trade. (p. 1)

She went on to predict:

The changes sweeping through electronic communications will transform the world's economies, politics and societies—but they will first transform companies. They will alter the ways companies reach their customers, affecting advertising, shopping, distribution, and so on; they will create new businesses; and they will change the way companies communicate with one another and with their staffs.

For this reason the corporate world had to embrace convergence if they were to survive in the new economy.

And embrace it they did. Believing their own copywriters, News Corp, Disney, Sony, WorldCom, and Vivendi started their march down the information revolution road to unstoppable profitability with vastly overstated expectations. These companies planned for a future based on a wildly optimistic, and ludicrously vague theory of communication. It imagined rapid social change emerging from a wired marketplace forged from the convergence of computers, television, and telecom technologies.

The same sense of digital inevitability began to permeate both government policy—the guidelines and subsidies that made the Web into a commercial medium—and corporate advertising, in which copywriters projected a bold rhetoric of an information age onto the multiscreen collective unconsciousness. Laptops, cell phones, and digital address books were sold to millions. The average family now spends proportionately more money on cultural, entertainment, and communication services to the home than ever before.

But the demand for information commodities cannot be infinite. In the saturated IT markets, cell phones and computer prices began to drop because most people who wanted them had them. Profit projections fell, and massive debts acquired the status of junk bonds, which is why doom and gloom invades the high-tech boardrooms of the nation. Indeed, although Amazon.com found it could sell books online, it could not make Americans into avid readers. With the disappearance of 6 trillion dollars from the stock market and an American economy in perpetual doldrums, commentators finally are struggling to understand just what went wrong in the 1990's.

It does not matter whether one reads *New Statesman, Le Monde, The Wall Street Journal,* or *Fortune,* the failures of the "information revolution" are now everywhere in evidence. As Canadian commentator Jeffrey Simpson (2002) suggested recently, the rise and fall of the information economy has become the morality tale of the millennium framed by "Monumental egos. A bristling new idea. Thrilling technology. The entrepreneurial spirit. But also greed, glitz, stupidity, recklessness, folly and ultimately failure." As Simpson (2002) explained, "Like Tolstoy's unhappy marriages, the disappointments and disasters of convergence differed in each case, but the end result was similar: the limitations of communication technologies to revolutionize our cultural practices."

Nowhere is the hubris of this hi-tech drama better exemplified than in the spectacular rise and fall of AOL-Time Warner's chief architect of synergy, Steve Case, who once stood as the lion king gazing out across the e-commerce jungle. As AOL's CEO, Case was one of the most effusive exponents of convergence and the man responsible for the merger of the old media empire of Time Warner and the new media empire of AOL. On January 17th, Case resigned, and on January 29, 2003 AOL-Time Warner announced losses of 98.7 billion dollars for the accounting year 2002, the largest ever recorded in American history.

Of course, we should have known better. As Kevin Robins (1995) stated, belief in the coming Information Age demanded a profound leap of faith into vague social theory: "All this is driven by a feverish belief in transcendence; a faith that, this time round, a new technology will finally and truly deliver us from the limitations and frustrations of this imperfect world" (p. 135). He went on to say: "There is a common vision of a future that will be different from the present, of a space or a reality that is more desirable than the mundane one that presently surrounds and contains us. It is a tunnel vision. It has turned a blind eye on the world we live in" (p. 135).

Since the "cyber-bubble" economy took a nosedive at the end of 2000, there has been a growing sense of realism about this convergent mediascape and a willingness to accept the limitations of a digital world still at war. Obviously, the rhetoric of converging technology was hideously vague and ungainly. Its promises all were based on poorly thought out and never tested promotional concepts. The media theory of its proponents was technological determinism of the worst sort. It mistook the possibility of the medium for the message while ignoring the specific cultural practices that embedded media use in the dynamics and social relations that conscribe contemporary households. Indeed, their puffery would leave us laughing now if it were not for the fact that it was precisely this rhetoric that galvanized the looming crisis of confidence in the hi-tech free-range capitalism it prophesied (Kline, Dyer-Witherford, & de Peuter, 2003).

Amid the shards of our wired utopia, the pundits are renouncing the promotional buzz words of the information age: convergence, synergy, interactivity, multimedia, artificial intelligence, flexibility, responsiveness. Some have sold their dot.com shares and donned a critical tone, mocking those euphoric promises of an wired world of peace and prosperity forged by the diffusion of computers, the commercialization of the Internet, and the globalization of media industries. Perhaps we should be content that their hubris has defined the morality play of the infant millennium. But that would mean ignoring the profound ideologic confusions that underwrote the digirati's prophesy that networked playgrounds would liberate the next generation.

GROWING UP DIGITAL

A 1998 Intel ad featured a group of pastel space suit–clad chip makers dancing gaily in the factory to rock music while they installed "fun" into the MMX chips. Intel's tale neatly recapitulates the origin myth of video gaming—the moment of realization that computers are not just destined for use in the workplace, but have a place in the streets, in the homes, and in the communities of the global information society as instruments of domestic entertainment and social communication. In a sequel ad, the dancing Intel workers move out of the factory and hit the Information Highway in their space capsule-like roadster to bring these playful machines to kids around the world. Their "MMX technology" is just one more exciting digital innovation on the road to interactive entertainment and global connectivity. Driving through the global marketplace, however, they discover with surprise that "kids already get it." Indeed, the happy throngs of postmodern youth have welcomed this networked virtual playground with enthusiasm. Like other promotional discourses on the Information Age, this ad offers a rapturous vision of the effect of new communication infrastructures being laid down in the wired society, ending with what might be called the "primal scene" of the information economy: future generations happily locked in the embrace of connected interactive media.

What often is overlooked in recent accounts of the information economy is how the public discourses on the computer revolution quickly became intertwined with the debates about mass-mediated childhood and children's video game play. *Time* magazine, greatly impressed with children's fascination with domestic computers, in 1981 declared the computer the "man of the year." *Time* quoted mathematician and computering educator Seymour Papert (1980), who promised that children not only were the pioneers, but that they also would be the main beneficiaries of this cultural revolution because computers facilitated active problem solving. Papert's pedagogy of constructivism was developed throughout his career promoting a technologically enhanced version of Piagetian developmental theory. In a series of books, he asserted his faith in computers as learning tools based on postulates about the medium:

That computers, like toys had the ability to fascinate and therefore motivate children by making learning fun

That they were intelligent and therefore adapted the assimilation of knowledge to the capacities and interests of the learner

That as a part of everyday play cultures, multimedia cultivated an autonomous zone free from parental control, in which, like toys, children constructed and bonded through self-made play interactions.

Papert's (1993) pedagogical theories promised that the national embrace of computers would quickly replace the paternalistic infrastructure of mass education with constructivist student-centered learning.

In 1994 president Clinton announced his National Information Infrastructure Initiative—the so-called "information superhighway" policy, which commercialized the Internet in an attempt to jump-start the information age. This policy set out to consolidate the already-existing network of fiber optics, copper wires, cable radio waves, and satellites into an integrated web comprising computerized channels of two-way data flows between computerized communication hubs. It was the day, he said, that America was taking a giant step into the Information Age. Three promises underscored Clinton's commitment to commercialized networked multimedia: (a) Networked media would galvanize creativity in the entertainment industry, (b) it would provide citizens with unlimited access to all kinds of information, and (c) it would reinvigorate schooling by providing potent new ways of teaching.

Gradually, many educators came to believe that computers were protean devices that could radically change how schools thought about and managed learning. Of course, other media also had promised to rock the cradle. Toys, comics, and TV in turn also were heralded as revolutions in youth culture. Although each became popular with children and found their way into schools, social change happened slowly, and schools adjusted their programs only marginally. So why were we to believe that computers were revolutionary pedagogical tools? The reasons, according to Henry and McLennan (1994), lay in the fact that multimedia represented the convergence of previous learning tools: television, books, toys, and films. As "new" media, multimedia were not an extension of historical processes of modernization, but a force for its overthrow and reversal:

> Unlike these earlier technologies, multimedia is interactive. It has the ability therefore to replicate some teacher/learner interaction. It also has the ability to link the student with tutors, his or her peers in other places, and with remote sources of information. (Telstra, 1994, p. 1)

Children's culture commentators such as Douglas Rushkoff also climbed on the digital bandwagon, extolling the control over learning processes. In *Media Virus*, Rushkoff (1994) quoted Timothy Leary in defense of his belief that computers were about to release a whole generation of children from the top-down control of the mass media: "The importance of the Nintendo phenomenon is about equal to that of the Gutenberg printing press. Here you had a new generation of kids who grew up knowing that they could change what's on the screen" (p. 30). The silicon apostles of the coming digital era claimed that Toffler (1981) was right. Because young people were to be the pioneers in this brave new digital world, we could look to them to understand what was happening argued Negroponte (1995), for their lives were the first to be transformed:

> We are not waiting on any invention. It is here. It is now. It is almost genetic in its nature, in that each generation will become more digital than the proceeding one. The control bits of that digital future are more than ever before in the hands of the young. Nothing could make me happier. (p. 231)

New media were already challenging the authority and paternalistic values of mass society, widening the generational divide between computer-literate youth and their parents, claimed the wired guru's. Even Japanese management guru Ken Ohmae (1995) speculated on the generational implications arising from this medium's rapid diffusion to youth in Japan. "Nintendo kids," Ohmae (1995) asserted, "are making new connections with the tens of millions of their peers throughout the world who have learned to play the same sorts of games and have learned the same lessons" (pp. 161–162). "The web of culture," he said, "used to be spun from the stories a child heard at a grandparent's knee. Today it derives from that children's experience with interactive multimedia." Commenting especially on the enormous popularity of video gaming in Japan, Ohmae (1995) noted "a cultural divide growing between young people and their elders." But he was enthusiastic about this break with tradition because he believed it would lessen the social isolation of the next generation and internationalize their attitudes. He went on to speculate:

> That experience has given them the opportunity, not readily available else-where in Japanese culture, to play different roles at different times, of asking the what-if questions they could never ask before. . . . Perhaps most impor-tant, Nintendo kids have learned, through their games, to revisit the basic rules of their world and even to reprogram them if necessary. . . . The mes-sage which is completely alien to traditional Japanese culture is that one can take active control of one's situation and change one's fate. No one need sub-mit passively to authority. (pp. 161–162)

This may be only the beginning, claimed Douglas Rushkoff (1996) in *Playing the Future*, wherein he boldly predicted that "interactivity" and "connectiv-ity" will become the forces of generational liberation. He claimed that com-puters were now so prevalent that they were already beginning to reverse the alienation and isolation created by the mass broadcast technologies of the past.

To understand the difference between interactive media and television one needs to realize that in playing video games, unlike watching television, users gain control over the flow of information from the screen:

> Thanks to video games, kids have a fundamentally different appreciation of the television image than their parents. . . . Rather than simply receiving me-dia they are changing images on the screen. (Rushkoff, 1999, p. 182)

Teenagers from around the world, he claimed, now assemble in "virtual communities," using networked multimedia to make their own culture, play-ing online games and socializing in chat rooms. For Rushkoff (1996), today's "screenager sees how the entire mediaspace is a cooperative dream made up of the combined projections of everyone who takes part" (p. 269).

> While their parents may condemn Nintendo as mindless and masturbatory, kids who have mastered video gaming early on stand a better chance of ex-ploiting the real but mediated interactivity that will make itself available to them by the time they hit technopuberty in their teens. (1999, p. 31)

Similarly enthusiastic about networked computers, Donald Tapscott (1998) emphasized the role that connectivity played in the liberation and leveling of the digital generation. Tapscott argued that today's kids are growing up in a society and economy very different from those of the boom-ers. Therefore, the way they are educated and prepared in schools must change to keep up with the world with which they are connecting. He argued that the only way out of the crisis in modern education is to "shift from broadcast learning to interactive learning." And the tool for achieving that shift was the Internet.

Tapscott (1998) believed that

> digital media is creating an environment where such activities of childhood are changing dramatically and may, for better or for worse, accelerate child development. Child development is concerned with the evolution of motor skills, language skills, and social skills. It also involves the development of cognition, intelligence, reasoning, personality and through adolescence, the creation of autonomy, a sense of self and values. . . . All of these are enhanced in an interactive world. When children control their media, rather than passively observe, they develop faster. (p. 7)

> The new media, because of its distributed interactive and many-to-many nature, has a greater neutrality. A new set of values is arising as children begin to communicate, play, learn, work, and think with the new media. More than ever before, a generation is beginning to learn. Call it generational learning. (p. 9)

The N-Generation, as Tapscott (1998) called them, already exhibit a strong preference for the interactive media instead of the older broadcast technologies that do not respond to their needs or their way of learning. He claimed that this is because "N-Geners" view it as a natural extension of themselves. It is in fact the specific medium that will follow and perpetuate the force of their youth, just as television has traced the lives of the boomers" (p. 31).

It was the networking of home computers that changed the one-way passivity of television audiences into a dynamic network of active learners. The Internet enabled these savvy young questers for knowledge to search the Web for the latest information and to self-organize into playful communities, even to set up their own Web sites and forge their own peer cultures. The Web was the ultimate tool of informal learning, Tapscott (1998) concluded. Freed from the top-down world of formal schooling, children established their own codes and styles of interaction in the digital playgrounds being provided online by far-thinking entrepreneurs in cyber-savvy organizations.

In short, kids did get the message of digital revolution. So it is hardly surprising that the one remaining star in the e-commerce firmament has been "interactive entertainment." Video game makers Sony, Nintendo, and Microsoft and their online gaming products continue to expand even while the rest of the dot.com world has drifted into a funk (Canadian Press, 2001). With the launch of graphically upgraded consoles and superfast graphic computers, U.S. game revenues swelled to $10.6 billion in 2001, a figure that surpasses the total annual box office receipts for movies and matches the amount spent on computers for schools. Although the National Information Infrastructure was meant to propel the American educational system into the information age, the real beneficiaries of interactivity are the digital entertainment industries. Ultima, one of the first PC games to move successfully online, has 125,000 subscribers who pay U.S. $10 monthly after their $40 to $70 initial costs to play Ultima Online (Kranz, 1999). The average Ultima Online player behaves like a member of a cult, logging 17 hr per week online, and frequently far more. Saved characters and items can be sold to other players or traded at ancillary Web sites for an amount up to and exceeding U.S. $3,000 (Gunter, 1999).

Indeed, the online entertainment market expanded rapidly throughout the 1990s as Doom and Counterstrike pioneered the multiplayer metagenre, which blended the shooter and the role-play adventures into an online war game experience. One of the most profitable of these networked games is Everquest. Currently, more than 350,000 individuals are paid subscribers at the price of approximately U.S. $10 per month, which grosses $3.5 million per month. This is in addition to the roughly U.S. $50 initial price for each game and $30 each for the three expansion programs, which brings in a revenue of $350 million per year.

CHILDREN'S MEDIA CULTURES IN TRANSITION?

> Once a single library held the knowledge of the world.
> Centuries later, data was still controlled by an elite few.
> Then Oracle freed everyone to work with databases.
> Today, Oracle is putting the knowledge of the world online.
> "It will forever change our markets and our culture" (says Oracle's CEO, Larry Ellison)
> Where do you learn about companies whose future is as limitless as our hunger to know?
> Exactly: Nasdaq.com. (Oracle Databases TV commercial 1998)

Negroponte (1995), Tapscott (1998), and Rushkoff (1999) portray the coming of "cyber gaming" as a revolutionizing force in children's lives overthrowing the authoritarian, centralized, elitist model of mass media in favor of emancipatory, decentralized, distributed, and populist "republic" of networked interactivity by which digital kids will feel most at home surfing the net and playing video games. After an analysis of several hundred magazine and television ads for this emerging genre of interactive entertainment, it is impossible not to notice the same Toffleresque tropes. Video game advertisers have portrayed interactive media as embodying the educational benefits of computers, the immersive liveliness of TV fantasy, and the social connectivity of telephones (Kline & de Peuter, 2002). In promotional missives to parents and teachers, interactive media have promised to enhance children's enthusiasm for learning, provide accessible resources for knowledge, and motivate young people with fun (Selwyn, Dawes, & Mercer, 2001). As illustrated in the Oracle ad, against a backdrop of feared mass media passivity, "interactivity" and "connectivity" are taken to be libratory because immersion in "virtual" worlds is touted to be both an intellectually challenging yet fun way to skill children for the inevitably wired future. Even sober educators, developmental psychologists, and children's media researchers rallied behind this utopian promise that video games would help children discover autonomy and a freedom in the pansophic world of cyberspace.

The author has listened to innumerable talks by optimistic researchers promising that free explorations of connected multimedia products such as online Web sites, encyclopedia, and educational games offered innumerable advantages and no disadvantages of past educational media: books, toys and films. Children, they claimed, explore these complex cyberworlds willingly, and therefore are motivated to learn better despite the marginal proof (Becker, 2000). They dismissed the violence of gaming, the cyberstalking in the chat rooms, the insistence of porn merchants, the banality of "cut and paste" homework assignments, the encounters with racism and hate sites, the perpetual Spam as incidental to the logic of networked computers, and the inherent "potentialities" interactive media bring to children's learning.

The author also has visited classrooms in which proud teachers showed him students aimlessly "texting" to each other about rock stars, surfing fanzines, or even playing video games in the classroom, as if these were ways of fulfilling the IT curriculum because no legitimate educational strategy has been developed for the use of the networked computers. Viewing digital culture through rosy lenses, the Information and Communication Technologies (ICT) enthusiasts not only ignored the various risks (and the costs), but willingly put the future of both schooling and children's leisure into the hands of the various global corporations and organizations that can afford to design and distribute interactive entertainment worldwide.

Perhaps the most protean feature of the information age lies in the discursive practices of the cybergurus who describe children's entertainment experiences with interactive media as if anything and everything was made possible by computerizing television. Video gaming is taken to be the exemplary interactive experience because gaming is assumed to be a dynamic, social, and self-motivated type of communication activity. In this digital version of the play ethos, gaming is endlessly enobling; making menued choices is the expression of creativity; any response to a simulated challenge is a strategic "action" based on a "decoding" of the problem; moving through virtual mazes is tantamount to exploring and mastering one's own

imaginations; the fantastical settings are providing exposure to other perspectives and points of view; and any kind of exchange between players en-
tails the consolidation of the online player community. These afficiando's
speak as if computers reinvented play. A graphic spatial representation is
now a "virtual reality"; audiovisual presentations of text, image, and sound
on the TV screen are "multimedia experiences"; and iconic representations
of characters are "computer presences" or "avatars." Most important, video
games are "immersive" rather than "escapist" because users can imagine
that they control the flow of fantastical images from the screen.

The author admires their linguistic creativity, but it must be remembered
that interactivity, interpretation, fantasy, and exploration are properties of all
communication media—even television. Television also is multimedia, pos-
sessing all the same audiovisual potentialities of moving images, music,
sound, and text. Television even allows a degree of control over the flow of
programming, although this is more true of the video game, in which control
includes the possibility of maneuvering and navigating through game spaces.
The navigational interface enables the player to make choices during the narrative or problem-solving action, creating the impression of control over the
flow of meaning. But choice is experienced as a matter of tactical decisions
executed within predefined scenarios whose strategic parameters are preor-
dained by the programming. The suspension of disbelief, however, is as
much a part of the video gaming experience as it is of all representational
forms because the choices must be preprogrammed into the game.

Perhaps it is more than just the optimist's faith in technology that needs
rethinking. Of all the forms of childhood communication activities, none is
more dynamic or ambiguous than game play. A group of children engaged
in role-play or sports provides a benchmark for the self-determining creative expressive events that most venerate with the word "play." To equate
two-way exchanges of digital information within computerized multimedia
networks with this idea of social play, as if the former exhausts the later, is
seriously to reduce the dynamism of social play. Put simply, the practices
of technological design and programming sets limits on the possibility of
culture making. Indeed, choosing a character or a weapon—rail gun or a
chain saw in a Quake Death Match—is hardly a matter of radical openness
or "real choice" experienced in playful encounters. In short, playing a video
game may be more flexible than watching TV, but it is not identical to a
group of kids in a park spontaneously discussing what game they should
play next.

Computer technology did create new possibilities for human expression.
No one will deny that interactive media provides the user with a greater degree of control over the flow of information, the cultural consumer with a
novel leisure product, or the gamer with a dynamic *spielraum* enabling social interaction with other players around the world. But this new cultural

trajectory has depended on the social institutions that designed and distributed gaming experiences as well as the resources and interest of those audiences that used them. Yet when one actually looks at what the educational game producers have invested in, one discovers that the design and distribution of interactive products has been constrained by marketing imperatives. It can cost between $2 and $10 million to produce a game, so although anything can conceivably be programmed into a computer, market economics is a constraining factor narrowing the potential diversity of interactive experiences to the games preferred by the most loyal and frequent buyers of games—youthful males (Kline, 1997). It is difficult to find evidence of those liberated subjectivities and egalitarian ethics in the actual virtual play spaces designed for young males seeking intensified and violent conflict and escapism (Provenzo, 1997).

It is not surprising, therefore, that on the other side of the information highway, Neil Postman's (1993) book *Technopoly* has provided what is perhaps the clearest expression of neoluddite skepticism about the potential of computers for kids. For Postman (1993), computers, like TV, fostered a mindless escapism that hastened the declining literacy and growing uncivility of the Nintendo generation. Postman (1993) lamented that another generation was about to be amused to death by vapid entertainment delivered through new electronic channels. The introduction of interactive media into their daily rituals, he argued, will continue to erode the "four hundred-year-old truce between gregariousness and openness fostered by orality and the introspection and isolation fostered by the printed word." Postman (1993) frowned upon the unrestrained enthusiasm for computers within educational circles, stating:

> In the most dramatic terms, the accusation can be made that the uncontrolled growth of technology destroys the vital sources of our humanity. It creates a culture without a moral foundation. It undermines certain mental processes and social relations that make human life worth living. (p. xiii)

Postman (1993) challenged the idea the computers are inherently educational, preferring to point to the commercial institutions and cultural practices that program and profit from it:

> Surrounding every technology are institutions whose organization—not to mention their reason for being—reflects the world view promoted by the technology. (p. 18)

In Postman's view, computer technology, like television before it, is part of broader cultural system in moral decline, which undermines the 400-year tradition of productive leisure fostered by the values and belief systems cultivated around "literate" childhood.

LEARNERS, SPECTATORS, OR PLAYERS?
RESEARCHING THE MEDIA-SATURATED
HOUSEHOLD

Their faith in technology and their ignorance of social history are the twin indications that the cyberenthusiasts have not bothered to think very carefully about the specific conjuncture of possibilities in which interactive media have been developed or how contemporary children use and are affected by this networked playground. This revolutionary rhetoric of convergence, it seems, has ignored some key lessons of communication theory taught by scholars such as Marshall McLuhan (1964). Of the various insights he offered, perhaps his most discussed and least understood is that the "medium is the message." This phrase often is taken as a jumping-off point for the digital technological hyperbole of the enthusiasts, who fail to appreciate McLuhan's (1964) paradoxical historical sensibility. New media were not necessarily good or evil, but they often did profoundly alter the course of a culture. Clarifying this aphorism, McLuhan (1964) stated that by this infamous phrase he implied no technological inevitability, but rather reminded us that "any understanding of social and cultural change is impossible without a knowledge of *the way media work as environments.*" The task of media studies was to examine carefully the bias of experience implicit in media, which as extensions of some aspect of ourselves, expanded our human potential for communication, generating unique, and sometimes contradictory, disturbances in our social institutions, arts, knowledge, attitudes, habits, and perceptions (McLuhan, 1964, p. 26). Historically, as McLuhan (1964) pointed out, television did not overthrow the literate culture that preceded it so much as it absorbed and reworked old forms of communication as contents and forms migrated into new media or were hybridized as they interacted with each other in the new electronic environment.

As the title of this chapter suggests, computers were developed within a cultural environment with well-established modalities of communication forged around three prior children's media: books, playthings, and TV. Taking literacy as the measure of civility, a modern conception of progressive childhood emerged in the early 20th century that made learning to read and write the essential agenda of children's intellectual development. As Brian Sutton-Smith (1986) has pointed out, toys and games also were to make play the "work of childhood." In becoming players, children were encouraged to participate in a socializing activity that became the sanctioned form of productive leisure—a healthy way for children to spend their idle time, to express their natural exuberance, and to have fun in a socially acceptable way (Sutton-Smith, 1986). It was against the ideology of toys and books as tools of progress that children's television entertainments came as a shock. Instead of educating children, broadcasting seemed to offer only passive entertainment, a flood of popular cultural experiences that attracted child spectators, but offered few of the redeeming qualities associated with the "productive" pursuits of play and learning.

McLuhan (1964) saw the contemporary child as torn between the literate culture of the book and the postmodern culture of mass media. Although not generally thought of as a play theorist, he was keenly aware of the growing importance of play cultures. For him, the child watching sports or game shows on TV was not just a passive viewer of an entertainment content, but also a participant in a play ritual. A game, he pointed out, is a very ancient tribal cultural form, a ritual occasion for social communication defined by rules and competition "contrived to permit simultaneous participation of many people in some significant pattern of their own corporate lives" (p. 210). The games a people play, he noted, are themselves mass "media that communicate specific cultural values and sentiments." In what might be his most prescient observation, he saw the broadcast media as amplifying the modalities of play in the postmodern culture. Yet he also recognized the underlying tensions created within cultural commentaries as people adjusted to these new modalities of communication, warning:

> We are today as far into the electric age as the Elizabethans had advanced into the typographical and mechanical age. And we are experiencing the same confusions and indecisions which they had felt when living simultaneously in two contrasted forms of society and experience.

Unfortunately, Marshall McLuhan's (1964) complex portrait of the emerging global village traumatized by colliding media cultures has been all but forgotten by those optimists who foretell our children's happy future from the "interactivity" of computers. Yet it was into this mixed and synergistic cultural context pulled in one direction by schools and in the other by electronic media that video gaming was first introduced during the 1980s. Although they were originally regarded as toys, interactive media have quickly shown themselves to be a highly convergent medium combining learning, play, and entertainment in a synergistic experience. As computers, they were programmable books that could deliver learning experiences in a more dynamic user-friendly way. Yet as high tech toys, computer games also could stimulate children's "productive play" and the history of sports, role-play, competition, and skills training that have become deeply embedded in children's culture. By linking players through online connections interactive, media were forging new channels of communal participation in play. As a text-based information distribution system, connectivity provided access to information databases that made books appear to be sluggish and forbidding ways of learning. In short, interactive media are a hybrid cultural form that combine the storytelling capacities of video and the information-processing capacities of computers with the active participation of toys. This hybrid medium has grown into a rapidly expanding digital entertainment network that complements and competes with other media traditions in children's lives. The aforementioned analysis suggests that it is the hybridization of cultural traditions rather than the convergence of technologies that is the most interesting feature of the interactive media environment.

Sonia Livingstone (2002) and George Gaskell (Livingstone & Gaskell, 1996) argued that it also is time to stop speculating about how new media impacted kids and to study empirically the actual use of these "new media" within the domestic context. Livingstone's (2002) account of the impact of new media shows why we must take seriously "the notion of the media environment" by providing a more realistic picture of how children incorporate various electronic information and entertainment sources into their daily routines within the media-saturated household.

Livingstone's (2002) study of media use in the home situates children's patterned use of new media within the underlying household social ecologies including the physical organization and social relations of family life. Time spent in mediated, as opposed to personal, communication is at a historical high in the United Kingdom. National policy and commercial environments obviously play an important role in the patterns of media technologies use in the home. For example, according to Livingstone (2002), the differences between Britain's "bedroom" culture (privatized media) and more traditional familial use patterns found on the continent deserve some attention, as do sociological factors because as in Himmelweit's original study, media use patterns are contingent on class, region, and gender. Therefore, for all the promises of universal education, ICTs remain a socially embedded cultural resource within contemporary British families.

The communication patterns of young people are diverse. They include social interaction, homework, leisure reading, playing, looking for information, and being entertained in various ways and through diverse media. Yet their use of old media such as TV, CDs, and books for entertainment is not largely altered by the incursions of the digital technologies. The new media too seem to have been incorporated into the old media cultural patterns, particularly social interaction and popular entertainments. The addition of video game play is perhaps the most significant new communication activity in the media-rich household, especially for boys. As Livingstone (2002) concluded:

> While adults wish children would gain from the encyclopaedic knowledge resources of the Internet, their children play fantasy games or follow their fa-

vorite television and sports stars, or discuss their lives—cautiously, playfully, or controversially—in chat rooms. (p. 241)

American researchers provide a similarly telling picture of the impact that new media have had on children's communication routines at home. Interactive media are found in the vast majority of American households, but the old media still pervade their day. The amount of TV viewing averages 2.45 hr, and has not decreased across the youthful population, which continues to read magazines and listen to music. Although the time spent using all media has increased with wired penetration of the household to 5.29 hr, a digital divide persists, with wealthier children owning PCs more, having more media in their bedrooms, and having access to the Internet, and with poorer children rely more on TV and video games for their electronic entertainment and being net consumers of all media for an hour longer (Kaiser, 1999). Time spent with media increases from 3.34 hr among the 2- to 7-year-olds to 6.43 hr for the 8- to 18-year-olds because children have tended to add up to 1 hr of new media use to their already stretched leisure schedules. New media are used more by boys than girls. Boys also clearly have access to and enjoy video game play more. Although they spend little time completing homework assignments online or researching their hobbies, young people have accepted interactive media as a comfortable place to spend just less than 1 hr of their leisure time each day (ACCP, 2000).

A similar story unfolds in Canada, where the number of wired households with children hovers around 79%. Indeed, the households of Canadian children are among the most wired in the world, and these children are well on their way to being among ICT's most avid users. In a recent Canadian study of more than 5,000 young people conducted by the Media Awareness Network (2001), researchers found that the young people still preferred television, which 81% report using every day, as compared with 43% who go on the Internet every day. Music and video games also are popular, with 48% of males, but only 16% of girls playing offline every day. Economic status and gender are important factors shaping how Canadian children gain access to and routinely use the net (Sciades, 2000). At home, the Internet is used primarily for downloading free music and software (Napster still was free), playing games, chatting, and cruising fan sites. The way children use the Internet, however, is gendered, with girls being more likely to prefer messaging and e-mail (68% vs. 45%) and chatting (42% vs. 32%) and with boys preferring gaming (56% vs. 37%). Gaming and downloading of music remain the most frequently reported use of the Internet. The least favorite activity of Canadian children is using the Web for educational purposes, which they do only when they are required to do so. Although 7% of the children reported using the Internet daily for homework, this was done mostly at school.

The author's own studies of media-saturated families in British Colum-bia[1] has more or less replicated Livingstone's (2002) studies finding that teens are spending up to 6.1 hr per day with electronic communication. Sim-ilar to youth in Europe, these teens have more scope to choose among more communication options than ever before. They have books, music, games, phones, and screens in abundance, often in their rooms. A visitor opening the door of teens' bedrooms in British Columbia will inevitably find books (94%), music (91%), TVs (42%) and Internet connections (30%). More than 80% reported having two or more media in their rooms (14% had six or more).

Despite these new communication options, music and television watch-ing have evidently not lost their appeal as traditional forms of entertain-ment, taking up the lion's share of young peoples leisure. Together, watch-ing TV and listening to music are the main forms of entertainment (24 hr per week). Downloading music on the net and listening to it on MP3 have supplemented the radio and phonograph. Moreover, as in the past, teens spend a lot of time maintaining social contact (8 hr/week for girls and 5 hr/week for boys). When young people use the Internet, it is largely to down-load music, to chat with friends, to cruise the fan sites, and increasingly to play online games (Kline, 2001). To the degree that cell phones and ICTs provide new channels for social interchange, they can provide a space for a favorite teen activity: conversations and hanging out. Although TV time is the same for both genders, boys report reading less than girls (see Fig. 9.1).

Although music, reading, hanging out with friends, sports, and of course television dominate the preferred activities of teens in British Columbia, boys do put video games at the top of their list. New "digital" media fill an-other 21 hr per week, with boys spending at least 1 hr per day more than girls with them, mainly using the computer or playing video games, increas-ingly playing games online. Girls report being less enamored with video games, but do explore the fan sites and send messages. The also are more likely to read books and enter chats. For most teens, ICTs seem to vie with the telephone as a medium for bonding with friends in chat rooms or online gaming dens.

The current study found a considerable "digital divide" between boys' and girls' access to new media. Twice as many boys reported having ready access to video games (43% vs. 17%), PCs (43% vs. 22%), and Internet con-nections (40% vs. 17%) in their rooms than girls. Access to media in their own rooms consistently related to their propensity to use them more (see Fig. 9.2).

---

[1]Data was gathered from 728 British Columbia teens in 2000. A full report on this study can be found at http://www.sfu.ca/media-lab/research/mediasat/secondschool.pdf.

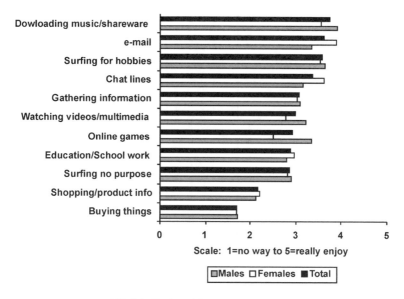

FIG. 9.1. Preferred Internet activities.

The digital divide reflects the gendered entertainment preferences established in children's play cultures. Boys prefer the action combat, strategy, and role-play games, whereas girls prefer the adventure, puzzle, and classic games (see Tables 9.1 and 9.2). Rather than change children's play cultures, digital media seem to be consolidating the same barriers that have long existed between the genders.

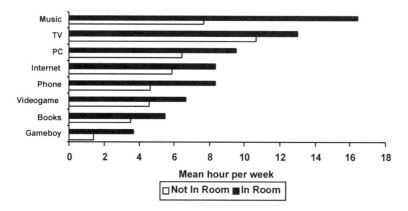

FIG. 9.2. Media in room/not in room and hours per week of play.

TABLE 9.1

Gender * What Are Your Favorite Types of Video Games (1st Choice) Crosstabulation

What Are Your Favorite Types of Video Games (1st Choice)

% Within Gender		Action/ Combat Games	Adventure Games	Classic Games (e.g., Chess, Card Games, Monopoly)	Gambling Games	Puzzles and Logic Games	Role Playing/ Interactive Fiction/ Fantasy Games	Simulation/ Strategic Planning Games	Sports and Competition Games	Total
gender	Male	39.4%	10.7%	.6%	.5%	.7%	15.0%	9.0%	24.2%	100.0%
	Female	16.8%	29.2%	13.8%	2.7%	6.7%	10.3%	4.2%	16.2%	100.0%
Total		29.3%	19.0%	6.5%	1.5%	3.4%	12.9%	6.8%	20.6%	100.0%

TABLE 9.2
Game Play Habit * What Are Your Favorite Types of Video Games (1st Choice) Crosstabulation

% Within Game Play Habit		Action/ Combat Games	Adventure Games	Classic Games (e.g., Chess, Card Games, Monopoly)	Gambling Games	Puzzles and Logic Games	Role Playing/ Interactive Fiction/ Fantasy Games	Simulation/ Strategic Planning Games	Sports and Competition Games	Total
game play habit	heavy gamer	38.4%	14.1%	2.9%	1.6%	1.6%	16.8%	9.5%	15.1%	100.0%
	avid gamer	30.6%	18.8%	4.8%	1.3%	2.7%	13.3%	7.2%	21.4%	100.0%
	occasional gamer	25.7%	20.4%	8.2%	1.3%	4.0%	11.4%	6.1%	22.8%	100.0%
	rare gamer	22.1%	22.6%	10.5%	1.9%	5.5%	10.3%	4.7%	22.3%	100.0%
Total		29.3%	19.0%	6.4%	1.5%	3.4%	13.0%	6.9%	20.5%	100.0%

With new media assimilated into established peer interaction and entertainment activities, it is in the popularity of video game play that the clearest indication is found that something is changing in the media-saturated household. The interactivity and connectivity has not so much transformed youthful entertainment cultures as it has supplemented its play options by building on boys' interest in war and conflict games, sports, and fantasy role-play. This is particularly evidenced in the analysis of the heaviest users of the new media environment—the avid heavy gamers who are more likely to play combat and role-play games and less likely to play adventure and sports games. The expansion of video game play has been achieved largely by the ability of the gaming industry to deliver these entertainment stalwarts in an attractive new way. It is important to reflect on the immersion, play control, and flow that gamers report as the active meaning-making experiences of these types of games. Simulation games, edutainment and puzzles are consistently among the least preferred genres (Kline, 1997, 2001).

Anyone trying to understand the media-saturated household needs to understand the trade-offs young people make when they choose between learning, entertainment, peer bonding, and play. These trade-offs speak to a wider set of social and emotional problems young people face at school, in peer groups, and in families. This study showed that the heaviest gamers are likely to trade off reading books and homework for screen entertainment, sleep for gaming, virtual play for active leisure and social interaction. Heavy gamers are most likely to report that they make friends by gaming, and that most of their friends are gamers, although in many cases they also report wanting to socialize with their friends in reality, but not being able to do so. The virtual sociability created in computer-mediated play is a phenomenon in need of study. Although friendship and entertainment seem to win over learning, it appears that for boys, playing games wins over all.

But it also is important to situate young peoples' use of mediated communication in its social context of family relations. Children's freedom to use media, however expanded, is not absolute, especially for the very young. The current data show that young peoples' active engagement with their media must be set carefully within the constraints of family and peer relations. The supervision of media by parents remains an important part of the way children gain access to and navigate the converging media environment, in terms of encouragement and modeling as well as constraints and rules (see Fig. 9.3). Children with more media in the bedroom are less likely to report supervision and more likely to engage in risky uses of the Internet. Family dynamics and parental attitudes, like peer relationships, are an important aspect of the analysis of contemporary play cultures.

Therefore, as in Britain and the United States, it has hard to find evidence that the diffusion of ICTs into the Canadian household has been educationally beneficial or socially leveling. Moreover, as this study shows,

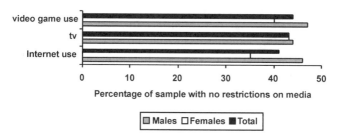

FIG. 9.3. No restrictions on media use.

more teens regularly use porn sites than use the Internet for homework or self-development on a daily basis. Meanwhile, theft of software, cyber-stalking, and unsolicited marketing have become serious issues, making both parents and young people wary of their use of ICTs. Around the world, inundated by porn site solicitations and concerned about Quake addiction, concerned parents are severing the electronic umbilical cord because these dreams of networked learning have dissolved into a XXX-wired playground. Disillusionment with the Web in Canada was evident in the fact that 200,000 subscribers logged off forever in the last 6 months of 2002. The reason they consistently gave was that they were worried about porn and security, or that they just never used the service because it did not provide value for themselves or their children (Crompton, Ellison, & Stevenson, 2002).

CONCLUSION

The problem with the spin-doctored promises made about the digital generation was the failure actually to examine how digital media have impacted children's culture. It is now known that these claims are overstated. Interactive media did not radically alter children's culture or displace television and books. In fact, the new media took their place alongside those other traditional "new" media, forcing trade-offs in some cases and hybridization in others. The convergence in children's media has resulted in a dynamic and constantly changing domestic entertainment environment, in which video game play has become an attractive alternative play form for many kids, especially boys. But it has not altered the course of history.

The threefold promise of democraticized access to information, powerful new opportunities for learning, and active leisure were never confirmed by those who bothered to look at how children actually use the new media. Ironically, on the same day that Steve Case resigned, newspapers reported that the legacy of our digital folly was still with us. Computers were still being ordered for Quebec schools although evidence had been found that computer-assisted learning was of little value (Sokolof, 2003). This does not mean that computers cannot be educationally useful. But it does mean that pedagogical use cannot be driven by a blind faith in technology. Although chat rooms and e-mail enjoy some popularity among digital kids, the primary driver of the Internet was the free music and games, which they now can and do play at school. Unfortunately, the investment in technologies were traded off against investment in educational software, and perhaps more problematically, against proven sports, music, and arts programs in the schools.

It is little wonder that studies of public opinion show many parents gradually becoming more concerned about their schools wasting money on computers and about cyberkids spending too much time playing on them. The new media have simply added to public confusion about children's culture, and to anxieties about media's contribution to school shootings and bullying, addiction, threats to the security, and the well-being of the digital generation. No one can predict the future by looking at technology alone, but surely as Sonia Livingstone (2002) pointed out, one thing can be prophesied: Public debates about the benefits and risks associated with media-saturated childhood will not disappear anymore than childhood itself.

REFERENCES

APPC Media in the home 2000: The Fourth Annual Survey of Parents and Children. Philadelphia, PA: The Annenberg Public Policy Center of the University of Pennsylvania. Accessed at http://www.appcpenn.org/mediainhome/children/

Becker, H. J. (2000a). Findings from the teaching, learning, and computing survey: Is Larry Cuban right? *Education Policy Analysis Archives, 8*(51).

Becker, H. J. (2000b). Pedagogical motivations for student computer use that lead to student engagement. *Educational Technology, 40*(5), 5–17.

Becker, H. J. (2000c). Who's wired and who's not: Children's access to and use of computer technology. *Future of Children, 10*(2), 44–75.

Bovill, M., & Livingstone, S. (2001). Bedroom culture and the privatization of media use. In S. Livingstone & M. Bovill (Eds.), *Children and their changing media environment: A European comparative study.* Mahwah, NJ: Lawrence Erlbaum Associates.

Cairncross, F. (1997). *The death of distance: How the communications revolution will change our lives.* Boston: Harvard Business School Press.

Canadian Press. (2001). *Role-playing computer fantasy rekindles debate over video game addictions.* Toronto: Canadian Press.

Crompton, S., Ellison, J., & Stevenson, K. (2002). Better things to do, or dealt out of the game? Internet dropouts and infrequent users. *Canadian Social Trends, 65*(Summer), 2–6.

Groebel, J. (1999). Media access and media use among 12-year-olds in the world. In C. F. U. Carlsson (Ed.), *Children and media: Image education participation* (Yearbook 1999, pp. 61–67). Nordicom, Goteborg University, UNESCO International Clearinghouse on Children and Violence on the Screen, Goteborg, Sweden.

Gunter, M. (1999). The newest addiction. *Fortune, 140*(3), 122.

Henry, D., & McLennan, K. (1994). *There are no brakes, so who's steering.* A paper on issues for educators presented at Griffith University 1994 Media Futures: Policy and Performance, Queensland, Australia: Telstra Corp Australia.

Kaiser Foundation. (1999). *Kids and media at the new millennium: A comprehensive national analysis of children's media use.* Kaiser Family Foundation. Accessed at http://www.kff.org/content/1999/1535/KidsReport%20FINAL.pdf

Kline, S. (1993). *Out of the garden: Toys and children's culture in the age of TV marketing.* London: Verso.

Kline, S. (1997). Pleasures of the Screen: Why Young People Play Video Games. *Proceedings of the International Toy Research Conference.* Angouleme, France.

Kline, S. (2001). *Media use audit for B.C. teens.* Accessed at http://SFU.ca/media_lab/risk/new/media_lab_research.htm/

Kline, S., & Banerjee, A. (1998). *Video game culture: Leisure and play preferences of BC teens.* Vancouver: Simon Fraser University, Media Analysis Laboratory.

Kline, S., & de Peuter, G. (2002). Ghosts in the machine: Postmodern childhood, video gaming, and advertising. In D. Cook (Ed.), *Symbolic childhood.* New York: Peter Lang Publishing.

Kline, S., Dyer-Witherford, N., & de Peuter, G. (2003). *Digital play: On the interplay of technology, markets, and culture in the making of the video game.* Montreal: McGill-Queens.

Krantz, M. (1999). Grab your breastplate! *Time Magazine, 153*(24), 63.

Leiss, W. (1991). *Under technology's thumb.* Montreal: McGill-Queens.

Livingstone, S. (2002). *Young people and new media: Childhood and the changing media environment.* London: Sage.

Livingstone, S., & Bovill, M. (1999). *Young people new media.* London: London School of Economics and Political Science.

Livingstone, S., & Gaskell, G. (1996). Children and young people's involvement with old and new media: The new Himmelweit project. In F. Guglielmelli (Ed.), *Reinventing television.* Paris: Association Television et Culture.

Livingstone, S., Holden, K., & Bovill, M. (1999). Children's changing media environments: Overview of a European comparative study. In C. F. U. Carlsson (Ed.), *Children and media: Image education.*

McLuhan, M. (1964). *Understanding media: The extensions of man.* Cambridge, MA: Mentor Books.

Media Awareness Network. (2001). *Young Canadians in a wired world.* Accessed at http://www.mediaawareness.ca/english/resources/special_initiatives/survey_resources/students_survey/students_survey_report.cfm

Negroponte, N. (1995). *Being digital.* London: Hodder and Stoughton.

Ohmae, K. (1995). Letter from Japan. *Harvard Business Review,* May–June, 161–162.

Papert, S. (1980). *Mindstorms: Children, computers, and powerful ideas.* New York: Basic Books.

Papert, S. (1993). *The children's machine: Rethinking school in the age of the computer.* New York : Basic Books.

Postman, N. (1993). *Technopoly: The surrender of culture to technology.* New York: Vintage.

Provenzo, E. F., Jr. (1991). *Video kids: Making sense of Nintendo.* Cambridge, MA: Harvard University Press.

Provenzo, E. (1997). Video games and the emergence of interactive media for children. In S. Steinberg & J. Kincheloe (Eds.), *Kinder-culture: The corporate construction of childhood.* Boulder: Westview.

Robins, K. (1995). Cyberspace and the world we live in. *Body and Society, 1*(3–4), 135–155.

Rushkoff, D. (1994). *Media virus! Hidden agendas in popular culture.* New York: Ballantine Books.

Rushkoff, D. (1999). *Playing the future: What we can learn from digital kids.* New York: Riverhead Books.

Sciades, G. (2000). *The digital divide in Canada.* Ottawa: Statistics Canada.

Selwyn, N., Dawes, L., & Mercer, N. (2001). Promoting Mr. "Chips": The construction of the teacher/computer relationship in educational advertising. *Teaching and Teacher Education, 17*(1), 3–14.

Simpson, J. (2002, August 3). When convergence ruled the world. *Globe and Mail*, A13.

Sokolof, H. (2003, January 30). Quebec school board first to equip all students with laptops. *National Post*, p. A4.

Sutton-Smith, B. (1997). *The ambiguity of play*. Cambridge, MA: Harvard University Press.

Tapscott, D. (1998). *Growing up digital: The rise of the net generation*. New York: McGraw-Hill.

Time Magazine, 3 January 1983. Accessed March 11, 2002 at http://ei.cs.vt.edu/~history/Time. MOTY.1982.html

Toffler, A. (1981). *The third wave*. New York: Bantam Books.

United States Federal Trade Commission. (2000). *FTC releases report on the marketing of violent entertainment to children*. Accessed March 26, 2000 at http://www.ftc.gov/opa/2000/09/youthviol.htm

U.S. Government. (2002). *Falling through the net IV: Towards digital inclusion*. National Telecommunications and Information Administration. Accessed March 24, 2002 at http://www.ntia.doc.gov/ntiahome/digitaldivide

Valkenburg, P. M., Krcmar, M., Peeters, A. L., & Marseille, N. M. (1999). Developing a scale to assess three styles of television mediation: "Instructive mediation," "restrictive mediation," and "social coviewing." *Journal of Broadcasting and Electronic Media, 43*(1), 52–66.

Walkerdine, V., Dudfield, A., & Studdert, D. (1999). *Sex and violence: Regulating childhood at the turn of the millennium*. Paper presented at Research in Childhood: Sociology, Culture, and History, University of Southern Denmark, Odense, October, 1999.

10

Learning With Computer Games

Jonas Linderoth
Berner Lindström
Mikael Alexandersson

Computer games are a part of many people's everyday activities and an expanding cultural phenomenon (Egenfeldt-Nielsen & Smith, 2000; Linderoth, Lantz-Andersson, & Lindström, 2002; Poole, 2000). This has brought expectations about the use of computer games in education for pedagogical purposes. A number of studies, projects, and conferences are concerned with the issue of computer games in education.[1] Games and simulations were used as learning resources long before the development of computer technology (Avedon & Sutton-Smith, 1971), and there is a long tradition of educators using games and simulations in their classrooms (Millians, 1999). However, the motives for using and developing computer games in education comprise a rather diverse, indistinct, and incongruous cluster of arguments. This diversity can be found both in the discussion of what specific learning objectives might be fulfilled by the introduction of computer games in education and in the ideas about how games contribute to learning (Linderoth et al., 2002).

With regard to what the usage of computer games enhance, a number of different abilities have been suggested, for instance, media and computer

---

[1]For instance the Computer Games in Education Conference held in Stockholm, June 2002, the Computer Games in Education Project established by the British Educational Communications and Technology Agency (http://www.becta.org.uk/technology/software/curriculum/computergames/) and the Games to Teach Project which is a partnership between Microsoft and Massachusetts Institute of Technology (http://cms.mit.edu/games/education/).

literacy, cognitive skills such as problem solving and spatial awareness, social skills such as the ability to collaborate, and the learning of content in
different subjects (Dawes & Dumbleton, 2002; Erstad, 2002). One learning
potential of computer games that has been described is the possibility of
detecting relations between symbols (Squire, 2002). Thus games are sometimes compared with books, films, or other means of storytelling. Games
then are described as media that may have some unique qualities that, in
contrast to older media, can be more productive for learning about a phenomenon represented in the game (Gärdenfors, 1999). The idea that computer games, more than other media, narrow the relation between a representation and the represented phenomenon also is suggested in the
research on games and aggressive behavior. For instance, Anderson and
Dill (2000) proposed that the players' identification with the avatar, the active participation, and the addictive nature of computer games constitute a
learning environment that may be more harmful (or powerful) than TV and
movies.

Concerning how learning with games occurs, diverse aspects and qualities of play have been emphasized to justify the effectiveness of using computer games as compared with traditional learning approaches. Play is
sometimes conceptualized as a form of socialization and cognitive growth,
primarily about development rather than enjoyment. The occurrence of
play then is seen as something good and productive by itself (Sutton-Smith,
1997). As Brougere (1999) pointed out, "The passage from the play experience in its singularity to learning content is sometimes very mysterious."
Another argument for the educational usage of computer games is that
games increase the learner's motivation, giving them the educational advantage of being more fun than other learning approaches.

The great diversity of the arguments for developing and using games as
educational tools makes it difficult to criticize the idea that games are suitable for educational practices. If evaluations do not show positive results of
learning, there is always another human quality that the advocates of educational computer gaming can claim is being positively affected.[2] The popular ideas that play and fun are essential for learning and development also
are hard to question, and the critic risks being defined as a boring Calvinist.

Some empirical studies have tried to scrutinize the educational benefits
that games may have by evaluating and comparing traditional learning approaches with the usage of games in education (Randel & Morris, 1992). Although this approach to educational games takes an analytical rather than
a rhetorical stance, it has a built-in normative agenda. Learning with computer games basically becomes a question of how curricular goals and ob-

---

[2]Compare the debate on the effects of LOGO programming on children's learning (Clements
& Meredith, 1992; Papert, 1987).

jectives can be promoted with the help of technology. Furthermore, it often is a question concerning the relative effectiveness of the technology. The issue of learning is basically limited to the acquisition (or not) of specific curricular objectives.

From a design perspective and as a practical enterprise, it is fully reasonable to follow this means–ends rationale. However, it can be argued that it is important, practically and theoretically, also to consider effects of a specific pedagogical intervention that are unintended and not foreseen. Such an approach provides a more refined basis for the development and use of, for example, a pedagogical technology. Because computer gaming is a part of young people's everyday practice, the issue of using these technologies for pedagogical purposes in educational institutions could benefit from an understanding of game playing as a social and psychological activity in this broader context. This should give a broader knowledge basis for discussing and using the technology to reach different curricular goals and objectives. The authors argue that sociocultural theories offer a framework for investigating learning with computer games in a more comprehensive manner.

A SOCIOCULTURAL PERSPECTIVE ON GAMES AND LEARNING

During the past two decades Vygotskian theory as a prototype for sociocultural theory has had a large impact on learning theory in particular and educational theory in general, challenging some basic premises of educational psychology and cognitive science. A central idea characterizes learning as a process of mastering different tools. Learning is not only a mental issue. These tools can be both physical (e.g., calculators and pencils) and psychological (e.g., mathematical models and concepts). Thinking, acting, and communicating are mediated by these tools. Individuals use different tools as resources, as mediational means to get along in the world. These tools, even if psychological, are not biological in their nature, but cultural (Säljö, 1999; Vygotsky, 1986; Wells, 1999; Wertsch, 1998). Wertsch (1998) pointed out that cultural tools have affordances[3] that make it possible for tasks to be performed that would have been impossible without these artifacts (p. 29).

---

[3]The concept of affordances, originally developed by J. J. Gibson, means what the environment offers an animal, the complementarity between animal and environment (Gibson, 1986). The concept has to some extent been redefined and is used sometimes just to define properties of an object. The concept is used here as Norman (2002) used it to define the "possible relationships among actors and objects." We find this definition appropriate when analyzing virtual environments, a phenomenon that was not a part of the original works of J. J. Gibson. [See also the chapter by Bergen, this volume.]

Sociocultural theory claims that learning cannot be seen as the result of education and instruction alone. It must be understood as an inevitable phenomenon that occurs in everyday activities (Säljö, 2000; Wells, 1999) as an appropriation of elements of social practices. This view of learning is developed in the theory of situated learning (Lave, 1999; Lave & Wenger, 1991).

Säljö (2000) pointed out that learning often is understood as something constructive and desirable, but noted that this hardly is an obvious conclusion. Many of the learning processes in modern society can rather be seen as destructive and dangerous. He concluded by saying that although it is common in research, "the study of learning and human development perhaps should not be reduced to certain psychological mechanisms that are assumed to have a positive significance" (p. 28).

Taking a sociocultural perspective on learning with computer games, the authors investigate what kind of learning processes can be found in the social and intellectual activity of playing computer games, both outside and within educational institutions. What do gamers learn, for better or for worse, while playing computer games? How do the players make sense of images, sounds, animations, and occurrences in the games? How are the games used as mediational means and for what purposes? All these questions and social theories of learning ought to be answered from a sociocultural perspective before claims are made about educational possibilities. To see what kind of possibilities a certain artifact has in the interest of education, there is a need to understand the properties of the artifact, to know what it affords.

METHODS FOR STUDYING LEARNING

In the theoretical perspective just outlined, the analytical focus should not be the effectiveness of games in educational practices but playing as a situated activity. The primary unit of analysis in this study was the interaction between participants during computer gaming and between participants and the technology. The methodological line of reasoning adopted in this work for the study of learning with computer games has been applied in studies of other learning with other kinds of technologies. Within the field of computer-supported collaborative learning (Koschmann, 1996a; Koschmann, Hall, & Miyake, 2002), the analysis of conversation and interaction is a rather common focus for the study of learning with information technology. The basic assumptions in this field have been described as a combination of social constructivist viewpoints and theories of situated learning within a more general sociocultural theoretical framework. The issues of concern in this field are those sketched earlier. Instructional efficacy is put aside to make way for the study of how people "do" learning and how instruction is "enacted" (Koschmann, 1996b). A method that researchers in this field use is termed "interaction analysis" (Jordan & Henderson, 1995), and can be described as a microsociological approach inspired by the works of ethnomethodologists such as Garfinkel (1984), conversation analysts such as Austin (1962), and the late Goffman (1981, 1986). The concrete analysis often is based on detailed transcriptions of audio or video recordings, in which the researcher focuses on such things as the structure of events, the spatial and temporal organization of the activity, turn taking, the usage of artifacts (Jordan & Henderson, 1995), how context is produced, and which discourses are used (Linell, 1998).

THE EMPIRICAL STUDY

Following this line of reasoning, an empirical study of children's interaction with computer games was conducted. The main purposes of the study were to produce knowledge about the possibilities of games as mediational means and to consider the educational possibilities of computer games as emerging media. The study addressed the issues of how learning occurs, and what is being learned in the situated activity of playing computer games. It is important to stress that the focus was not only on the process of learning as a form, but also on what meanings subjects give to their game-playing activity in terms of experiential aspects of their interactions. In this, the authors stress the phenomenological argument that learning for the subject must always have an experiential content. The subject must be learning something—a topic, a problem, a perspective, an issue, an attitude, a certain value, a behavior, or a capability (Edelman & Tononi, 2001; Marton & Booth, 1997). The research objective was to show what this something is, what the subject's learning object is.

Design

Following the tradition of computer-supported collaborative learning studies, children's collaborative interaction comprised the unit of analysis. Video recordings of 22 gaming sessions generated 25 hr of video data. The recordings were performed using a stationary camera, with the researcher only occasionally present in the room, thus minimizing the camera's effects on the interaction. A total of 35 children (18 boys and 17 girls) participated in different constellations. The children ranged in age from 6 to 12 years. The setting and the sort of computer games used in the sessions varied from edutainment and simulation games in schools to multiplayer video games in home environments.

After an initial analysis of the total material, 11 unique sessions were chosen for further analysis. The other 11 sessions tended to contain data on the same children, or certain games were overrepresented in the material. The chosen sessions were transcribed in detail using columnar transcripts (Jordan & Henderson, 1995). All the children as well as their parents gave their approval for participation in the study. Children used only games their parents allowed them to play.

Part of the sessions were chosen for further analysis on the basis of the authors' first readings of the excerpts. Episodes were chosen in which the data showed what the children took for granted in their sense-making processes. From these episodes, the authors searched for structures in the children's assumptions and expectations. The main analytical focus was to see how they made sense of the objects represented with images, texts, sounds, and animations. Once the main result was found (see below), the authors went back to the transcripts to see whether they could find more episodes that could fit under their discovered patterns of interaction to strengthen the result. The excerpts chosen for this discussion describe episodes found to be the most illustrative examples of the result.

Overview of the Sessions

As background for the results, an overview of the four sessions from which the excerpts were taken is presented.

Session 1. Build Cars With Mulle Meck. In this session two boys, Ola (8 years old) and Per (8 years old) played the game on a PC for 45 min. The session took place in a corridor outside the children's classroom. The gaming situation was not part of the regular school activity, but prescribed by the research project. Recording was done with one stationary camera. The teacher was never present, and the researcher checked the session only occasionally.

The game can best be described as a car-building simulation. The player controls the character Mulle, who is a single male living in the forest with his dog, and builds cars out of scrap from his personal junkyard and things he finds in the game world. The back story of the game is that Mulle longs to get to the place where the road ends at the ocean. The player constructs cars and tests their properties by driving in a virtual world (two-dimensional, birds-eye perspective). While playing the game, the player receives different car parts that gives the car a variety of properties. Thus big tractor tires are needed to get through muddy parts of the road, strong engines to get up steep hills, and so on. Building with some car parts such as engines and tires represents "real" car building. The use of other parts gives a more fictional frame. For instance, roller-skates can be used instead of wheels on the player's car.

Session 2. Theme Hospital. In this session a boy, Bo (11 years old), and a girl, Annika (11 years old), played Theme Hospital on a PC for 60 min. The session took place in a storeroom of the children's school. The gaming situation was not part of the regular school activity, but prescribed by the research project. Recording was performed with one stationary camera. The teacher was never present, and the researcher checked the session only occasionally.

The game is a humorous hospital simulation with fictional diseases. The player, who is the hospital manager, has the task of building and running a profitable establishment. By building different rooms in the hospital (isometric perspective), hiring different employees, and handling a number of different dimensions (or variables), the objective is to produce a certain surplus. If the player succeeds, he or she can go to the next level and build a bigger, more advanced hospital.

Session 3. The Kingdom of Sweden (Svea Rike). In this session two boys, Thomas (11 years old) and Lars (11 years old) played The Kingdom of Sweden on a PC for 60 min. The session took place in a storeroom of the children's school. The gaming situation was not part of the regular school activity, but prescribed by the research project. Recording was performed with one stationary camera. The teacher was never present, and the researcher checked the session only occasionally.

The game is a turn-based strategy game with a couple of small "arcade-like" minigames within. The player is controlling a noble family in Sweden, and the player's objective is to gain reputation points for his or her family. The game starts in the year 1523. Each turn simulates 4 years, and the game stops in 1818. If enough reputation points are gained, the player is elected king of Sweden. Reputation points are gained by acquiring many provinces and recruiting many scientists and intellectual persons to one's family. The means of doing this are trade, diplomacy, and warfare with other countries (Denmark, Poland, Russia, and Prussia), but the player's opponents in the game are the other Swedish noble families.

Session 4. Perfect Dark. In this session two sisters, Bea (6 years old) and Elin (8 years old) played Perfect Dark on a Nintendo 64 console for 60 min. The children played the multiplayer option. They were sometimes on the same team fighting against bots and sometimes on opposing teams. The session took place in the children's room at home. Recording was performed with one stationary camera. On two occasions, a parent was called upon. The researcher overheard the session from next door.

The game is an agent-style action adventure with the possibility of playing a multiplayer scenario on a split screen. With the multiplayer option, one to four players can be either for or against each other when playing. The players also can have bots, so-called simulants, in their teams. The basic way of gaining points to win is to defeat members of the other team without getting one's own avatar killed.[4]

RESULTS

The analysis showed that there was one pattern of interaction, which the authors believe has broad implications for understanding learning processes with computer games. The excerpts were chosen as representative examples of this interaction pattern. They illustrate the main finding and the result described in this chapter. The findings showed that the children developed their own conceptual tools to communicate the affordances of different game features to each other during the sessions. This way of making sense of the gaming situation also was produced when children used concepts from a computer game discourse as intellectual tools. The focus for the children was thus on the possible relations between themselves as agents and the game features as objects (see footnote 3), not on the represented phenomena. As illustrated in the excerpts, this meant that they treated the game itself as an object of learning. In these cases, the games did not become conceptual tools for the children's understanding of something outside the gaming situation. Instead, they developed concepts to handle the concrete situation in a very local manner.

Goatscares and Cleningchaps

In session 1, Ola and Per play very effectively. Ola, who is in charge of the mouse during the whole session, has the Mulle Meck game at home. Throughout the session, he uses his knowledge of the game to progress as effectively as possible. This means that he actively seeks the car parts that he knows will be crucial to overcoming some of the obstacles. One obstacle in the game world is cows and goats standing in the middle of the road so that Mulle cannot pass them. A horn is needed to honk at the cows, but the goats are more stubborn, so to pass them, a megaphone is needed that Mulle can use to shout at the goats. The megaphone can be used to scare both the cows and the goats out of the road.

---

[4]"Avatar" is the term for an actor whom a player controls in a game or a chat environment. Originally meaning "the incarnation of a God," Krishna is, for instance, an avatar of the higher deity Vishnu. If an actor is controlled by artificial intelligence, it is called a "bot."

FIG. 10.1. Mulle at his junkyard.

In the first excerpt Mulle's friend Figge, a local scrap merchant, has been at Mulle's farm with some new parts for the car. Figge shows up rather randomly during game play, and sometimes the only way to get a key part for one's car is to wait for Figge.

Excerpt[5] 1 From Session 1

1.
   Ola clicks on the garage gate, and Mulle rolls out his car to the yard in front of his farm. Mulle says, "Let's roll it out." In the yard, there is a pile of new car parts.

2. Ola [imitating a phrase that Mulle sometimes says]: "Let's hope we get gorgeous car parts" [interrupted by Per who laughs].
   Mulle says, "Figge must have been here with new car parts."

3. Ola [in an excited voice]: "The ambulance!"
   One car part is in the shape of an ambulance coach.

4. Per: "There's our, so we can find our thing."

---

[5]In all the excerpts, the information is structured in two columns. The first column contains the speech. The second column contains information about other events relevant for the interaction.

Ola uses the mouse cursor in the shape of a mechanics glove to lift the new parts into Mulle's garage.

5. Ola: "Why is it that we never get the horn?" [hesitates] "Why do the doodah-horn never appear?"

6. Per: "Take a regular horn."

7.   Ola does not answer Per. Instead, he lets Mulle go into the garage and starts to rebuild the car.

Ola seems to search for something. He expresses his hope in line 2 that a certain part will show up. He changes his focus when he sees the ambulance. Per is encouraging, saying that this is the thing they need to find another thing (he probably is referring to the rocket engine, a car part that is difficult to gain). Thus Per seems to be aware of the fact that they are searching for a particular car part they need to overcome obstacles to get to other parts in the virtual world. Which part they need is, however, unknown to him. He assumes after Ola's excited statement in line 3 that it is the ambulance. Ola expresses his disappointment. He is searching for the "doodah-horn," a concept he has made up himself to communicate what the missing part is. It is related to the horn (Fig. 10.3), but it is not a horn. Because the children already have one horn, Per suggests that they can take the regular horn instead. Later in the session, Ola comes back to the theme of the missing, highly desired car part.

Excerpt 2 From Session 1

1. Ola: "Do you know what we should have?"
2. Per: "No."
3. Ola: "The goatscare."
4. Per: "Yeah, right, you can scare the dog with it, right?"
5. Ola: "The billy-goat."
6. Per: "Oh, I mean the billy-goat."

The object that scares the goats is the megaphone (Fig. 10.2). Because excerpt 1 suggests that Ola is searching for a part related to the horn, one can assume after excerpt 2 that it was the megaphone for which he was searching. These objects are related to one another because they have similar but not identical affordances. The horn affords scaring cows off the road, whereas the megaphone affords scaring goats as well as cows.

The Doodah-horn in excerpt 1 becomes a goatscare when Ola communicates his desire to Per in excerpt 2. The concept of megaphone is not some-

FIG. 10.2. The megaphone.

FIG. 10.3. The horn.

thing that Ola uses as a conceptual tool when making sense of the game. Instead, the image gains meaning in accordance to its local affordances within the game. From a sociocultural perspective, this is a process by which Ola develops a conceptual tool (Säljö, 1999) to plan his activity during the game session. The rationale for construing this concept is his need to think and communicate about the missing car part that affords scaring goats. Thus the developed conceptual tool is named "goatscare."

This way of making sense of a represented phenomenon is similarly exemplified in session 2. In this session, Annika, who has played Theme Hospital before, instructs Bo about one of the game's features.

Excerpt 3 From Session 2, Turn 406

   1. Annika: "You can press on one of those cleaningchaps and get a tip. Yes he walks there by himself."

The cleaningchap is the handyman that can be hired in the game. He fixes broken things in the players' hospital, but most of the time his job is to clean up after patients. As in the case with the megaphone, children develop their own conceptual tools to communicate something. Goatscares and cleningchaps refer to some function that the "thing" has in the game. The underlying rationale for the conversation then is what something does and what one can do with it in the game, not what the feature represents.

Spin-Weapons and Sandpaths

Other results indicate that the communicative and conceptual tools constituted by children are built upon some visual characteristic of the graphic object to which they are referring. The affordances still are a part of the focus for the children, but some known aspect of the visual representation becomes the rationale for naming the conceptual tool. In session 4, the two sisters play against each other in a split-screen multiplayer scenario for the game Perfect Dark on Nintendo 64. Elin, the older girl and usually the winner, has used a pair of guns that she thought looked cool.

Excerpt 4 From Session 4

1. Elin: "Yes I won; no I died. These   The children's avatars are firing at
   guns are useless. They are no   each other. Elin loses the battle.
   good these pistols, right Bea?"

2. Bea: "Yes."

3. Elin: "No doubt they are no good;
   they are useless."

4. Bea: "Yes, but not the spin-
   weapon; it was that you
   meant was bad, but the other
   . . ."

5. Elin: "No, no, the spin-weapon isn't
   useless; it is good."

In this excerpt the usefulness of a certain weapon is discussed. Elin looses the battle and claims that this is because of the "useless" guns. Later they discuss another weapon and by comparison agree that "the spin-weapon" is good. Again, what a thing offers is central for making sense of the game. The concept "spin-weapon," which in the game is called "skedar reaper," however, is based on the experience of an animation of a part of the weapon that rotates when fired. This is a unique feature of this weapon; no other weapon in the game does this. When referring to the guns, Elin simply said "these," perhaps because they looked similar to a number of other

FIG. 10.4. The skedar reaper.

guns and lacked some unique visual feature. Still, in both cases, it is the local affordances that are being communicated. The guns are useless, but the spin-weapon is good. As game objects, they afford losing and winning.

In the same excerpt, there are more situations in which the children develop their own concepts using visual aspects of the game.

Excerpt 5 From Session 4

1. Elin: "Are you still in the sandpath?"
2. Bea: "Yes."
3. Elin: "Bea, I'm going to the sandpath now; stay there."

As in the case with the spin-weapon, the part of the virtual environment called the sandpath varies from other places in the game because it is only here that the floor is of sand. This part is a landmark for the children throughout the whole session. They use it as a means of orientating themselves within the game. In the excerpt, the children's avatars have not found each other. Thus they have not challenged each other. The conceptual tool of the sand-path is developed as a collaborative tool for coordinating their movements so there can be some action in the game. They are ironically collaborating to be able to compete with each other. This also can be seen as a way of communicating affordances. By telling each other that their avatar is in the sandpath, they also tell that the sandpath affords a meeting that can result in winning or loosing points (see Fig. 10.5).

Excerpts 1 to 5 are just examples of a more frequent pattern of interaction in the data material. Some other concepts that the children develop in the 22 sessions are double-gun, leader-shell, and port-one-player. Taken together, these observations show that children develop concepts as tools

FIG. 10.5. The sandpath.

for handling the situation at hand. In this process, the affordances, or what one can do with things in the game, seem to be of great importance. Thus the children do not always have to classify what an image represents to give the image a meaning. As Gibson (1986) suggested when discussing the affordances of objects, "If you know what can be done with a graspable detached object, what it can be used for, you can call it whatever you please. . . . You do not have to classify and label things in order to perceive what they afford" (p. 134). This is exactly what the children in the excerpts are doing, seeing the possibilities and constraints of different game features, acting in accordance with the affordances they perceive, and when the need to communicate these affordances emerges, calling the object whatever they want. Thus they can make a goatscare out of an image of a megaphone.

The aforementioned findings show that sounds, images, occurrences, and the like in computer games make sense to participants in game activities according to the game's formal rules. The children develop conceptual tools that primarily are functional within the local context of the game. They do not stand for something else, outside the game. The authors also claim that some of these locally developed concepts are "built into" computer game culture. Learning these concepts thus becomes an issue of appropriating this cultural discursive practice.

Clocking and Conquering Worlds

Another result of the analysis is a pattern of interaction that can be seen as related to the aforementioned findings. Sometimes children use what can be called a "computer game discourse" to construct meaning during the game sessions. They then use conceptual tools that are part of a more or less informal practice of computer gaming. Sometimes this gaming discourse is mapped in a creative way. For instance, Ola in excerpt 6 claims that he has "clocked" Mulle Meck. "Clocked" or "rolling over" are terms that come from the time when the scoreboards on games looped when you reached a certain score. Clocking a game then meant that the counter started at zero again, but also that one has finished a game.

Excerpt 6 From Session 1

1. Ola:	"I have clocked this game at home."
2. Researcher:	"Clock . . . how can you clock Mulle Meck?"
3. Ola:	"There are no car parts left."
4. Researcher:	"Are there now car parts left to fetch?"
5. Ola:	"No."
6. Researcher:	"How can one know that then?"

7. Ola: "For example, there's no doodah there." [points at the screen]

8. Researcher: "So this is clocked now?"

9. Ola: "Perhaps."

It is interesting that Ola says he has clocked Mulle because the developers claim that this game is an "adventure that never ends." Although there is a back story in the game, there are no cues indicating that the game is finished. Yet finishing games is an essential part of computer game culture, and Ola manages to find a way of mapping this meaning onto the game. Thus a conceptual tool that refers to something within the game system has become a part of the game culture. Other players have developed it in other contexts. Throughout computer game history it has become a part of the way we talk about games. The concept is here used as a means of communicating a game experience that is rather different from the original meaning of "clocking" a game.

Another concept that is part of computer game discourse is the idea of referring to the virtual game space as a "world." Worlds then are used to point out the available game environment. Like the concept of clocking games, it has its origin with the earliest computer games. Thus a hospital as well as Scandinavia can be called worlds in game situations. In excerpt 7, Annika comments on the game. This occurs when the children have managed to win the first level and are building their second hospital.

Excerpt 7 From Session 2

1. Annika: "I think this was really hard."
2. Bo: "What?"
3. Annika: "This world is hard, or this hospital."

Another situation in which the word "world" points to the wholeness of the available game environment is found in session 3. Two boys are playing The Kingdom of Sweden. During the session, they try to conquer land to Sweden. Excerpt 8 shows that it has gone well for them for a while.

Excerpt 8 From Session 3

1.   The children's troops are in a pitched battle with Denmark, and their cavalry defeats some Danish troops.

2. Lars: "Oh, yes."
3. Thomas: "Damn! We are conquering the world now."
4. Lars: "Just him left." [points at a solider representing Danish infantry]

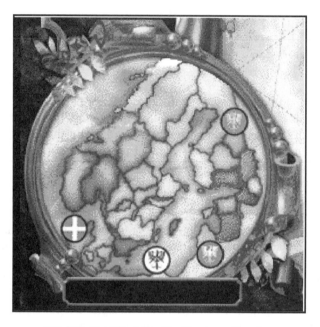

FIG. 10.6. The "World" in The kingdom of Sweden.

In this game, the province one can conquer is Scandinavia and some surroundings (Fig. 10.6), not the entire world.

Although this way of talking of a world is similar to the concept of clocking in excerpt 6, "world" is a term with a common, everyday meaning. Thus the activity here becomes illusory because one may think that the children actually are using the word with its everyday meaning. The most trivial conclusion then would be that they understand Scandinavia as being the whole world. This may seem rather far-fetched, but much of the popular debate about the dangers with games is based on this way of arguing.

CONCLUSIONS: GAMES AS THEMABLE ARTIFACTS

The finding that there are patterns of computer game interaction in which children do not treat game features as representations and symbols does not mean that there can never be situations in which a gaming experience could be a resource or a mediational means for something outside the gaming situation. But it indicates that it is not necessary to see a game as a representation to make sense of game play, an observation that to some extent can be seen as supported with theoretical arguments. In the literature on conventional games, there has been a similar line of reasoning. In his essay Fun in Games, Goffman (1961) analyzed the nature of gaming activities. He started by pointing out the flexible character of the material used for a game:

> For example, it appears that whether checkers is played with bottle tops on a piece of squared linoleum, with gold figurines on inlaid marble, or with uniformed men standing on colored flagstones in a specially arranged court square, the pairs of players can start with the "same" positions, employ the same sequence of strategic moves and countermoves, and generate the same contour of excitement. (p. 19)

Goffman propounds that the nature of a game activity is to treat the game material in accordance with the rules of the game. What becomes relevant for the players is not the aesthetics of the game, nor the representations, but the internal relations between different aspects of the game. He pins down his argument in a distinct way when citing a chess example given by Kurt Riezler:

> The queen is not a real queen, nor is she a piece of wood or ivory. She is an entity in game defined by the movements the game allows her. The game is the context within which the queen is what she is. This context is not the context of the real world or of ordinary life. The game is a little cosmos of its own. (Riezler, 1941; cited in Goffman, 1961, p. 27)

Using the concept of affordance, this means that participants in a game activity are interested primarily in the affordances that keep the rules. They see the possible relations between themselves as agents and different objects in the game, which are allowed without breaking the temporary agreement between the participants.

Goffman's claims are made about conventional games, not computer games, but similar arguments have been made for computer games. For instance, Juul (1999, p. 33) pointed out that computer games "do refer to a large amount of cultural texts and thoughts, but computer games carry a basic artificial quality that makes it hard to see them as signs of *something else*." Instead, Juul (1999) suggested that the output of games consists of two "layers": the game material such as images and sounds and the rules that combine the material in different ways. Computer game players, he continued, often are not more interested in the theme of a game than Kasparov is in the shapes or names of the chess pieces. In a later article, Juul (2001) ameliorated this point, arguing that the rules in a game can be themed in a number of different ways, with the game still remaining the same game. He takes the example of chess that has been repackaged in different guises, with the pieces depicted as figures from Star Wars or Simpson's, and suggests the term "themability" as referring to this aspect of games.

The empirical results of this study fit this theoretical line of reasoning well. The findings empirically confirm that it is reasonable to discuss computer games as "themable" artifacts. The pattern of interaction accounted for in this study is very similar to Riezler's chess example. But it is important to emphasize that even if the interaction pattern of children communicating the affordances in the game were frequent, it was not the only one. There were other ways that children made sense of the games. For instance several examples show how the aesthetics of the game became a rationale for making decisions.

A Final Remark on Games in Education

As the findings from this study show, it cannot be taken for granted that images, sounds, texts, and animations in a game will be understood as representations. The fact that children can develop their own conceptual tools to communicate the affordances of a game system instead of using the offered symbols in the theme of the game as resources for sense making has far-reaching implications for the idea of games in education.

The study results show that the children's experiences during the sessions have a very local meaning. The affordances of the features in the game seem to be most important for the player. Thus the assumption that games by their nature carry qualities that narrow the relation between representation and represented phenomena is not substantiated. This means that there is no support for some of the common beliefs about the possibilities of computer games as educational media, at least when the educational outcome is supposed to be the learning of specific curricular topics represented in the theme of the game. Still, learning occurs during game play because the children learn the skill of handling games and developing local conceptual tools in game environments. This learning could be called a computer game literacy. Whether this learning object is positive in terms of intended learning objectives or not is a completely different question that must be judged against curricular goals and objectives.

One of the central points made in this chapter is that children constitute this object as they interact with each other and with the computer game. However, if the computer game should be used as an educational medium in an educational setting (i.e., in a classroom environment), an explicit, intended object to be learned must exist. The intended object of learning, as seen generally from the teacher's perspective, is somehow realized in the classroom as a particular way of organizing the learning process. This chapter proposes that communication plays a central role in the construal of experience, that it does not just represent experience, as widely perceived. Rather, it more importantly constitutes experience. Seen in this light, communication plays a central role in learning through computer games. How the intended object of learning is being constituted through communication when interacting with computer games is crucial to understand if computer games are expected to become suitable for educational practices. It is possible that experiences from gaming sessions can become intellectual tools for making sense of the intended object of learning.

As this study indicates, however, images, sounds, texts, and animations in the games should not be understood as representations, but more as material that can become a representation. How computer games can be used as educational tools must therefore be studied further.

REFERENCES

Anderson, C., & Dill, K. (2000). Video games and aggressive thoughts, feelings, and behavior in the laboratory and in life. *Journal of Personality and Social Psychology, 78*(4), 772–790.

Austin, J. (1962). *How to do things with words.* Oxford: Oxford University Press.

Avedon, E. M., & Sutton-Smith, B. (1971). *The study of games.* New York: Wiley.

Brougere, G. (1999). Some elements relating to children's play and adult simulation/gaming. *Simulation and Gaming, 30*(2), 134–147.

Clements, D. H., & Meredith, J. S. (1992). *Research on Logo: Effects and efficiency.* The Logo Foundation. Accessed April 30, 2003 at http://el.media.mit.edu/logo-foundation/pubs/papers/research_logo.html.

Dawes, L., & Dumbleton, T. (2002). *Computer games in education project report.* Accessed August 1, 2002 at http://www.becta.org.uk/technology/software/curriculum/computergames/report.html.

Edelman, G. M., & Tononi, G. (2001). *The universe of consciousness.* New York: Basic Books.

Egenfeldt-Nielsen, S., & Smith, J. H. (2000). *Den digitale leg—om børn og computerspil.* Köpenhamn: Hans Reitzels Forlag a/s.

Erstad, O. (2002). Handlingsrummet som öppnar sig: Berättelser från ett multimedialt praxisfält. In R. Säljö & J. Linderoth (Eds.), *Utm@ningar och efrestelser: IT och skolans lärkulturer.* Stockholm: Prisma.

Gärdenfors, P. (1999). *Media och berättande.* Accessed September 29, 2002 at http://www.itis.gov.se/studiematerial/kopia/pdf/334.pdf.

Garfinkel, H. (1984). *Studies in ethnomethodology* (2nd ed.). Oxford: Blackwell.

Gibson, J. J. (1986). *The ecological approach to visual perception.* Hillsdale, NJ: Lawrence Erlbaum Associates.

Goffman, E. (1961). *Encounters: Two studies in the sociology of interaction.* Indianapolis: Bobbs-Merrill.

Goffman, E. (1981). *Forms of talk.* Philadelphia: University of Pennsylvania Press.

Goffman, E. (1986). *Frame analysis: An essay on the organization of experience.* Boston: Northeastern University Press.

Jordan, B., & Henderson, A. (1995). Interaction analysis: Foundations and practice. *The Journal of the Learning Sciences, 4*(1), 39–103.

Juul, J. (1999). *A clash between game and narrative.* Unpublished master thesis, University of Copenhagen, Copenhagen.

Juul, J. (2001). *Play time, event time, themability.* Paper presented at the Computer Games and Digital Textualities, Copenhagen.

Koschmann, T. D. (1996a). *CSCL: Theory and practice of an emerging paradigm: Computers, cognition, and work.* Mahwah, NJ: Lawrence Erlbaum Associates.

Koschmann, T. D. (1996b). Paradigm shifts and instructional technology. In T. D. Koschmann (Ed.), *CSCL: Theory and practice of an emerging paradigm* (pp. 1–23). Mahwah, NJ: Lawrence Erlbaum Associates.

Koschmann, T. D., Hall, R., & Miyake, N. (2002). *CSCL II, carrying forward the conversation.* Mahwah, NJ: Lawrence Erlbaum Associates.

Lave, J. (1999). Lärande, mästarlära, social praxis. In K. Nielsen & S. Kvale (Eds.), *Mästarlära: Lärande som social praxis* (pp. 49–65). Lund: Studentliteratur.

Lave, J., & Wenger, E. (1991). *Situated learning: Legitimate peripheral participation.* Cambridge, England: Cambridge University Press.

Linderoth, J., Lantz-Andersson, A., & Lindström, B. (2002). Electronic exaggerations and virtual worries: Mapping research of computer games relevant to the understanding of children's game play. *Contemporary Issues in Early Childhood, 3*(2), 226–250.

Linell, P. (1998). *Approaching dialogue: Talk, interaction, and contexts in dialogical perspectives.* Philadelphia, Amsterdam: John Benjamins Publishing.

Marton, F., & Booth, S. (1997). *Learning and awareness.* Mahwah, NJ: Lawrence Erlbaum Associates.

Millians, D. (1999). Simulations and young people: Developmental issues and game development. *Simulation and Gaming, 30*(2), 199–227.

Norman, D. (2002). *Affordances and design.* Accessed August 9, 2002 at http://www.jnd.org/dn.mss/affordances-interactions.html.

Papert, S. (1987). Computer criticism vs. technocentric thinking. *Educational Researcher, 16*(1), 22–30.

Poole, S. (2000). *Trigger happy: The inner life of videogames.* London: Fourth Estate.

Randel, J. M., & Morris, B. A. (1992). The effectiveness of games for educational purposes: A review of recent research. *Simulation and Gaming, 23*(3), 261–277.

Säljö, R. (1999). Learning as the use of tools: A sociocultural perspective on the human–technology link. In K. Littleton & P. Light (Eds.), *Learning with computers: Analyzing productive interaction* (pp. 144–166). London: Routledge.

Säljö, R. (2000). *Lärande i praktiken: Ett sociokulturellt perspektiv.* Stockholm: Prisma.

Squire, K. (2002). Cultural framing of computer/video games. *Game Studies, 2*(1). Accessed November 24, 2003 at http://www.gamestudies.org/0102/.

Sutton-Smith, B. (1997). *The ambiguity of play.* Cambridge, MA: Harvard University Press.

Vygotsky, L. S. (1986). *Thought and language.* Cambridge, MA: MIT Press.

Wells, G. (1999). *Dialogic inquiry: Toward a sociocultural practice and theory of education.* Cambridge, England: Cambridge University Press.

Wertsch, J. V. (1998). *Mind as action.* Oxford, UK: Oxford University Press.

HOW TECHNOLOGY
INFLUENCES PLAY

11

Tangible Interfaces in Smart Toys

Mark Allen

Smart toys first appeared fewer than 10 years ago, and they were considered in some quarters of the toy industry to be the new rock 'n roll. Likewise, the study of haptics—the sense of touch—has been receiving increased attention over the past decade as the basis for a revolutionary form of computer interface. Although in many ways smart toys and haptics research are quite distinct, this chapter reviews the multidisciplinary research being carried out by the author that attempts to build some connections between them. A general overview of current research is presented, followed by a description of a new experimental rig and example case studies enabled by the equipment.

SMART TOYS, HAPTICS, AND PLAY

Smart toys can be defined as those that have embedded electronics, leverage some form of computational power, and appear to have a capacity for adapting their interactivity to the abilities of the player. These toys either are linked to a personal computer via an umbilical cord or accommodate onboard computer chips, and use sensors and electronic circuitry to enhance play. Chip-enabled animals, robots, and dolls can be "trained" by a child, whereas toys connected to a personal computer generally enhance a child's play via an interface medium or a computer peripheral (e.g., a digital camera).

Recent smart toys include Furby, Shelby, Poo-Chi, Interactive Yoda, Interactive E.T., Interactive Barney, and Me Barbie. The list grows daily. Forrester Research predicted that 80% of new toys in 2002 would be smart toys (Hodges, 2000), and the smart toy market was expected to grow to $2 billion by 2003 (United Internet Technologies Newsletter, 2001). This represents a large growth sector in the toy industry, and the drive toward technology suggests that smart toys are here to stay.

Tamagotchi was the first artificially intelligent toy, making its U.K. debut in 1996. It was created by Ban Dai, a Japanese company, and took the form of a small egg. The Tamagotchi was programmed to be nurtured by a child. The more it was fed and cared for, the stronger it became, and if neglected it eventually died. The interface comprised a series of buttons and a small view screen. In 1997, Furby made its appearance. Made by Tiger Electronics, and distributed by Hasbro, Furby was a squat, furry, surreal-looking creature with moving parts. It could speak and generally was more advanced than Tamagotchi. Furby owners "taught" the toy English by speaking to it, and the Furby appeared to mature as a result of stimulation by feeding or touching. In 1999, Sony moved the benchmark to a higher level with the introduction of AIBO, a robotic dog. Interactive Yoda, also from Tiger Electronics, debuted in 2000, introducing movie characters into the realm of smart toys. Yoda instructed the user in the use of a light-sabre and the way of The Force.

Currently, the greatest limitation of smart toys is the underdevelopment of artificial intelligence and speech recognition technologies. The toys have no ability to learn, so they are bound to predefined actions and speech. The Furby, rather than learn English, simply unmasks words already stored in its memory. Likewise, Interactive Yoda answers questions from a predetermined library of phrases. Current artificial intelligence technology is too costly to be implemented in a toy, but this will change as computational power and speed capabilities increase, resulting in cheaper technology, increased functionality, and a richer play experience. From an industrial design point of view, most smart toy design and development have been centered on the visuals, audio, and electronics. There is little evidence of haptic design. The physical child-to-toy interface usually is via a digital button, which is either on or off, and thus unable to allow for varying pressures. The capabilities for the sense of touch and its ability to produce pleasure and fun appear to have been overlooked.

Touch aids our identification of nearby objects by providing us with information about their shape, size, and weight. It also reveals a surface's texture and mechanical consistency, two properties that may not be visually obvious. Touch may well be considered one of the least well understood of our five senses (Weisenberger, 2001). The word "haptic" comes from the Greek *haptesthai*, which means "to touch." Human haptic perception uses three distinct systems (Roland & Mortenson, 1987):

1. Touch sense arises from stimulus to the thousands of mechano-receptors contained within the skin and produces tactile perception of heat, pressure, vibration, slip, and pain.
2. Kinesthesia is sensed by end organs located in muscles, tendons, and joints, which are stimulated by body movements, limb position, and applied forces. These contribute to the analysis of weight, size, and shape.
3. Cognitive processes analyze the information provided by the sensory and motor systems.

Touch is unique within human sensory perception in that it is not localized. The skin can be characterized as one large receptor surface for the sense of touch (Sherrick & Cholewiak, 1986) because touch sensations can be produced anywhere on the body's surface. However, when we touch an object, the hand usually is the organ of stimulation. Although during multisensory exploration the hands are considered to support an object while it is being viewed, significant amounts of information still are being passed through touch. With immovable objects, the eyes examine the front while the fingers may explore the rear (Newell, Ernst, Tjan, & Bulthoff, 2001).

Tactile acuity, or sensitivity, differs over the body. It is greater on the hands and fingertips than on the limbs and the trunk. Areas on the somatosensory cortex correspond to different areas of the body, and it has been found that some areas of the skin are represented by a disproportionally large area of the brain, the homunculus. The fact that these mapped areas are related to how sensitive the body part is to tactile stimulation indicates that brain function is adapted to the organism's needs. Experiments have shown that the map changes when the signals to the cortex are modified. For example, the loss of a finger results in a reduction of the cortex area devoted to that part of the body (Kaas, Merzenich, & Killackey, 1983). Similarly, areas mapped on the somatosensory cortex can be expanded by increased simulation of the respective area of skin (Jenkins & Merzenich, 1987). The sensory homunculus is therefore not a static mapping, but can be modified through experience. This ability of the nervous system to change is called neural plasticity.

Another unique quality of the sense of touch is that it is bidirectional. Touch input has been widely used in information systems, computers, and toys. On the other hand, tactile output has been underused. For example, the first commercial force-feedback computer gaming joystick appeared only in 1995. Currently, few devices detect the amount of pressure exerted by touch.

Another attribute of touch is that it remains the most alert of the senses in sleep, and is the first to recover on awakening. Montagu (1977) found that the distance senses of sight and hearing both attain their full development later than the proximity senses of touch, taste, and smell. Touch can be construed as the most reliable of the sensory modalities. When the senses conflict, touch usually is the final arbiter. When reaching out to touch an object that can be seen but not felt, one probably will decide that it is the visual system that has been deceived. This is not to say that touch is better than vision, but rather that they are complementary sources of information (Lederman, Klatzky, & Pawluk, 1993).

Psychophysical research has shown that adults take fewer than a couple seconds to identify most common objects using only touch (Klatzky, Lederman, & Metzger, 1985). Lederman and Klatzky (1987, 1990) observed subjects' hand motions and concluded that there were a number of distinct movements, which they termed "exploratory procedures." They found that the exploratory procedures implemented depended on the qualities of the objects the subjects were asked to identify. Texture was identified using mainly lateral motion and contour following, whereas enclosure and contour following was used to judge shape. This motion of the hands in identifying objects is described as active touch. Passive touch is experienced when an object is pressed into the skin.

Historically, haptic research has its roots in robotics and tele-operations. Over the past 10 years, the driving force has been tangible user interfaces in the computer industry, medical surgical simulations, and virtual reality in the high-tech entertainment industry. Haptic studies have concentrated on speed and accuracy in performing a task, for example, tactile stimulation identification (Craig, 1985); on a child's ability to identify familiar objects haptically (Alexander, Johnson, & Schreiber, 2002); and on haptics as a means of data input and output. Generally, little research has focused on children and haptic perception during play.

Garvey (1993) characterized play as spontaneous, voluntary, pleasurable, and without extrinsic goals. Play is an essential activity of childhood, the way children learn about themselves, their environment, and the people around them. Play with toys has been shown to aid the development of mental problem solving, enabling a child to move to higher levels of thought (Ellis, 1973; Freyberg, 1973; Peplar & Ross, 1981; Piaget, 1962). Preschools in the United Kingdom promote physical and motor skills development of children through various activities. One of these activities uses "touch bags" or "feely boxes." Everyday objects are hidden inside, and the children are encouraged to explore the various textures and identify the items. However, once children enter school, the emphasis is on academic achievement, and little value seems to be placed on free play either by parents or teachers (Manning, 1993, 1998).

There is a body of research exploring the development of children's motor skills through play. Gallahue (1993) proposed that children progressively acquire motor skills in four phases. The sequence in the appearance of the phases is universal although the acquisition rate varies from child to child. Children who have not mastered the various motor skills before entering school may be frustrated later in recreational activities. Understanding the process of fundamental motor skills, exploration, and play should help toy manufacturers design appropriate toys. Hutt (1966) conducted an experiment to distinguish the features between exploration and play. Although not specifically focused on the sense of touch, the study indicated that audio and visual responses would elicit increased contact with an object. When manipulating objects, children rapidly shift between exploration and play, making it difficult to determine when one stops and the other starts (Weisler & McCall, 1976).

A study by Piaget and Inhelder (1956) on the nature of exploration found three stages:

1. Children 3 to 4 years old generally were involved in random exploration, holding the object or touching parts found accidentally.

2. Children 4 to 6 years old were more active in their examinations, but were not always systematic.

3. Among 6- to 7-year-old children, exploration followed a general plan. Abravanel (1968) and Zaporozhets (1969) concluded that this age group changed from predominantly palm contact to using finger tips during exploration because of progress in their fine motor skill development. Generally, girls tend to be more advanced in fine motor skills, whereas boys have the advantage in gross motor skills (Cratty, 1986).

EXPERIMENTAL METHOD AND EQUIPMENT DESIGN

A preliminary study by the author and his colleagues, begun in September 2000, was primarily video based. The aim was to create a framework from which to develop further experiments because no study had observed the use of touch and smart toys. At an after-school club, 20 children, ages 5 to 9 years, were observed during free play. Toys with varying degrees of electronic interactivity were left in an adjacent playroom, to which the experimental group was given unlimited access. The role of adults in child play is a point of debate among play theorists (Smilansky & Shefatya, 1990; Sutton-Smith, 1990; Sutton-Smith, 1998; Trawick-Smith, 1994). The teachers did not spend time in the play area, except to carry out their usual tasks. This was seen to be necessary to avoid modification of the children's usual play behavior. The children were given no instructions on the toys' functionality. They were free to exchange experiences from identical toys at home. A miniature camera, of which none of the children were aware, captured 7 hr of video evidence of free play.

During the final session, a structured but informal question session was held involving 14 of the children and their teacher. The teacher was primed concerning the limitations of the toys. For example, when Poo-Chi was singing, it was unable to react to being fed its bone. The children usually were unaware of these functional idiosyncrasies, assuming that the toy was broken. They made comments such as "Something is wrong; it has never done that before!" While the children were talking to their teacher, the toys were subtly placed in the child's hands and any responses were noted. The children either held and manipulated the toy or placed it on the table. The teacher continued encouraging the children to talk about the feel of the toys.

During this study, three observations were made:

1. The children tended not to interact directly with the smart toys, but rather remotely by placing them on a flat surface. This was attributable partly to the design of the toys. For example, moving parts made the toys difficult to hold.

2. A disparity was found between the child's verbalized favorite toy and the one the child found most haptically stimulating. For example, Furby and Gizmo were essentially identical toys, except that the latter had arms. Gizmo was not selected as a favorite toy, but received more attention and direct contact during free play than Furby.

3. The children did not discover the full functionality of the smart toys. When asked to show the teacher what a toy could do, apart from an occasional fanciful description, they were able to demonstrate only low-level interactivity. It also was observed that if the reaction of the smart toys was significantly different from that anticipated by the child, the toy was soon discarded.

Inevitably, the data gathered in this study were qualitative. The aim was to highlight issues to be addressed in subsequent experiments. The transcription of video data requires substantial time, which is exacerbated by the rapid shifts between exploration and play. The haptic data gathered from video also lack accuracy. It often is impossible to determine clearly where and how hard a child touches and holds a toy, introducing further subjectivity into the transcription. The number of variables had to be reduced, including the removal of all extraneous stimuli, whether these were sensory or media influences. Some of the data also were highly ambiguous. For example, when the children were asked about the feel of a toy, they talked about the fact that it was on television the previous afternoon, or that they generally liked the color. Conventional reduction of the variables would have controlled the task to such an extent that the child would not have been playing anymore, and as a result, all external validity of the study would have been lost. However, this approach had positive aspects, including the absence of an adult observer and the unlimited time for free play.

Nevertheless, it was important to examine the haptic effects in isolation from the other senses. After consultation with teachers and a psychologist, the final design specified an autonomous "feely box" of the kind described earlier. The experimental rig consisted of the box and five specially constructed tactile spheres (Fig. 11.1). The feely box was used to keep the tactile spheres in a confined area, which simplified the observation mechanisms. The box had two apertures in the front allowing access for the child's arms. These apertures were designed to be slightly smaller than the diameter of the tactile spheres to inhibit their removal. Sleeves were attached inside the apertures to stop users from peering inside. The feely box housed a miniature camera, which captured both internal activity of the child's hand movements and, via a polarized periscope, the children's faces for gender determination and emotional analysis, for example to determine whether actions were the result of pleasure or frustration. The feely box was designed so that the children had access only to the tactile spheres. A microphone was included to create an audio recording of the children's comments.

The five tactile spheres were designed to be heavy and large enough to induce double-handed interactions. Each sphere had two removable silicone hemispherical covers, which were specially molded to facilitate various permutations of texture, feature, and feedback. Under the silicone were 32 sensors capable of detecting deflections measuring a fraction of a millimeter in the outer surface. Each of the spheres also had a feature formed of a single node molded into the surface. Feedback was given through a micromotor with an off-center weight vibrating the area directly under the area pressed. The feedback was produced for the length of time the appropriate area was pressed. Because each of the five spheres always had a

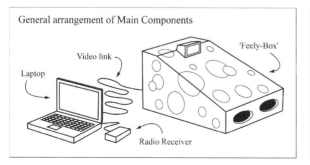 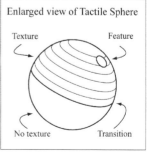

FIG. 11.1. Experimental rig.

smooth hemisphere, the surface of the spheres was divided into four zones: no texture, transition, texture, and feature. The "no texture" zone was smooth, and the "transition" zone was the joint between the smooth hemisphere and the textured surface. The "texture" zone was either furry or comprised a series of ribs molded into the silicone.

The data from each sensor was captured by an onboard microprocessor and transmitted via narrow-band radio to a receiver. Radiotelemetry was the preferred means of data transfer because it ensured that no umbilical cords were attached to the tactile spheres. These could have created a perceived orientation. The receiving microprocessor collated the data from the five spheres and transferred it to a laptop computer at a predetermined rate. It was possible to collect the data from each sphere 10 times a second, although during the experiments, it was set at one fourth of a second. The laptop simultaneously captured the tactile force data and the video stream. The feely box was fully autonomous. No adult observers were required in the vicinity of the box, and the laptop and radio receivers were removed from the play area so as not to give an indication that the children were being observed or that an experiment was in progress.

Later, the radiotelemetry data was filtered through software that logged the time and forces for each of the 32 sensor areas, corrected data errors, and created base-lined data. The process of creating subjectivity-free spreadsheets from the collected data was practically instantaneous. The radiotelemetry plots indicated regions of interest, and the respective video and audio data were checked for any significant tactile activities. For example, a force spike on the plot may have been the result of a sphere being bounced, hit with another sphere or a hand. Finally, a variety of visualizations were created in a graphic form as representational three-dimensional movie animations that could be stepped through frame by frame.

Time is an important factor in play (Christie & Wardle, 1992), so the play time, ranging from half an hour to 2 hr per session, was defined by the scheduled play time at the various venues. Because play is spontaneous, it was important not to force it or make it appear to be a task. The main study took place at four different venues, incorporating a total experimental group of 50 children 5 to 8 years of age. The experimental procedure was simple. The feely box was left with a variety of smart toys in the play area without any explanation. The children were allowed to interact freely with the box. The system was in record mode for the full duration of the play time.

CASE STUDIES

The following case studies are examples from the research undertaken during the free play sessions. The first case study compares the relative tactile activity expended on the spheres with the texture, feature, and feedback of each. The second case study examines the activity on the surface of individual spheres, then reviews a study of an informal interview session comparing verbal preferences, exploration, and play duration. Finally a few anecdotal observations regarding isolated phenomena that occurred over the course of the study are included.

Case 1

As suggested by Hutt (1966), an increase in child activity would be expected from novel objects: the greater the novelty, the greater would be the expected contact times. This was shown to be true. The duration of the activity was high with the spheres that produced feedback, and the sphere with a feature and feedback attracted still more attention. The results indicated that there also was a correlation between duration and the applied force. If the child suspected or was aware that a particular object in the feely box vibrated, a greater force was applied to the entire surface than to the nonreactive tactile spheres. The spheres were designed to produce feedback when a force of 2.5 N was applied, although in practice the spheres routinely experienced forces in excess of 10 N. The spheres that had no feedback were subject to lower forces. Some smart toys incorporate hidden buttons in the hand or belly areas to maintain natural aesthetics. The forces required to operate Interactive Yoda and E.T., for example, range between 5.6 and 11 N. During exploration and play with the tactile spheres, when there was no awareness of buttons or a possible reaction, the forces applied by the children often did not attain the required magnitude for them to discover the existence of the features in the two toys mentioned. This may partially explain why the children did not find the full functionality of the toys during the pilot study. The conclusion drawn from this case study indicates that the cognitive value, specifically the haptic cognition, of some smart toys is low. Buttons should be designed to require lower forces for activation, or some cue, either visual or haptic, should be provided to suggest areas of particular interest in the play experience.

Case 2

Activity levels at the four surface zones were compared. For tactile spheres that had texture and a feature with feedback, the activity around the feature was significantly higher than on any other area of the surface. Where texture and a feature were combined, with no feedback, the feature attracted the most activity. The texture and feedback combination, without a feature, showed substantial activity over the whole textured surface as the child attempted to extract a response from the sphere. The conclusion is that there is a distinct hierarchy. The greatest influence was the stimulus from the feedback, followed by the feature. Of least significance was the texture.

Case 3

This case study supports the conclusions of Abravanel (1968) and Zaporo-zhets (1969), who determined that there is a change from the use of palms to the use of fingers in children ages 6 to 7 years. The 5-year-old children grasped a sphere with a single hand and bumped it around. If they acciden-tally found something of interest, they explored that. When older children were encouraged by peers to find the vibrating ball, two predominant meth-ods of eliciting the feedback were noted, particularly in the case of the sphere with texture and feedback, but no feature. The children either sys-tematically ran their fingers over the surface, pressing intermittently until they discovered the area that produced the feedback, or they randomly pressed down on the sphere with open palms or resorted to placing their hands on top of one another and pressing down with as much force as they could muster. Naturally, the force measured under the hands far exceeded that required to induce the feedback. If the children did not perceive a reac-tion, the sphere then was rotated slightly and the two-handed force arbi-trarily applied again. The conclusion from this case study was that a gen-eral change from palm to finger manipulation is linked to increasing age. However, momentary regressions occurred, in which the child replaced precision with force.

Case 4

During the final session, a short informal interview was held. The aim was to compare verbal choice against recorded exploration and play. To reca-pitulate, the five tactile spheres all possessed one smooth hemisphere. The second hemispheres had no texture; texture, feature, and feedback; texture and feature; texture and feedback; a furry feel. The children each were pre-sented randomly with two of the spheres until every permutation was com-plete, after which they were asked their preference. The video and radiote-lemetry data were used in parallel: the video data to determine when the children were exploring or playing and the radiotelemetry data to collect empirical data on force and duration of contact. Hutt (1966) observed that exploration was accompanied by an intent facial expression. The explora-tion was characterized by repeated sequences of touch, and the play phase by brief, nonrepeated actions that varied in sequence, and by a decline in the intent facial expressions (Power, 2000).

The choices verbalized by the girls in the experimental group were dom-inated by the furry sphere, whereas the boys were divided equally between the furry sphere and the sphere with a feature and feedback. The exploration time was similar for the three textured spheres, irrespective of feedback and whether the child eventually rejected it. The furry sphere received little exploration time, less than half the time devoted to the textured spheres. The fur appeared to be instantly recognizable and seemed to require little further exploration. The smooth sphere received a little more attention than the furry sphere, approximately half that of the three textured spheres. The girls took more than 20% longer than the boys during exploration to verbalize a preference. Although the sphere with a feature but no feedback received a significant amount of exploration time, the children showed almost no interest in playing with it. When asked, the girls stated a preference for the sphere with fur, although the two spheres with feedback received more play time. The play with the various spheres was accompanied by laughter, for example, when the feedback was found or hands were run through the fur.

OBSERVATIONS

As researchers develop theories on play, it is becoming clear that play is more complex than originally proposed. Examples of this complexity have appeared during the current research. A group of 5-year-old children in a reception class assumed that the spheres in the feely box must be able to talk because the four smart toys placed alongside the box were able to talk. They spent most of the session trying to find the mouth or a way of extracting speech from the spheres.

As a precursor to the feely box experiment, a separate study was conducted to determine whether children would show a preference for electronic or smart toys over traditional toys. A segment of the experimental groups was shown two transparent acrylic balls and one of the tactile spheres. Without touching the objects, the children were asked which they preferred. The first sphere contained a defunct electronic circuit board, the second a handful of beads, and the last one of the tactile spheres. The sphere with the electronics was an overwhelming favorite. Although it was a nonfunctional piece of electronics, the children figured it would be able to do something for them, such as play music. The sphere with beads was their second choice, and the least interesting was what the children took to be just another rubber ball. Clearly, this was determined by a perceived "wow factor." A similar observation made by Singer (1994) suggested that once the child realized the electronics were nonfunctional, the ball would be discarded.

In the case of the feely box experiment, there were several surprising and inventive responses. One 8-year-old girl was described disruptive, with a short attention span. The author was asked whether she should be removed from the experimental group. However, during the course of the experiment, the girl repeatedly asked to return to the feely box. Once there, she clearly was able to distinguish each of the five spheres. Replacing them in the same position as they had been when she left, she continued where she had left off with her storytelling. The story involved a mother, father, and three siblings, one of which clearly did not want to go to school.

A group of 7- and 8-year-old boys assumed that there had to be more to the feely box than just five spheres, and after a brief discussion among themselves, concluded that the box was clearly an elaborate bowling alley. They defined rules for turn-taking and a method to decide a winner. This supports observations made in studies by DeVries (1998), suggesting that at this age children begin imposing game structures on noncompetitive motor skill activities. It was interesting to observe that the boys did not use the sphere with fur. Recorded data showed that throughout the entire experiment, the furry sphere did not get bounced, although it possessed the same structural capacity as all the other spheres.

During the informal interview, the various spheres were placed in the feely box by the interviewer. The child placed the first sphere in one hand and the second sphere in the free hand. During the course of the exploration, the spheres always remained in, or were returned to, the same hands in which they had first started. Only once in 160 events did the spheres finish up in the opposite hands.

By the fifth day, each of the experimental groups showed signs of decline in the interactions with the feely box. An instructor at one of the holiday clubs used for the study casually inquired of the children playing around the feely box why they were not particularly interested in it. The children expressed their view as "We did that yesterday," adding that the spheres in the box were unchanged from previous days (which was not in fact the case). It was clear from the audio data from earlier play sessions that the children described to one another the differences between the spheres. This raises questions regarding haptic memory in children and its decay rate. Haptic memory has not yet received much attention, and as a consequence, still is not well understood. The feely box used in the author's experiments was white with large colored spots, and this remained the same throughout the studies. An interesting strand of further work could include changing the external facade of the feely box, perhaps retaining the same tactile spheres over the course of a few play sessions, to monitor whether the children's haptic perception was altered.

FURTHER STUDIES AND CONCLUDING REMARKS

Further research could include the following, among other possibilities:

1. Quantitative modification of the feedback, for example, to determine whether creation of an activation period once the feedback is induced results in the children touching another surface region and returning to the original activation point once the vibration stops?

2. Qualitative modification of the feedback by an increase in the intensity or frequency of the vibrations to see whether this elicits greater interactivity by the user. Another qualitative change would involve dislocating the feedback from the area pressed to observe whether the child is attracted to the stimuli or just receiving a response.

3. Addition of an audio or visual dimension to make the reaction for the tactile manipulations bisensory. Is there a significant increase in haptic activity attributable to the multisensory nature of the reactions from the tactile spheres?

4. Creation of a longitudinal study to examine haptic perception changes as children make the transition into formal schooling. Does the emphasis of the current school curriculum on academic achievement inhibit continued development of fine motor skills? Is there a long-term effect on tactile acuity with toys that do not promote tactile play?

5. Incorporation of the analysis technology into existing toys, either in the feely box or unrestrained activity, to examine whether there are areas on the toys that receive more or less tactile interaction, both in duration and pressure, than the original toy designers considered.

The complexity of the multidimensional data calls for the design and development of further tools to aid in the analysis. This is a common problem in all data collection and processing systems, but the large volume of data generated in these studies exceeds the limits of most standard software packages. This situation would be exacerbated if the data transfer rate were set at 10 events a second rather than the rate of 4 used in this series of studies. Currently, the nonstandard software used is quite powerful, but it is not particularly user friendly. The data collection, error checking, and transcription into spreadsheet format have been automated. However, the specific analysis (e.g., extraction of gender- or even child-specific data) has been performed manually.

The final observation from this research relates to the physical interface between the user and the technology. The human skin is analog, in that it allows for varying forces, both as input and output. These forces are determined by mechanical and psychological factors. If a button needs to be pressed with a predetermined force, tactile perception makes the appropriate adjustments. The magnitude of a force also is determined by the psychological state of the user. How often has a computer's delete key been hit harder and faster in a state of frustration although this did not make the computer work better? These studies do not seek to explain the psychological reasons behind the observations, but it is clear that duration and force of physical contact convey more than a simple on/off action. Smart toys attempt to create more natural interactions through adaptive play and their responses to nurturing, but the actual interface is unnatural. The haptics community has awakened to the fact that imitating the skin is the way forward in tangible user interfaces. Toy designers continue to develop artificial intelligence and natural speech recognition technologies, but until they examine natural interfaces and ways of harnessing the natural haptic abilities of children, toys will continue to fall short of the mark.

The research reported in this chapter has two aims. First, it seeks to develop an understanding concerning the haptic perception of children, and ultimately to improve the cognitive value of smart objects. This in turn may promote creative play and the continued use of manipulative learning based on the primary skill of direct locomotion/manipulation, touch, and natural feedback. Second, it seeks to improve links between industrial designers, psychologists, and engineers, hopefully to promote a more holistic, multidisciplinary approach to the research of the subject. For every question answered through our studies of child haptics, new questions are uncovered. This clearly is, as play researchers have been discovering over the centuries, the work of a lifetime.

REFERENCES

Abravanel, E. (1968). The development of intersensory patterning with regard to selected spatial dimensions. *Monographs of the Society for Research in Child Development, 33*(2, serial #118).

Alexander, J. M., Johnson, K. E., & Schreiber, J. B. (2002). Knowledge is not everything: Analysis of children's performance on a haptic comparison task. *Journal of Experimental Child Psychology, 82,* 341–366.

Christie, J. F., & Wardle, F. (1992). How much time is needed for play? *Young Children, 47,* 28–32.

Craig, J. C. (1985). Attending to two fingers: Two hands are better than one. *Perception and Psychophysics, 38,* 496–511.

Cratty, B. J. (1986). *Perceptual and motor development in infants and children* (3rd ed.). Upper Saddle River, NJ: Prentice-Hall.

DeVries, R. (1998). Games with rules. In D. P. Fromberg & D. Bergen (Eds.), *Play from birth to twelve and beyond* (pp. 409–415). New York: Freeman.

Ellis, J. J. (1973). *Why people play.* Upper Saddle River, NJ: Prentice-Hall.

Freyberg, J. T. (1973). Increasing the imaginative play of urban disadvantaged kindergarten children through systematic training. In J. L. Singer (Ed.), *The child's world of make believe* (pp. 129–154). New York: Academic Press.

Gallahue, D. L. (1993). Motor development and movement skill acquisition in early childhood education. In B. Spodek (Ed.), *Handbook of research on the education of young children* (pp. 24–41). New York: Macmillian.

Garvey, C. (1993). *Play* (enlarged ed.). Cambridge, MA: Harvard University Press.

Hodges, J. (2000, December). *Toyland gets smart.* Business2.0. Retrieved from Business2.0 database.

Hutt, C. (1966). Exploration of play in children. *Symposia of the Zoological Society, 18,* 16–81.

Jenkins, W. M., & Merzenich, M. W. (1987). Reorganisation of neocortical representations after brain injury: A neurophysiological model of the bases of recovery from stroke. *Progress in Brain Research, 71,* 249–266.

Kaas, J. H., Merzenich, M. J., & Killackey, H. P. (1983). The reorganisation of somatosensory cortex following peripheral nerve damage in adult and developing animals. *Annual Review of Neuroscience, 6,* 325–356.

Klatzky, R. L., Lederman S. J., & Metzger, V. A. (1985). Identifying objects by touch: An "expert system." *Perception and Psychophysics, 37,* 299–302.

Lederman, S. J., & Klatzky, R. L. (1987). Hand movements: A window into haptic object recognition. *Cognitive Psychology, 19,* 342–368.

Lederman, S. J., & Klatzky, R. L. (1990). Haptic classification of common objects: Knowledge driven exploration. *Cognitive Psychology, 22,* 421–459.

Lederman, S. J., Klatzky, R. L., & Pawluk, D. T. (1993). Lessons from the study of biological touch for haptic robot sensing. In H. Nicholls (Ed.), *Advanced tactile sensing for robots.* In World scientific series in robotics and automated systems, vol. 5 (pp. 193–200). Singapore: World Scientific Publishing.

Manning, M. L. (1993). *Developmentally appropriate middle level schools.* Wheaton, MD: Association for Childhood Education International.

Manning, M. L. (1998). Play development from ages eight to twelve. In D. P. Fromberg & D. Bergen (Eds.), *Play from birth to twelve and beyond* (pp. 154–162). New York: Freeman.

Montagu, A. (1977). *Touching: The human significance of the skin* (2nd ed.). New York: Harper & Row.

Newell, F. N., Ernst, M. O., Tjan, B. S., & Bulthoff, H. H. (2001). Viewpoint dependence in visual and haptic object recognition. *Psychological Science, 12*(1), 37–42.

Peplar, D. J., & Ross, H. S. (1981). The effects of play on convergent and divergent problem solving. *Child Development, 52,* 1202–1210.

Piaget, J. (1962). *Play, dreams, and imitation in childhood.* New York: Norton.

Piaget, J., & Inhelder, B. (1956). *The child's conception of space.* London: Routledge and Kegan Paul.

Power, T. G. (2000). *Play and exploration in children and animals.* Mahwah, NJ: Lawrence Erlbaum Associates.

Roland, P. E., & Mortenson, E. (1987). Somatosensory detection of microgeometry, macrogeometry, and kinesthesia in man. *Brain Research Reviews, 12,* 1–42.

Sherrick, C. E., & Cholewiak, R. W. (1986). Cutaneous sensitivity. In K. Boff, L. Kaufman, & J. Thomas (Eds.), *Handbook of perception and human performance* (Vol. 1, pp. 12.1–12.58). New York: Wiley-Interscience.

Singer, J. L. (1994). Imaginative play and adaptive development. In J. H. Goldstein (Ed.), *Toys, play, and child development* (pp. 6–26). New York: Cambridge University Press.

Smilansky, S., & Shefatya, L. (1990). *Facilitating play: A medium for promoting cognitive, socioemotional, and academic development in young children.* Gaithersburg, MD: Psychosocial & Educational Publications.

Sutton-Smith, B. (1990). Playfully yours. *TASP Newsletter, 16,* 2–5.

Sutton-Smith, B. (1998). *The ambiguity of play.* Cambridge, MA: Harvard University Press.

Trawick-Smith, J. (1994). *Interactions in the classroom: Facilitating play in the early years.* Upper Saddle River, NJ: Prentice-Hall.

United Internet Technologies Newsletter. (April, 2001). Accessed November 29, 2003 at http://www2.uitlive.com/investor/pr/wbwb041701.html.

Weisenberger, J. M. (2001). Cutaneous Perception. In E. B. Goldstein (Ed.), *Handbook of perception* (pp. 535–562). Somerset: Blackwell.

Weisler, A., & McCall, R. B. (1976). Exploration and play: Resume and redirection. *American Psychologist, 31*, 492–508.

Zaporozhets, A. V. (1969). Some of the physiological problems of sensory training in early childhood and preschool period. In M. Cole & I. Maltzman (Eds.), *A handbook of contemporary Soviet psychology* (pp. 86–120). New York: Basic.

12

Preschool Children's Play With "Talking" and "Nontalking" Rescue Heroes: Effects of Technology-Enhanced Figures on the Types and Themes of Play

Doris Bergen

Many of the newest toys designed for young children incorporate technological enhancements, such as computer chips that make toys "talk" or "act" in certain ways. Although these technology-enhanced toys have become increasingly popular with parents and children, there is little research on how children play with such toys. Thus, little is known about how these toys may or may not affect children's play. Parents, toy makers, and early childhood educators all have questions about the potential positive and negative impacts of such toys, which may have highly salient "affordances" (characteristics that suggest their use). It is presently unknown whether such toys reduce or add to play creativity, channel play in prosocial or antisocial ways, positively or negatively influence children's cognitive, social–emotional, or language development, or affect the way children play with traditional toys (Bergen, 2001).

According to Gibson (1979/1986) and Gibson and Pick (2000), the environment and the child (or any organism) cannot be studied independently because the affordances of the environment and the child's perception of the affordances comprise a mutually dependent system. Affordances are opportunities for action within a given environment and are specific to individuals. An affordance may not be perceived if there are physical or developmental constraints (e.g., the child does not have physical skills) or there are perceptual constraints (e.g., the child does not notice the affordance). Because affordances permit and restrict actions, children acquire information by detecting invariants. Thus learning becomes a process of differentiation.

Gibson's views are gaining importance in the design of educational technologies because designers hypothesize that the constant interplay between perceiving and acting that technological environments afford leads to children's discovery of information. Both computer programs and technology-enhanced toys have affordances that differ from those of traditional toys. Designers of technology are beginning to realize the importance of analyzing how these affordances influence children's play interactions. Whether technology-enhanced toys elicit differentiated behaviors in children as compared with behaviors elicited by toys without technology affordances (but with other affordances) was the major question of interest in this study.

Whereas there have been a few studies of young children's play with computers, research investigating children's play with toys that have computer chips added to initiate sounds, talk, or actions is almost nonexistent. Studies of preschoolers'computer play generally show that when children encounter computer software for the first time, they go through the following stages: discovery, involvement, self-confidence, and creativity (Haugland & Wright, 1997). For children, computer use often is a social activity. For example, Heft and Swaminathan (2002) found that the preschoolers in their study setting observed and acknowledged other children, commented on other children's actions, shared and helped one another, and had conflicts over turn-taking. Boys used the computer more than girls. When girls were paired and worked together on computer-related tasks, however, they often performed more successfully (Yelland, 1999). Early literacy development with the aid of computers has shown some success (Segers & Verhoeven, 2002), and the use of computers to enhance the play of children with disabilities also has been studied (Hitchcock & Noonan, 2000; Parette, Heiple, & Hourcade, 2000). The findings show that structured approaches to helping children learn computer skills can be successful.

Only a few studies have combined computers with toys. A recent study that combined computer play with a technology-enhanced interactive plush toy, which gave directions and feedback to children, found that most children preferred human help to learn the computer games and ignored the toy's help unless their attention was drawn to it (Luckin, Connolly, Plowman, & Airey, 2002). In general, once they knew what to do with the computer program, the children did not refer to the "talking" toy's suggestions.

The play of children with nontalking rescue heroes also has been the subject of a few studies. These studies investigated how the affordances of these action toys affect the way the toys are used. For example, if a toy has an axe, a potential "weapon," is it also likely to be used to knock down a wall to "help" someone escape from a fire? Which of these actions is most likely to occur? Kline (1999) conducted a structured qualitative study of rescue heroes toys to examine how boys communicated the rescue scripts after they had seen a video of the toys in action. Seeing the "prosocial" actions on video did reduce somewhat the more violent themes that the boys played earlier, but there was a wide variation in the children as to how much they played with the toys, how imaginative their play was, and how prosocial their themes of play were. Somewhat similar findings were evident in a study by Guisset (2002), which concluded that "external features [i.e., affordances] are not enough to promote prosocial behavior" (p. 9). The researcher attributed the pervasiveness of more violent play to the fact that the prosocial video was seen only briefly, whereas "war games are deeply rooted in the culture of children" (p. 9).

Whether the themes of children's pretend play focus more on prosocial "helper" actions when these replica figures of "helper" personnel (fire and police) are used is especially of interest since the September 11 disaster in the United States, in which such personnel were highly evident. Many parents bought rescue toy fireman and policemen after this terrorist attack, presumably to allow children to play these helper roles. The primary question of interest in the current study was whether the technology-enhanced rescue heroes, which encourage children to activate the buttons that make the figures "talk" about rescue themes and initiate environmental sounds and pictures that suggest such themes for play, would be played with differently than the "nontalking" figures, which have affordances that may suggest a wider range of actions. The study investigated the ways that "talking" (computer-chip enhanced) and "nontalking" rescue heroes might affect the types and themes of the play of the preschool children. Because the toys are typically played with by boys, another question of interest was whether girls' reactions to the toys would be similar to that of boys. Whether the presence of two other types of affordances (a peer and a rescue heroes video) might be influential in promoting and extending prosocial themes of play were also of research interest. Influences of other environmental opportunities such as toys and videos provided in the home and television images of the World Trade heroes also were explored.

RESEARCH QUESTIONS

The following questions were the focus of the study:

1. Do children play differently with technology-enhanced rescue heroes ("talking") and those that are not technology-enhanced ("nontalking")?
2. Do boys and girls use different toy figures, play actions, and themes with rescue heroes?
3. Do children who see videos of rescue heroes have different play actions and themes?

4. Do children have different actions and themes if they play alone or with a peer?
5. Do children use World Trade disaster themes in play with rescue heroes?

METHOD

Toys Used in Research

Because the data collection phase of the study was funded by Fisher-Price, the toys and the video used were provided by the company. The three toys used in the study were a male firefighter, a female firefighter (both European American), and a male police officer (African American), for whom there are talking and nontalking versions. The talking toys had backpacks with computer chips and two activation buttons, one of which elicited words from the toy (e.g., "tornado") and one of which elicited sounds and pictures on a screen (e.g., the roar of a tornado and a view of it). There was only one implement (a small axe) that could be removed from one of the figure's hands. The nontalking toys also had backpacks, which included an implement that could be activated by pressing a lever. The male fireman had an axe; the female fireman had a water spray gun; and the policeman had a handcuff. A small set of unit blocks also were on the table with the toys to provide a "traditional" alternate activity choice and a potential prompt for the World Trade disaster rescue or other rescue themes to be enacted. A short segment of the rescue heroes video focused on snowstorm disasters showing rescue heroes flying in a plane to help people, rescuing a child who had fallen through pond ice, and helping snowbound people from a house and off a cliff also was used.

Design of the Study

In this study, 64 children (32 boys and 32 girls), ages 3½ to 5 years, played with the toys and the blocks in two sessions about 1½ to 2 weeks apart. The settings were rooms outside the children's classrooms at their preschools, with most of the children playing for 15 to 20 min each session. The children were from five Head Start, two private child care, and five university child care classrooms. Approximately 30% of the children were African American. There was a range of socioeconomic levels in the families of the children. After parental permission was obtained, the children were assigned randomly to research conditions that combined three independent variables: talking/nontalking toys (T/NT), rescue heroes video/nonvideo viewed after first session (V/NV), and play alone or with peer of opposite gender (A/P). After their agreement to play with the toys and be video-taped, the children were videotaped with a lap-held camera. The intent was to have the children play for 20 min. However, the children who wished to leave earlier were allowed to do so. The mean time was 17 min for the first session and 16.7 min for the second session. The videotapes then were coded according to the dimensions of interest. Intercoder reliability for the amount of time spent in various types of play averaged 87%, with a range of agreement from 62% to 100%. The parents also completed a questionnaire about their children's play with replica figures.

Information From Parent Questionnaires

The parent questionnaires provided information about the children's previous experiences and showed that 24% of children had rescue heroes, 52% had other action figures, and 63% had other pretend figures. The children had watched rescue heroes videos or the TV program in 46% of the homes, and 39% of the children had seen World Trade Center images on television. Although 57% of the parents talked to their child about fire and police heroes at the World Trade disaster, the parents reported that only 29% of the children had used disaster themes in play. Not surprising, analysis by gender of parents' reports showed that there were significant differences between the boys and girls in the types of toy figures they had. The parents of the boys reported that their children had more rescue heroes (only one girl had such a toy) (χ^2 [$df = 1$] = 14.254; $p < .001$), and more action figures in general ($\chi^2 = 8.658$; $p < .01$). On the other hand, the parents of the girls reported that their children had more other pretend figures (χ^2 [$df = 1$] = 24.952; $p < .001$). The boys also were more likely to have seen rescue heroes videos or TV (χ^2 [$df = 1$] = 21.967; $p < .001$). There were no significant differences in the themes of play relative to the home experiences with the various types of toys, however. There also were no significant differences between parental reports on the exposure of boys and girls to World Trade images or discussions of such events.

RESULTS

Actions Afforded by the Toys and Blocks

The affordances (i.e., opportunities for actions perceived and engaged in by the children) of the talking toys, nontalking toys, and blocks elicited relatively similar actions, especially after the first few minutes of the first session. Table 12.1 shows the types of actions afforded by the toys at each time period. With the exception of the screen/button pressing, which was an

TABLE 12.1
Percentages for Types of Actions With Toys by All Subjects

	Time 1 (%)	Time 2 (%)
Actions Specific to Rescue Heroes' Salient Affordances		
Looks/inspects	78	38
Lines up	33	22
Pushes screen/talk button	50	47
Hold/uses implements	80	74
Backpack off/on	48/42	39/34
Exchanges backpacks or implements	11/9	13/9
Presses backpacks simultaneously	13	8
Shoots, sprays, or chops	70	66
Actions Specific to Replica Figures' General Affordances		
Makes toy walk/sit	16	20
Makes toy step, climb, or slide	19	9
Makes toy fly/jump	17	16
Makes toy talk	44	45
Makes toy do unique actions	44	45
Engages in pretend action	58	52
Labels toy (e.g., fireman)	28	27
Describes toy (e.g., a girl)	30	28
Uses words/sounds to accompany actions	52	42

affordance exclusive to the talking toys, the types of actions in which the children engaged with both types of toys were wide ranging. Table 12.2 shows the types of actions afforded by the unit blocks that also were present at each time period. Tables 12.3, 12.4, and 12.5 show the actions that were significantly different for the T/NT, M/F, V/NV, and A/P groups. As would be expected, some of these actions were directly related to the affordances of the toys, whereas others were actions related to other fac-

TABLE 12.2
Percentages for Types of Actions With Blocks by All Subjects

Actions Specific to Block Affordances	Time 1 (%)	Time 2 (%)
Uses blocks without construction	41	20
Separates blocks from toys	11	19
Builds block tower	34	33
Builds block building	28	44
Builds other block structure (e.g., wall)	52	45
Labels block structure	34	38
Knocks down block structure with toy implements	27	22
Includes blocks in pretend play	50	63

TABLE 12.3
Significant Differences in Actions Afforded
by Talking/Nontalking Toy (T/NT) Conditions

Differences	Chi-Square (df)	Significance (p)
T exchanged backpacks more at time 1	7.860 (1)	<.01
T activated backpacks simultaneously at time 1	5.143 (1)	<.05
T exchanged implement (axe) more at time 1	6.621 (1)	<.01
NT shot implements more at time 1	10.656 (1)	<.001
NT held/used more implements at time 1	7.815 (1)	<.01
NT labeled toys more at time 2	6.488 (1)	<.01
NT described toys more at time 2	4.947 (1)	<.05
NT built more with blocks at time 2	4.063 (1)	<.05
NT knocked down blocks with toys more at time 2	5.85 (1)	<.05
T repeated rescue heroes' language more at times	13.166 (1)	<.001
1 and 2	7.585 (1)	<.01
T talked more to researcher at time 2	8.576 (1)	<.01
NT made toys do more unique actions at time 2	5.107 (1)	<.05

TABLE 12.4
Significant Differences in Actions Afforded by Gender
as Well as Video/Nonvideo Viewed (V/NV) Conditions

Differences	Chi-Square (df)	Significance (p)
Girls played more with blocks without construction at time 1	4.146 (1)	<.05
Girls labeled block constructions more at time 1	4.433 (1)	<.05
Girls talked to researcher more at time 1	4.433 (1)	<.05
V used more words/sounds to accompany action at time 2	7.75 (1)	<.01
V built more buildings at time 2	4.063 (1)	<.05

tors. For example, a number of actions of children with peers differed from those of children alone. There also were some significant differences in the children's use of language by condition.

Differences and Similarities in Play With the Talking and Nontalking Toys

Overall, there were few differences in the children's types of play with the two types of toys. Table 12.6 shows the percentage of time the groups were engaged in various types of play: exploratory, practice, pretend. With regard to percentage of time spent in types of play, the T/NT groups showed a significant difference in only one area: At time 1 the children who had the nontalking toys spent more time in practice play with the toys and blocks

TABLE 12.5
Significant Differences in Actions Afforded by Play Alone
or With Peer of Opposite Gender (A/P) Condition

Differences	Chi-Square (df)	Significance (p)
A lined up toys more at time 1	5.741 (1)	<.05
P labeled block structures more at time 1	4.433 (1)	<.05
P knocked down more block structures with		
toys at time 1	6.488 (1)	<.01
A held/used implements more in time 2	3.925 (1)	<.05
P made toys talk more at time 2	5.107 (1)	<.05
P described toys more at time 2	4.947 (1)	<.05
P pretended more with toys at time 2	10.573 (1)	<.001
P labeled toys more at time 2	9.600 (1)	<.01
P knocked down blocks more at time 2	5.85 (1)	<.05
P used more of own language to accompany	5.333 (1)	<.05
play at times 1 and 2	10.256 (1)	<.001
P used more rescue hero language at time 1	5.107 (1)	<.05
P used more language unrelated to play at	14.076 (1)	<.001
times 1 and 2	6.926 (1)	<.01
P talked more to researcher at time 1	4.433 (1)	<.05
A more often used no language at time 1	4.010 (1)	<.05

TABLE 12.6
Mean Percentages of Time Spent in Types of Play

	Time 1	Time 2
Mean of total time spent by each child (min)	17	16.7
Percentage of time in exploration with toys (%)	13.5	4.4
Percentage of time in practice play with toys (%)	29.6	32.5
Percentage of time in practice play with blocks	11.9	13.5
Percentage of time in practice play with toys and blocks	8.9	7.9
Total percentage of time in practice play	50.4	53.9
Percentage of time in pretend play with toys	11.7	6.2
Percentage of time in pretend play with blocks	3.6	9.0
Percentage of time in pretend play with toys and blocks	4.9	8.6
Percentage of time in theme pretend play with toys and blocks	3.6	2.6
Percentage of time in theme pretend play with toys	7.3	7.0
Total percentage of time in pretend play	31.1	33.4
Total percentage of time in pretend play with themes	10.9	9.6
Disengaged	3.8	5.5
Onlooking	2.0	1.0

together ($F[1, 63] = 8.238$; $p < .01$). This was probably because of their efforts to use the implements these toys had (axe, handcuff, water spray) to
knock down block towers, catch blocks, or pound on blocks. Although the
children with talking toys spent slightly more time in exploration at both
sessions, this difference was not significant.

TABLE 12.7
Themes of Pretend Play

Themes	Time 1 (%)	Time 2 (%)
Number of themes	3–9, 2–17, 1–30, 0–44	3–9, 2–25, 1–26, 0–39
Percentage of rescue heroes themes	34	39
Percentage of family/general helper themes	8	13
Percentage of general violent themes	28	20
Percentage of other themes	22	33
Percentage of World Trade themes	0	1.6

Of special interest was the thematic play of the children. Thematic play was categorized as in terms of the following types: rescue hero theme (e.g., helping put out fire, saving someone from drowning), family/general helper theme (e.g., mom/dad/child walking to home, building roads, and traveling), general violent theme (e.g., fighting, name calling), other themes (e.g., jumping on trampoline), and World Trade themes (e.g., specific to disaster). The overview in Table 12.7 shows the number of different theme types the children used during pretend (even brief themes are included). There were no significant differences between the children who played with the talking and those who played with the nontalking toys in the amount of time spent in theme play. However, the children who played with the talking toys were more likely to have a rescue hero theme at both the first and second play sessions (χ^2 [$df = 3$] = 10.178; $p < .05$; χ^2 [$df = 4$] =10.504; $p < .05$).

Differences and Similarities in Play Between Boys and Girls

There were no significant differences in the percentage of time the boys and girls spent in practice or pretend play. However, the boys spent more time in theme play ($F[1, 60] = 274.76$; $p < .05$). If the peer pairs had been grouped by the same gender, the differences may have been greater. However, the children who played alone also showed this pattern, with boys engaging in more thematic play.

Differences and Similarities Between Video and Non–Video Watchers

The children who saw the video between sessions did not spend a longer time playing or using themes in play. Apparently the video was not sufficiently long or pervasive to influence the themes of play or its extent. How-

ever, these children did use more words and sounds to accompany their actions and built more buildings after they had seen the video (time 2).

Differences and Similarities Between Children Who
Played Alone and Those Who Played With Peers

The children in the peer condition spent a significantly longer time playing
during both periods. They spent less time in exploration at both times, and
more time in practice play with toys and with blocks at time 1. They pre-
tended more with toys at time 1, and more with blocks and with toys and
blocks at time 2. They also showed less disengagement at time 1. However,
the children who played alone were more likely to play with all three toy
figures than the children playing with a peer. In the alone sessions, almost
all the children played with all three toys, but in the peer sessions, each
child usually selected one toy or one child immediately took two toys. Most
of the children in the peer group did play with all the toys at some point,
however. At time 1, there was a significant difference in that boys in the
peer group more often used all three figures or had one or two male figures,
whereas the girls more often had the female figure and/or the female and
one male figure (χ^2 [$df = 6$] = 16.662; $p < .01$). Some of the children tried to
get more toys or to switch toys, but often the other child resisted. Interestingly, the girls who had picked the female toy often kept that toy the entire
period, even when asked to exchange.

Presence of World Trade Center Themes

Only one child (a boy) specifically used a World Trade theme during play,
and this theme was of the disaster rather than the "helper" aspect. Both his
mother and preschool teacher reported that he had replayed the crash
scene many times during the months after the disaster occurred.

DISCUSSION AND CONCLUSIONS

Both the talking and nontalking toys had some salient affordances that elicited particular behaviors (e.g., button pressing; activation of handcuff), but
after an initial exploratory period, most of the children used the toys in generally similar ways, especially during their practice and pretend play. The
children with technology-enhanced toys repeated some phrases and
sounds that the toy made and initially activated the sound/talk mechanisms, but in their practice play most of them used actions and language
narratives similar to those of the children with the nontalking toys. In their
pretend play, they all used language relevant to the themes of the play.

There also were few differences in the amount of time they played in different modes. Thus, there was little evidence in this study that technology-enhanced toys of this type were overly directive of the children's play. Rather, the children's play presented a fairly typical picture of play choices. In the approach used for this study with the video stimulus, only a few children showed evidence of replication of specific video themes. This may be attributable to the single and brief exposure to the video and to the time lag between the two data collection sessions. Whether greater exposure to rescue hero videos would elicit greater adherence to the themes suggested by the toys is currently unknown, although anecdotal records from parents do suggest that the videos influence play.

Having the toys at home increased theme and pretend play somewhat, but in general the children's past experience with various types of toys was not a major influence. However, a few children who had home experience with rescue heroes seemed to move almost immediately to practice or pretend play without any exploration period. The World Trade disaster influence was clearly evident only in one child. Because these children were from the Midwest, the disaster and "helper" figures may have been less vivid than for children in the East. The results may have differed if the study had been conducted in New York.

The presence of a peer (even of opposite gender) increased the quality of play in numerous ways. There were more actions, pretend themes, block/toy pretend, and labeling or describing of the toys. The peer's presence also increased the length of the session and amount of time spent in pretend. Thus, the best affordances of play with toys in this study appeared to be the addition of another child! This sample exhibited very few gender differences. This may be attributable to the mixed gender pairs used in the study. If the peer pairs had been of the same gender, this may have increased stereotypic differences in play behavior. The tapes do reveal that some of the boys and girls played differently with the toys. However, the actions of many children of both genders were similar.

Generalization of findings in this study is limited because of the artificial conditions in which the children played and the possible influence of setting variability. However, the study does shed some light on the ways children play with technology-enhanced toys of this type. It remains to be seen whether the influence of the more demanding interactive toys (e.g., robotic types that give vivid directions to children) would have more influence on the children's actions. This study suggests that more research is warranted to investigate the effects of technology-enhanced toys on play. The collaboration between a toy maker and a university researcher made this study possible. There should be more collaborations of this type, especially because technology-enhanced toys are becoming increasingly popular.

ACKNOWLEDGMENTS

The author thanks Fisher-Price, Inc., who funded the research data-gathering phase, and especially Kathleen Alfano, Director, Fisher-Price Child Research Department, for her support and encouragement in making the study possible. Sincere thanks also go to the graduate assistants, Jessica Burnham and Patrick Frato, who supervised the data collection and coding phases, and to the undergraduate research assistants, Katie Reinke, Brooke Fox, Rachel Meyer, Mike Keidel, Leslie Smutz, Kristen Olson, Julie Tiemeier, Arron Terrill, and Anna Stachel, who participated in data collection and/or data coding. Without their dedicated assistance, the study could not have been accomplished.

REFERENCES

Bergen, D. (2001, Summer). Technology in the classroom: Learning in the robotic world: Active or reactive? *Childhood Education, 77,* 249–250.

Gibson, E. J., & Pick, A. D. (2000). *An ecological approach to perceptual learning and development.* New York: Oxford University Press.

Gibson, J. J. (1979/1986). *The ecological approach to visual perception.* Hillsdale, NJ: Lawrence Erlbaum Associates.

Guisset, F. (2002). *Study of the influence of video on play with "rescue hero" figures.* Unpublished manuscript.

Haugland, S. W., & Wright, J. L. (1997). *Young children and technology: A world of discovery.* Boston, MA: Allyn and Bacon.

Heft, T. M., & Swaminathan, S. (2002). The effects of computers on the social behavior of preschoolers. *Journal of Research in Childhood Education, 16*(2), 162–174.

Hitchcock, C. H., & Noonan, M. J. (2000). Computer-assisted instruction of early academic skills. *Topics in Early Childhood Education, 20*(3), 145–158.

Kline, S. (1999). *The role of communication in supporting prosocial "play scripts" in young boys' imaginative play with action hero toys: A pilot study of rescue heroes.* Technical Report, Media Analysis Laboratory, Simon Fraser University, Canada. Accessed at http//www.sfu.ca/media-Lab/rearch/rhreport.html, 29 pages.

Luckin, R., Connolly, D., Plowman, L. P., & Airey, S. (2002, August). *With a little help from my friends: Children's interactions with interactive toy technology.* Paper presented at the International Toy Research Association Conference, London.

Parette, H. P., Heiple, G. S., & Hourcade, J. J. (2000). The importance of structured computer experiences for young children with and without disabilities. *Early Childhood Education Journal, 27*(4), 243–250.

Segers, E., & Verhoeven, L. (2002). Multimedia support of early literacy learning. *Computers and Education, 39,* 207–221.

Yelland, N. (1999). "Would you rather a girl than me?": Aspects of gender in early childhood contexts with technology. *Journal of Australian Research in Early Childhood Education, 1,* 141–152.

13

"Hey, Hey, Hey! It's Time to Play": Children's Interactions With Smart Toys

Lydia Plowman

TOYS THAT TALK

The prospect of a talking doll was made possible by Edison's invention of the phonograph in 1877. By 1890 Edison had built a factory to manufacture talking dolls that encased a miniaturized version of the phonograph so that the dolls appeared to sing nursery rhymes. Although large numbers were produced, the doll was not successful. It was very expensive; the voice mechanism wore out prematurely; and, like the more recent My Real Baby and My Dream Baby mentioned later, the dolls were too heavy. The ambition to create a talking doll dates back at least as far as the 18th century, when mechanical toys and automata were popular as part of a quest for artificial life (Standage, 2002; Wood, 2002). Other talking dolls, such as Dolly Rekord, were developed during the early part of the 20th century, but the mechanical recordings on which they relied were not robust, and it was not until electronic voice synthesis became possible that they became more reliable. In the interim, Mattel produced Chatty Cathy in the 1960s, operated by pulling a cord in the doll's back to make it talk, and Worlds of Wonder produced a talking teddy bear, Teddy Ruxpin, in 1985.

The new generation of talking toys has capitalized on developments in computing and speech technology to produce smart dolls that not only talk but also appear to have some capacity for learning. Speech is a popular manifestation of computationally augmented interactivity because it gives the illusion of a rapport between a plaything and its user, and voice is a powerful indicator of social presence (Reeves & Nass, 1996) and intelligence. For the simulation of even partially convincing levels of intelligence, dolls and toys have needed a link to a PC for maximum functionality, as was the case for the Microsoft Actimates used in the current study, instead of relying on the mechanical devices of Chatty Cathy and Teddy Ruxpin. Mattel's Talk With Me Barbie Doll, launched in 1997 and marketed at $90, needed to be connected to a full-size PC. Children were able to select their own name and a range of topics to discuss with Barbie from a CD-ROM. The choices then were beamed from the computer to the infrared receiver in the doll's necklace and stored in its memory. The Barbie Doll then could talk to the child without the need to be attached to a desktop computer (Eng, 1997).

Hasbro's My Real Baby, introduced in 2000 and retailing at $99, used techniques developed by Rodney Brooks, a robotics and artificial intelligence specialist at Massachusetts Institute of Technology (MIT). According to the instruction leaflet, the doll

> responds to you in a true-to-life way, with different facial expressions, emotion-like responses, sounds, words and sentences. . . . The more you play with My Real Baby, the more she seems to "learn." Her vocabulary changes, progressing from cute baby sounds and babbling to simple words and phrases, then up to 4–5 word sentences. The way she responds to you during an activity will vary depending on how much she has learned and what mood she is in!

There was much anticipation for this product, as there had been for Edison's doll, but the mechanics necessary for movement made the dolls heavy and unwieldy. They required frequent replacement of batteries, and the functionality of the interactive features was unreliable, leading a customer on the amazon.com Web site to post the following review:

> This is my last battery operated doll purchase, I am going back to dolls that do nothing and are soft to hold and [my daughter] can make believe she is doing all the mommy things . . . without spending a hundred dollars and buying lots of batteries. (Mrs Kim, a school bus driver from Hillsborough NJ)

My Dream Baby was a similar doll, marketed at about the same time and produced by MGA Entertainment. This doll went through stages from lying down to crawling and then walking, had language that developed in parallel with these functions, and also was capable of limited speech recognition. These dolls, along with Talk With Me Barbie Doll and the Actimates, were withdrawn from the market because the costs of extensive research and development resulted in a higher retail price than the domestic market would tolerate.

ARTHUR AND D.W.

"Hey, hey, hey! It's time to play" are words spoken by one of the toys in this study. Originally produced in 1998 at $99, the Microsoft Actimates can talk, although they do not have speech recognition technology. These toys are not generic dolls, but were based on Arthur and his sister D.W., two aardvark characters from the Marc Brown stories and cartoon series. They were familiar to more than three fourths of the children in the study. From a marketing point of view, the use of existing characters means that the toys come with established personalities and characteristics, so children know how the toys are likely to respond. Because they have a velour finish, they are similar to traditional soft toys (Fig. 13.1), and unlike the dolls, the sensors and batteries do not make them heavy and unwieldy. Adults expressed some distaste for dolls such as My Real Baby and My Dream Baby because they simulated human babies, but both children and adults found Arthur and D.W. more agreeable.

Arthur and D.W. are 60 cm tall and have a vocabulary of about 4,000 words, motors to provide movement, and an electronic chip to recognize inputs. Because the toy cannot respond intelligently to spoken input, it depends on gestural interaction. If a child squeezes its hand or wristwatch, the toy will ask questions. If its toe is squeezed, it will suggest a game.

FIG. 13.1. Using the toy (Arthur) in conjunction with the PC and CD-ROM.

Games include the child estimating a time (5, 10, 15, or 20 seconds) by squeezing the toy's hand when the time is up and saying the alphabet (backward and forward) and tongue twisters. In addition to being used in this stand-alone mode, the toys can be used in conjunction with specially encoded CD-ROMs that feature language and number games.

Playing with the toy and the software simultaneously in this way requires a PC pack accessory. A radio transmitter that resembles a modem connects to the computer's game port and enables the toy to communicate with a PC using radiofrequency technology. Adding the PC pack increases the toy's vocabulary to 10,000 words, enabling it to "talk" to the child, commenting on their interaction with the software and offering advice and encouragement. While engaged in the software activities, children are able to elicit help and information from the toy by squeezing its ear. If children have difficulty progressing through a game, or persist in making the same mistake, the toy reminds them of this.

YOUNG CHILDREN, PLAY, AND TECHNOLOGY

The debate on the relation between technology and young children's emotional, social, and cognitive needs is polarized, with those who consider computers to be detrimental to health and learning on one side, and evangelists who promote the role of computers in children's lives on the other (Plowman & Stephen, 2003). Although computers can represent a medium for children's social and intellectual development (Papert, 1996; Pesce, 2000), Healy (1998) insisted that the early years are a "busy time for the brain," and that using computers before the age of 7 years subtracts from important developmental tasks. She argued that learning to use computers exhausts cognitive resources that could be applied to other types of learning. The predominant view of those opposed to computers is that because computer activities are screen-based, they are not as effective as manipulatives (artifacts that can be handled) in developing understanding and skills in the early years. Computers are therefore not developmentally appropriate (Haugland, 2000).

Anxieties extend to technologies such as smart toys. Levin and Rosenquest (2001) claimed that electronic toys produce limited and repetitive interactions, expressing concerns for the healthy play and development of young children. They refer to a time not long ago when most of the toys available for sale were generic rattles, dolls, trucks, and blocks that helped children to be the "creators and controllers of their play and helped parents play in imaginative give-and-take ways with their infants and toddlers" (p. 243). These authors claimed that individualized and open-ended opportunities for creating play are greatly hampered by programmed responses and embedded scripts, and that the use of such toys not only limits play, but also limits the child's imagination and development. They maintained that there is a need to "develop strategies for stemming the tide as these toys flood homes and classrooms" (p. 245).

The Alliance for Childhood promotes a similar view. In *Fool's Gold: A Critical Look at Computers in Childhood*, Cordes and Miller (2000) called for an immediate moratorium on the further introduction of computers in early childhood, except for special cases of students with disabilities. They recommended a refocusing on "the essentials of a healthy childhood" (e.g., play, book reading, and direct experiences of nature and the physical world) and requested that the U.S. Surgeon General produce a report on the hazards computers pose to children. Robotic dolls are called the "worst toy idea of the year" in a press release issued by the Alliance for Childhood (2000). The pressure group believes that programmed toys distract children from "real play," fool children into thinking the toys are alive, manipulate their thoughts and reactions, and prompt unhealthy emotional attachments. Such toys are described as a straitjacket on play.

Play is widely believed to be the main mechanism for children's learning and central to certain aspects of development (Ariel, 2002; Lindon, 2001; Singer, 1994, among many others) including self-confidence, collaboration, and the practice of skills, as well as making sense of the world, developing a sense of self and other, expressing emotions, and taking the initiative. This relation between play and learning usually is seen as benign, but it becomes problematic when particular toys become a focus for concern (e.g., if they are seen as perpetuating gendered behavior or promoting violence) because toys have a central role in the lives of young children. Children are seen as vulnerable, and therefore capable of absorbing the undesirable values promoted by such toys, leading many adults to be nostalgic for traditional homemade or simple versions (Best, 1998). Exposure to technological innovations such as television and computers has provoked similar types of anxieties for the well-being of children (Buckingham, 2000; Luke & Luke, 2001; Valentine & Holloway, 2001). Combine technology and toys and there is a potent mix, particularly if parents feel guilty about buying these toys for their children.

Educational value frequently is used as a marketing device for these interactive toys, and even the use of the word "smart" to describe them implies a level of intelligence in the toy that will transfer to its user. Statements that products "give your preschooler a heads up on reading" (Read With Winnie, Fisher-Price) and "provide infants with the foundation for successful language learning" (The Babbler, Neurosmith) feed parents' anxieties about the extent to which they feel able to offer learning opportunities to their children. The promotional literature frequently refers to the role of "leading psychologists" or "education experts" in the design process in the belief that parents' guilt about buying technological toys and not spending enough time with their children can be assuaged if the toys are educational in purpose.

Few people would challenge the Alliance for Childhood's premise that play and interaction with other children and adults is central to children's development, but its stance on the dangers of technological toys is not supported by research evidence. Claims that programmed toys inhibit children's "real play," manipulate their thoughts, and lead to unhealthy attachments require closer examination. Levin and Rosenquest's (2001) critique is motivated by one anecdote of a child's interactions with an electronic Rock-n-roll Ernie toy. This chapter describes an empirical 18-month study investigating young children's uses of smart toys and draws some different conclusions. In particular, this study examined whether children's opportunities for creating play are hampered and described their interactions with the toy.

CACHET

Computers and Children's Electronic Toys (CACHET) was a research project that investigated the use of interactive toys during 2001–2002. The focus was on studies conducted in homes and after-school clubs. Other more controlled studies were conducted in a school classroom (Plowman & Luckin, 2003). The main aim of the research was to consider the toys' mediation of the child's activities and the new forms of interaction engendered by these toys.

The Microsoft Actimates can be used either on a stand-alone basis or in conjunction with a standard desktop PC fitted with a radio transmitter, and their properties include both wirelessness and manipulability. Because Arthur and D.W. can be played with on their own or in conjunction with the compatible CD-ROM, its use in both scenarios was studied. The home studies involved 12 children (6 girls and 6 boys) ages 5 and 6 years. These children were visited three times over a period of approximately 2 weeks. Half of the children received the toy first and were given the CD-ROM at the midway visit. The other half used the CD-ROM first and were given the toy at the midway visit. In all cases, the children kept both items for the second week of the study and thus had the opportunity to play with the toy in conjunction with the PC, enabling the researchers to explore the three-way interaction between the child, the toy, and the computer. Pairs of children often used the toy in the school and after-school clubs, but it was used mainly by individuals in their homes, although occasionally a sibling or friend joined in.

Parents completed a diary over the 2-week period to provide background information and data on the use of the items while the researcher was absent. The children's play with the toys was not prescribed, but at the start of each loan period, the researchers ensured that the children knew how to access the help facility, and that they could ask Arthur or D.W. for a hint if they needed some help to play the game. There was no control over how often or how long the children used the toys or software, and video recordings were made on an opportunistic basis.

PLAY

Kathleen, a 7-year-old who had access to both toys for a short while, produced a daily schedule for the toys' activities (Figs. 13.2 and 13.3). She clearly anthropomorphized the toys, but the emphasis on bed time and waking up time was partly attributable to their time-telling features (the toy could be programmed as an alarm clock, and squeezing the watch prompted it to tell the time). These technological features were integrated into her play, but she combined them with the nontechnological, so the toys were dressed in other clothes and put to bed in the same way as traditional soft toys.

Suzy also put the toy to bed, but explained that D.W. did not sleep beside her because she feared dropping it on the floor and breaking it, a concern that may be attributable to the technological features of the toy or simply to the fact that it was on loan. James is recorded in the parental diary as having made up a bed for Arthur beside his own at bedtime, and Mark also chose to sleep with Arthur at night. John's parents commented in their diary that he was "intrigued" by the toy. They thought he had "bonded" with it as he carried it around the house with him even when it was not activated.

This type of attachment behavior was limited, however, and there was little evidence of the toy's participation in "free flow" play activities (Bruce, 1991), possibly because the children knew the toy was on loan and would have to be returned. For most of the children, it was just a toy, and some preferred to play with it not switched on, taking the toy to the table to join in with the rest of the family or making a bed for it next to their own. These nurturing behaviors do not constitute evidence for "unhealthy attachments" to the toys given that this type of play was not sustained beyond a few days, and that such behaviors would be interpreted as normal play in

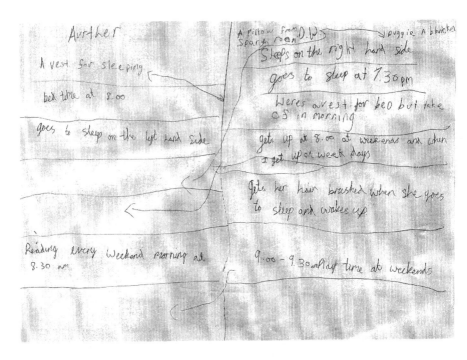

FIG. 13.2. A daily schedule for Arthur and D.W.

Aurther	A pillow from **D.W.** Duggie A blancket spare room
A vest for sleeping	Sleeps on the right hand side
bed time at 8.00	goes to sleep at 7.30 pm
goes to sleep on the left hand side	Weres a vest for bed but take of in morning
A pillow from spare room	gets up at 8.00 at week ends and when I get up on week days
	gets her hair brushed when she goes to sleep and wakes up.
Reading every weekend morning at 8.30 am	9.00-9.30 am Play time at weekends

FIG. 13.3. An approximation of the preceding figure.

214

the context of traditional soft toys. None of the parents raised any concerns about these play activities.

Kathleen's merging of the toys' technological and nontechnological features was characteristic of several children's play activities and, like John, some children preferred to play without using the interactive functions. In such scenarios, even if the concept of "real play" (Alliance for Childhood, 2000) were meaningful, it is not possible to distinguish the elements of play that are "real" from those that are "not real," and there is insufficient evidence to conclude that the toys constrain the child's imagination or inhibit play. The researchers found that the children enjoyed the tactile nature of the toys more than their so-called interactivity.

Episodes that found the children engaged in imaginative encounters beyond the programmed repertoire were unusual, and it was more common for the children to be dismissive of the toy. For children such as James, whose parents recorded that he took the toy to bed with him, but who displayed evident boredom with it when the researcher was present, this could be explained as a performance for the benefit of the adult onlookers.

The children played with the toys on their own terms, except when they felt dragooned into interaction on a research visit, as the following three exchanges demonstrate:

Researcher: "Do you like this game?"
Toy: "Ready, go."
Researcher: "Is this one of the games you like?"
Toy: "Ready, go."
Researcher: "Rob?"
Rob: "No."

Toy: "Here's a good one, ready? Peter Piper picked a peck of pickled peppers. Now it's your turn."
Researcher: "You say it now."
Aileen: "No."
Toy: "To try a different game, squeeze my ear."
Aileen: "I don't want to do that one again."

Toy: "Squeeze my ear to make a new silly sentence. Ready? The lumpy Eskimo eats mud pies with the snoring gorilla. Ha, ha, that's funny!"
Researcher: "Did you think that was funny?"

Rosie: "No."
             (Edit)
Toy: "To make more rhymes, squeeze my hand. To play a differ-
             ent game, squeeze my toe."
Rosie: "I don't want to play with her anymore."
Researcher: "OK, that's fine. So, Rosie, did you like D.W?"
Rosie: "No."

Whether children were interested in the toy or not, they routinely referred to it as "he" or "she." This anthropomorphism is not surprising given
that Arthur and D.W. have names and a combination of cognitive features
(appearing to remember dates, knowing when a child encounters problems
with the CD-ROM) and behavioral features (some movement, talking). The
toys also are based on cartoon characters that combine facial features associated with animals with human attributes such as clothes, spectacles,
wristwatches, and hands. In this respect, the toys are like many soft toys
that combine animal and human features, and these characteristics appeared to be more significant in determining anthropomorphism than the
technological features such as speech.

Although some of the children seemed to infer a degree of sentience in
the toy, parents' comments suggested that this did not translate to a
greater degree of dialogue or other forms of interaction with it. Some children knew batteries powered the toy, although younger children tended to
think it had feelings and could think and talk on its own. Interview questions elicited the extent to which children attributed human characteristics
to the toys. There was considerable diversity of views, partly because children of this age find it difficult to articulate opinions of this kind, but there
was no evidence that the children had been fooled into thinking the toys
were alive. Invited to suggest ways in which the toy could be improved, several children mentioned that they would like it to be able to walk, perhaps
because this is seen as an indicator that a figure is animate. This is consistent with experiments conducted by van Duuren and Scaife (1996) in which
5-year-old children considered a robot to be more capable of thought than a
computer because children at this age associate a capacity for motor behavior with brain functioning.

Arthur and D.W. present a curious mix of toy and technology. Parents
did not often refer to their children *playing* with the toy although they did
refer to them playing with the games on the CD-ROM. This seemed to be
partly because the scripted interactions limited free-flow play. But rather
than this leading to a situation in which "the child's own budding imagination" was "overpowered" (Alliance for Childhood, 2000), the evidence from

the transcripts suggests that this was not the case. Children played with the toys in unpredictable ways. Sometimes they chose not to engage and quickly became bored, whereas at other times they integrated the toys into their daily domestic schedules, showed them to their friends, and engaged in the sorts of play activities associated with traditional soft toys.

CLAIMS FOR LEARNING

In the scenario that has the child and the toy jointly playing the educational games on the CD-ROM, the toy is referred to in the accompanying literature as "your child's computer learning buddy." The marketing emphasizes the toy's educational value, and itemized skills are listed on the box in which the toys are sold. These include cooperation and following directions, logic and critical thinking, creativity and imagination, memory building, word and sound recognition, self-esteem, exercise and physical activity, telling the time, dates and holidays, and classification and rhyming. With the addition of the software and PC pack (and the toy's increased vocabulary), further skills are added: story comprehension, problem solving, social skills, spelling and parts of speech, science, history and geography facts, math and money concepts, music, and rhythm.

The box invites children to "join bright and friendly Arthur on an amazing learning adventure!" The accompanying leaflet uses the authority of a developmental psychologist to reinforce its claims for enhanced learning:

> Fun functions to help your child learn . . . the ideal learning partner for children. "The Actimates interactive learning system grows with a child, . . . uses fun, challenging games and activities to help children master time concepts, language skills and more," said the developmental psychologist and lead designer in developing the Actimates learning system.

Although the parents found the ways that the toy and the software interacted to be an impressive feature, the children seemed to take it for granted. All the children seemed to enjoy the software, regardless of ability or age, but the low level of interest in the toy appeared to be age-related because parents reported much more interest in the toy from younger siblings. The children who had the toy first tended to lose interest in it once the software had been introduced. The toy then was played with only occasionally, if at all. If the toy was introduced after the software, the toy was played with infrequently because the software had already been explored and the help features generally were not needed. In this software-then-toy sequence, it also was the case that the toy was seen mostly as an adjunct to the software and rarely played with away from the PC. The home study children were slightly older than those in the reception class and after-school clubs, and this may account for parents' comments on how quickly children's interest in the toy had waned and its greater popularity with younger children, although all were well within Microsoft's suggested age range of 4 to 8 years.

The toy was promoted as an "interactive learning partner," and suggestions made by the toy to help with the games on the CD-ROM were a unique feature. Nevertheless, the children rarely asked the toy for help, although they were fully aware of this function because they needed to be active in seeking help. The technology was not intelligent enough to recognize all their errors, and its speech was too primitive to provide adaptive feedback. If the toy provided hints or tips, the children did not seem to notice or they ignored it. The children generally preferred to ask an adult. Most of their queries were concerned with interpreting what the toy or a character in the software had said. If the children asked for help and succeeded in their task, they generally demonstrated pleasure at the toy's praise, but they were not taken in by the constantly positive and flattering feedback provided by the toy and soon found this irritating.

The claims that the toy represents a "child's computer learning buddy" appear to be unrealistic considering the ways that children dismissed or ignored the help feature. The toy's verbal and gestural responses are far too limited to simulate finely tuned human guidance, and the toy has no memory of its interactions with the child, an important aspect of providing tailored help.

Video analysis (Luckin, Connolly, Plowman, & Airey, 2003) showed that young children are able to make the connection between two different interfaces and to coordinate the experience they receive through their convergence. Children as young as 4 years were not disconcerted when faced with feedback and interaction possibilities from different artifacts. Given that children cannot interact with the toy intuitively by talking to it, but must rely on strange gestures such as squeezing the toy's ear or squeezing its foot, this may seem surprising. (These interactions are further complicated because the toy works in different ways depending on whether it is operating in freestanding mode or in conjunction with the computer.) The children in the study were able to understand the mechanics of the toy interface, and all could engage at an operational level of controlling the mouse and understanding the relation between the mouse and the screen cursor.

Ultimately, the educational value of these toys probably is no more or less than the educational value of many soft toys. Although the toys engage the child in games and activities, their interest value seems to be short-lived, and the toys are not generally integrated into the child's play once their functionality has been the subject of an initial exploration. The unique selling point of the interaction between the CD-ROM and the toy is largely overlooked by children. Although this study did not aim to measure learning gain, some measures of the standard proxies for learning such as engagement, motivation and time on task are available from the diaries and interviews. According to these, it is unlikely that any short-term learning gain would be sustained because interest in the toy diminished over a relatively short period.

THE CONVERGENCE OF TECHNOLOGY AND PLAY

Young children's play generally is considered a physical activity (dressing up, sand and water play, tumbling and climbing) rather than a digital one. However, this distinction between digital and embodied play may be eroded by the new generation of technologies with tangible (i.e., touchable) interfaces. Many of the fears about children's use of technology are based on a concept of technology that is now out of date. Seen as detrimental to children's development because of their fixed, screen-based nature, it is assumed that information and communication technologies cannot be used by young children for creative and collaborative play or to engage all of their senses. These concerns apply to the use of desktop computers, and have less currency as computing technology becomes embedded in a range of everyday objects. The Actimates exhibit a hybrid technology that challenges some of these assumptions.

The concept of "interactive" toys has been applied mainly to products using familiar forms (cuddly toys, balls, rattles, dolls, or construction bricks) that are computationally enhanced. It is this technological interactivity that is assumed to confer educational value. This belief rests on a skills-based notion of the value of familiarity with technology for future schooling and employment (Facer, Sutherland, Furlong, & Furlong, 2001) and is, more generally, a symptom of the increased curricularization of family life (Buckingham & Scanlon, 2003). The imperialism of a schools-based approach to learning has extended even to children's play with computer games. This play now is validated as educational (Gee, 2003; McFarlane, Sparrowhawk, & Heald, 2002; Prensky, 2001), and computer games are promoted as a vehicle for stealth learning.

It is commonplace to refer to computers as tools for learning and this is reinforced by the dominant metaphor of the office, desktop, and workstation. In this mode, interaction is functional and focused on computers tethered to the desk, with the screen used as a locus of interaction. As technologies become increasingly domesticated, leisure-oriented developments in speech and gesture are used to produce toys and other artifacts that interact in different ways (Bergman, 2000). In this mode, interaction becomes more social in nature, including the ability to express and recognize emotions (Picard, 1997). These changes could increase the scope for richer interactions while simultaneously making technological interactions simpler because "when media conform to social and natural rules, no instruction is necessary" (Reeves & Nass, 1996, p. 8).

This combination of functional and social interaction is embodied in the toys and may have contributed to the ambivalence with which the children in this study viewed them. As a tool, the functional interaction is represented by the tutorial relation used to provide help and guidance and the explicit educational value. As a toy, the social interaction is provided by it representing a partner for silly games, jokes, and riddles. The situation becomes more complex when the software with which both the child and the toy interacts is considered. The toy offers a corporeal figure with whom the child can verbally and physically interact, whereas the screen-based software provides functional interaction.

Although the speech function, a main selling point for the toys, is critical for delivering the sense of social presence and intelligence promoted in its marketing, many of the children in the study found that the talking became monotonous or irritating and preferred to switch it off. Given its 10,000 word vocabulary, the toy can verbally interact with the children at a basic level, but rather than contribute to extended child–toy interaction and role-play, the spoken interaction seems to detract from this possibility. The extent to which a toy can talk has come a long way since Dolly Rekord, Chatty Cathy, and Teddy Ruxpin, but although the Actimates' powers of speech impressed adults, they did not have this impact on children. Although initially captivating, the toy's vocabulary presents only an illusion of reciprocity because the toys do not have speech recognition, the ability to "understand" and respond to spoken words, or speech synthesis, the ability to sequence prerecorded phrases in meaningful ways. Speaker-independent technology means that toys are easy to use straight from the box, but the vocabulary is fixed and not easily upgraded. Speaker-dependent technology must be trained to recognize an individual child's voice and thus is not suitable for young children, although it offers the benefits of vocabularies tailored to a child's specific circumstances (Soule, 2000). Incorporating these features into toys is difficult for the very reason that children are unpredictable users and do not respond well to programmed interaction.

The Actimates' talk is too limited for the suspension of disbelief necessary to imply personality, and it is unlikely that smart toys will be able to simulate the role of a buddy or to appear really smart until speech technologies have met some of these manufacturing challenges. Those who are fearful of technology's detrimental effects on children probably would become more concerned in this scenario, but it is worth remembering that the

Turing test of intelligence posed more than 50 years ago (Turing, 1950) depends on the simulation of speech for an answer to the question "Can machines think?" The test examines a human participant's ability to tell whether the responses to diverse questions are provided by another person or by a computer. If the human participant is unable to discriminate responses over time, then Turing claims intelligence can be ascribed to the computer. The quest to simulate intelligence through the use of speech has not been solved, and it continues to be the subject of scientific competitions and research.

This study of children's interactions with toys that have a very limited speech repertoire shows that there did not appear to be anything dangerous or inhibiting in their interactions. Children made their own choices, using the technology in ways that suited their own purposes, and there was no evidence to suggest that these toys made either a beneficial or detrimental difference in the children's ability to engage in child-led imaginative play. This statement could be applied equally to many other toys because the technological nature of Arthur and D.W. was not really the defining characteristic. The age of the children and their perceptions of how they appeared to adults seemed to be a stronger indicator of interactions with the toy than its interactivity. This provides a corrective to the fears that technological toys are psychologically damaging to the children who use them, particularly to their ability to engage in imaginative play.

ACKNOWLEDGMENTS

Exploring and Mapping Interactivity With Digital Toy Technology, known as CACHET, was funded by the U.K. Economic and Social Research Council and the Engineering and Physical Science Research Council (Award no. L328253009). The research team was Rosemary Luckin, Sharon Airey, and Daniel Connolly. The project Web site is available at http://www.ioe.stir.ac.uk/CACHET/.

REFERENCES

Alliance for Childhood. (2000). *Robotic baby dolls named worst toy idea of the year.* Press release, 22.11.2000.
Ariel, S. (2002). *Children's imaginative play.* Westport, CT: Praeger.
Bergman, E. (2000). *Information appliances and beyond.* San Francisco: Morgan Kaufmann.
Best, J. (1998). Too much fun: Toys as social problems and the interpretation of culture. *Symbolic Interaction, 21*(2), 197–212.

Bruce, T. (1991). *Time to play in early childhood education*. Sevenoaks, England: Hodder & Stoughton.

Buckingham, D. (2000). *After the death of childhood: Growing up in the age of electronic media*. Oxford: Polity Press.

Buckingham, D., & Scanlon, M. (2003). *Education, entertainment, and learning in the home*. Buckingham, England: Open University Press.

Cordes, C., & Miller, E. (Eds.). (2000). *Fool's gold: A critical look at computers in childhood*. College Park, MD: Alliance for Childhood.

Eng, P. (1997). This Barbie even knows your name. *BusinessWeek, 14*(7), 1997.

Facer, K., Sutherland, R., Furlong, R., & Furlong, J. (2001). What's the point of using computers? The development of young people's computer expertise in the home. *New Media and Society, 3*(2), 199–219.

Gee, J. (2003). *What video games have to teach us about learning and literacy*. New York: Palgrave Macmillan.

Haugland, S. (2000). Early childhood classrooms in the 21st century: Using computers to maximise learning. *Young Children, 55*(1), 12–18.

Healy, J. (1998). *Failure to connect: How computers affect our children's minds—for better or worse*. New York: Simon & Schuster.

Levin, D., & Rosenquest, B. (2001). The increasing role of electronic toys in the lives of infants and toddlers: Should we be concerned? *Contemporary Issues in Early Childhood, 2*(2), 242–247.

Lindon, J. (2001). *Understanding children's play*. Cheltenham, England: Nelson Thornes.

Luckin, R., Connolly, D., Plowman, L., & Airey, S. (2003). With a little help from my friends: Children's behaviours with interactive toy technology. *Journal of Computer-Assisted Learning, 19*(2), 165–176.

Luke, A., & Luke, C. (2001). Adolescence lost/childhood regained: On early intervention and the emergence of the techno-subject. *Journal of Early Childhood Literacy, 1*(1), 91–120.

McFarlane, A., Sparrowhawk, A., & Heald, Y. (2002). *Report on the educational use of games*. London: TEEM/DfES.

Papert, S. (1996). *The connected family: Bridging the digital generation gap*. Atlanta: Longstreet Press.

Pesce, M. (2000). *The playful world: How technology is transforming our imagination*. New York: Ballantine.

Picard, R. (1997). *Affective computing*. Cambridge, MA: MIT Press.

Plowman, L., & Luckin, R. (2003). *Exploring and mapping interactivity with digital toy technology: Summary of findings*. Report to ESRC/EPSRC, February 2003. Accessed at http://www.ioe. stir.ac.uk/CACHET/publications.htm

Plowman, L., & Stephen, C. (2003). A "benign addition"? A review of research on ICT and preschool children. *Journal of Computer-Assisted Learning, 19*(2), 149–164.

Prensky, M. (2001). *Digital game-based learning*. New York: McGraw-Hill.

Reeves, B., & Nass, C. (1996). *The media equation: How people treat computers, television, and new media like real people and places*. Cambridge, England: CSLI Publications & Cambridge University Press.

Singer, J. (1994). Imaginative play and adaptive development. In J. H. Goldstein (Ed.), *Toys, play, and child development* (pp. 6–26). Cambridge, England: Cambridge University Press.

Soule, E. (2000). Designing toys that talk—no child's play. *Electronic News, 12*(11), 2000.

Standage, T. (2002). *The mechanical Turk: The true story of the chess-playing machine that fooled the world*. London: Allen Lane.

Turing, A. (1950). Computing machinery and intelligence. *Minds and Machines, 59*, 433–460.

Valentine, G., & Holloway, S. (2001). Technophobia. In I. Hutchby & J. Moran (Eds.), *Children, technology, and culture* (pp. 58–77). London: RoutledgeFarmer.

van Duuren, M., & Scaife, M. (1996). "Because a robot's brain hasn't got a brain, it just controls itself": Children's attributions of brain-related behaviour to intelligent artefacts. *European Journal of Psychology of Education, 9*(4), 365–376.

Wood, G. (2002). *Living dolls*. London: Faber & Faber.

14

Adaptation of Traditional Toys and Games to New Technologies: New Products Generation

M. Fabregat
M. Costa
M. Romero

Nearly everyone agrees that play and toy vehicles for free time enjoyment are fundamental elements for the integral development of the person during infancy and youth. This concept has been demonstrated by many research projects over the years (Almonacid & Carrasco, 1989; Blakely, Lang, & Hart, 1991; Martinez & Muñoz, 2002; Ramsey, 1990; Rivière, 1991; Rosel, 1980a, 1980b; Schneekloth, 1989). Nevertheless, the benefits that come from playing are not, even today, within the reach of all. Much work still must be done to ensure that the design of toys takes into account the end user, considering all of childhood diversity. The objective of this research was to expand the study of possible adaptations that can be made to traditional toys to guarantee that all children, independently of their capacities, can enjoy playing together with toys designed to be accessible for all children. This objective could be attained by taking advantage of the great potential offered by new technologies.

Although there are many other possibilities, this study has focused on the incorporation of an obstacle and direction detection system (GPS) to electronic play vehicles. This type of adaptation was judged to be the most adequate for facilitating the use of toy motor bikes, tricycles, and cars for children with a total or partial visual handicap, who were the subjects of our study. This study focused on toy electronic vehicles because they promote movement and spatial exploration most directly. Both abilities need to be enhanced, according to the experts on children with visual handicaps.

DISABLED CHILDREN AND PLAY

It is not necessary to find a reason to justify play. Playing is positive in it-self, independently of the end to which it contributes. Playing is an enjoy-able, voluntary, creative, imaginative, and fun activity. For that reason alone, energy should be invested in achieving the creation of toys for every-one. Nevertheless, play activities also are excellent means for the transmis-sion and acquisition of values and abilities. The spontaneous motivation that accompanies play reduces the effort expended in learning to a mini-mum. Playing also helps to reduce laziness, fears, and the resistance that some children feel when confronted with certain situations. It is an excel-lent tool for working with the development of many abilities that should be acquired during the first years of life. Experts in the evolutionary develop-ment of visually impaired children advise, for example, that it is necessity to stimulate the start of walking in an especially intense way during the early stages of development. They also insist on indicating that it is impor-tant to facilitate the independence of action necessary for the child to ac-cess the first experiences of communication, movement, spatial orientation, and the sense of touch. Many games and toys contribute to this.

Some specifics that characterize the development of children with visual handicaps (a delay in aspects related to personal autonomy, social behav-ior, difficulties in the spontaneous motor imitation, less motivation toward the exterior world) allow the definition of the areas that should be stimu-lated with such children, especially during early education. All of them, as will be seen shortly, have been taken into account during the development of this project for the design of two different prototypes.

Ages 6 months to 3 years

Acquisition of the ability to walk and speak at the same time that other cognitive notions (e.g., space, time, habits) are developed
Increase of motor possibilities
Knowledge of objects and their properties
Knowledge of spatial relations
The first social habits: food, bathroom, dress

Ages 3 to 6 years

Development of autonomy, first social experiences
Symbolic conduct (play, imitation, and representation)
Language

Knowledge of objects and their characteristics of grouping (order, classification and manipulation of them)

Spatial relations (up–down, inside–outside, backward movement, representation)

Psychomobility

Dress habits, food, bathroom, housework

Play stimulates curiosity for surroundings, favors communication and socialization, and offers opportunities for the development of creativity and imagination. If, during infancy, children with visual handicaps are offered the possibility to play independently and freely, like any other child, they will be able to improve verbal expression, social abilities, fine and gross motor skills, and auditory acuity. Above all, they will feel capable of exploring their environment. They also will be able to discover new sensations without fear and complete the sensory impressions and images that are limited because of their visual impairment. In this way, they will be able to acquire basic abilities for daily life, encounter strategies for resolving practical problems, and receive fundamental training in controlling future situations (Martin, 2001). As Bruner (1978) indicated, playing is a way to minimize the consequences of one's own actions, and thereby to learn in a less risky situation. A child learns about his surroundings through play. Following the reasoning of Almonacid and Carrasco (1989), play for a child is synonymous with living.

Lucerga, Sanz, Rodríguez-Porrero, and Escudero (1992), in their document Pretending Play and Visual Disability, cover the aspects that the most relevant authors consider specific to the play activities of children with visual handicaps. They point out the tendency to play more simple and repetitive games, to play less spontaneously and creatively, to engage in more concrete and less imaginative play, to exhibit a lesser degree of aggressive manifestations, to have little interest in objects, to depend on adults, and to experience difficulty understanding spatial elements. It is most important then to concentrate specifically on these points when designing projects that seek to make playtime more accessible and appealing to children with special handicaps.

The "play for all" philosophy that served as the basis for the current investigation departs radically from the possibility of creating specific toys for children with handicaps. The release of products for "special audiences" would be an absolute failure in terms of mutual play, isolating rather than integrating children with special needs in relation to other children. The adaptation of playtime products for children with different characteristics permits different children to grow together, meet each other, understand each other, and share common experiences.

This idea comes from the principle known as "universal accessibility," from the paradigm of "design for all." Although much has been done to ensure the participation of handicapped people in all social spheres, there still are many objectives that remain unaccomplished. As Gomez (2003) pointed out, the demand for a design for all applies equally to the condition of goods and services offered to citizens through the market and to those available through the public sector. A person with a disability, like any other citizen, must be guaranteed the possibility of freely choosing the same products and services available to the public. For this reason, these products and services must be conceived using the universal design criteria.

Each child, whether characterized by a handicap or not, is unique and needs adequate resources according to his or her specific characteristics. If it is desirable that all toys and games be created respecting the principle of universal design, it is true that even today many playtime products do not comply. For this reason, there still is a need to select products from the marketplace before ensuring that they will be accessible for the child who will use them. Several general guidelines can be followed in deciding how to adapt products, and also in selecting playtime products for children with visual handicaps.

AIJU toy guide 2002 selection tips

Toys should have a simple and realistic design easily identified by touch.

They should include objects and parts that are easy to handle.

They should have sound effects and different textures.

They should not include too many small parts, or at least the parts should be quick and easy to classify by touch.

They should have vivid and contrasting colors, so that children with some vestige of vision can perceive them.

They should be compact and not fall apart easily.

AIJU toy guide 2002 suggestions for making adjustments:

Text or instructions should be translated into Braille, raised, or replaced with voice recordings.

Sound, raised surfaces or textures should be added to replace or accompany visual stimuli.

The board for board games should have a raised part, and the counters or pieces should be made more secure (with Velcro, protruding parts, etc.) to prevent them from being moved involuntarily.

When toys are used for symbolic play with several parts, it can be a good idea to stick them together to prevent them from falling apart.

Finally, it is important to mention that some interesting publications specialize in playtime activities for visually handicapped children. These publications provide details about the possibilities offered by commercially available games and toys, suggesting modifications when they are necessary. These publications include the following:

Toy Guide for the Stimulation of Visual Perception—
Spain
Toy Guide for Differently-Abled—TIA, USA
Toy Guide for Kids With Special Needs—Australia
The Toy Catalogue England
Guide to Toys for Children Who Are Blind or Visually
Impaired—BTHA, England
AIJU Toy Guide—Spain

These publications suggest that appropriate toy products addressed to visually impaired children develop fine and gross motor skills, eye–hand and ear–hand coordination, cause and effect relation understanding, communication and language, physical exercise, and socialization. The information provided in these and other specialized bibliographies was studied carefully during the research process, with the idea of guaranteeing an optimum level of adaptation for both the product and the end users.

ADAPTATION OF TRADITIONAL TOYS AND GAMES TO NEW TECHNOLOGIES: NEW PRODUCTS GENERATION

Institutions Participating in the Research

Three different organizations participated in the research: the Technical Institute of Toys (AIJU) with its multidisciplinary group of toy, infancy, and market experts, the Spanish Association for the Blind (ONCE), and the toy company FAMOSA.

The Technical Institute of Toys was created in 1985 with the objective of contributing to the toy sector by encouraging research, technological innovation and diversification of the possibilities for toys during the different stages of life, diffusion of the benefits from play, and improvement in the quality of playtime products. The Department of Pedagogy at the Technical Institute of Toys has for many years been developing research projects that link play with special education needs. The potential of toys as a tool of intervention in the contexts of prevention and rehabilitation has been analyzed, connecting new technologies with playtime activities and participating in European research networks focused on the creation of products for everyone. The main objectives have been to assess businesses so they learn to take into account the needs, characteristics and preferences of the user before creating new products or improving current products already in their catalogs. Increasingly, AIJU aims to be the link for putting businesses into contact with end users. All this previous work has enabled the development of a specific method for creating playtime products for the user. This method also was used during the current research. The Department of Pedagogy collaborates with a panel of more than 5,000 families, more than 500 teachers of children of different ages who participate in the current research, and a national network of toy libraries where the products are tested as required.

The PROFAMOSA group is an important international toy manufacturer made up of various smaller companies, each specializing in different phases of the production and creation chain. They have branches in different countries in Europe and the rest of the world. One of these branches, Onilco Innovation, which focuses its work on the research and development stages, has been directly involved in the current project.

FAMOSA offers a wide range of products: dolls (of different types aimed at different ages), accessories for the dolls, items used for play on the beach or at the swimming pool, toys for artistic play, board games, miniature toys, toy vehicles, musical toys, and the like.

The first type of toy benefiting from the results of the research was the electric toy vehicle. However, the company and the experts participating in the research aim to extend and apply the research to the remaining products, carrying on the work so that all children (with or without disabilities) may enjoy play and benefit from playing together with the same toys. The research team considered it important not to forget the needs of production because a good idea must always be feasible as well as surprising and different.

The Spanish Association for the Blind (ONCE) is a nonprofit corporation with the mission of improving the quality of life for the blind and the visually handicapped in Spain. An institution with a social character, ONCE is dedicated also to people who have been affected by different handicaps that works with the state administration through the ministries of economy, finance, labor, and social and interior matters. Alicante's Espiritu Santo College, part of ONCE, ceded the use of its facilities and collaborated in the development of the research. The experts at ONCE provided the project with their valuable experience and knowledge concerning everything connected with the visually impaired.

Why Toy Electric Vehicles?

Without a doubt, all toys help to improve the fundamental aspects of infant development. In this research, priority was given to the necessity, as suggested by the experts, to stimulate in visually handicapped children movement as well as control and recognition of environment. Almonacid and Carrasco (1989) have indicated that those among the latest in achieving walking autonomy are blind children and, to a lesser extent, visually handicapped children. According to the authors, whereas children with full sight begin to walk before the age of 1½ years, visually handicapped children generally achieve the ability to walk only later. Children who are completely blind usually require more than 1½ years to learn to walk. This fact must be kept in mind when the limitation of autonomy is considered as well as the learning of early skills related to movement, spatial relations, and the like. Playing with vehicles especially reinforces these kinds of abilities, and it also encourages imagination and oral expression (through pretend play); spatial orientation; all-around movement coordination; auditory, hand–eye/hand–ear, and foot–eye coordination; balance; early walking and driving experiences; reaction speed; and independence to explore. Moreover, it provides the child with a wide variety of stimuli that help to enlarge the benefits of play time: tactile stimuli (from handling different elements of the vehicle, playing with the manipulative parts, fitting pieces together, touching buttons, turning circular objects, and so on), auditory stimuli (from buttons with sounds or the sounds produced from movement), and visual stimuli (during the exploration of the environment or from the lighting elements).

A great variety of products form part of the "play vehicle" typology. For this reason, an exhaustive market search preceded the investigation. The planned analysis of products available on the market allowed the researchers a maximum variety of products for the testing sessions, guaranteeing a representative sample of the real situation and the presence of the highest possible number of companies from the sector in their research. The vehi-

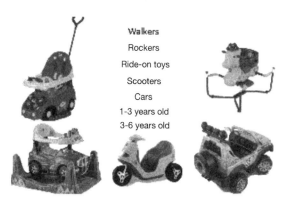

Walkers

Rockers

Ride-on toys

Scooters

Cars

1-3 years old

3-6 years old

cles were classified in two basic age groups (1 to 3 years and 3 to 6 years) in keeping with their dimensions and the type of play offered. This classification directed the design method of the fieldwork. Sixteen vehicles, classified in four categories, were finally selected and evaluated by children, parents, and experts.

METHODS

Given the fact that the objectives of the research required a deep analysis of opinions and behaviors, it was decided that the methodology would be oriented toward a qualitative focus. Obtaining details provided by the evaluation of children, parents, and specialists was given preference over the possible collection of many quantitative evaluations.

Thus, the research was structured in four phases: The first stage involved a comparison and classification study of the different toy vehicles that can be found on the market. To identify the pros and cons of these vehicles, their characteristics, the difficulties of their use, and so forth, the following three different studies were conducted:

1. Usability test for electronic toy vehicles with handicapped and nonhandicapped children.

Twelve observation sessions were conducted in which six technicians from the pedagogical department participated. All the 16 selected toys were used in the sessions by children with visual disabilities, children with slight visual impairment, and children without visual disabilities. Altogether, 97 children 1 to 7 years of age tested the selected toys. The possibilities of use were evaluated for each of the vehicles, and potential differences in the use depending on the level of visual impairment were analyzed. Information was obtained concerning the suitability of the vehicle size for each age, the difficulties for accessing the vehicle, suitable speed, stability, the comfort and security of the seats, and the type of activation system.

Children's Age (n = 97)	Partial Visual Impairment (n)	Total Visual Impairment (n)	No Visual Impairment (n)
1 to 3 years	16	16	16
3 to 6 years	16	16	17
Total	32	32	33

2. Study of electronic toy vehicles by professors specialized in visual handicaps

Eighteen in-depth interviews were conducted with specialist teachers of children who had vision difficulties, all belonging to ONCE. From their knowledge concerning the development of disabled children, they answered questions about how to improve the vehicles and the elements they considered necessary for future products. This information allowed the ideal product to be determined.

	n
Experts' Gender	
Men	4
Women	14
Total	18
Pupil's Age (years)	
1 to 3	31
3 to 6	42
6 to 9	28
9 to 12	26
>12	24

3. Study of electronic toy vehicles evaluation by families with handicapped or nonhandicapped children

A series of in-depth interviews were conducted with 36 parents who had children 1 to 14 years old (disabled and nondisabled). These parents provided valuable information in relation to their purchase criteria, their frequency of using the products, their motivations, the advantages and disadvantages of each product, and so forth. They also helped in the search for the ideal product in terms of design, activation systems, colors, labels, and play theme.

Parents' Gender	*Family With Visually Impaired Children (n)*	*Family With Nonvisually Impaired Children (n)*
Male	4	2
Female	14	16
Total	18	18

Children's Age (years)	*Visually Impaired (n)*	*Nonvisually Impaired (n)*
1 to 3	11	6
3 to 6	7	12
Total	18	18

The second phase involved looking at the results obtained in the first phase to establish guidelines for guaranteeing that the products created were accessible and suitable for use both by visually impaired children and children with no disabilities. During this phase, the design criteria that guaranteed the production of accessible toy vehicles were established. This stage also included the development of the novel "electronic" systems to be incorporated into the vehicles.

The third and current stage consisted of testing the prototype designed in the second phase. Some details currently need redefining for improvement of the vehicles. Plans call for the definitive results to be ready at the end of 2003.

Finally, the fourth stage concerning the launch of the end product is projected for January 2004.

RESULTS

The same conclusions were not always reached because the opinions of the children, parents, and teachers did not always coincide. However, this served the intention of the research exactly: to find out the three realities and, with the information from all three groups, to prepare the final briefing for the design of the new toy vehicle product for all. For example, the children greatly enjoyed the products that incorporated a spring movement. However, the teachers advised against this type of activity because it tended to be converted into a stereotypical movement, completely unbeneficial for children's habits.

The following sections briefly enumerate some of the conclusions obtained from the testing of the selected products with the three target groups participating in the research.

Children

First, it was deemed necessary to modify and simplify the activation systems of the vehicles. This also was essential for simplifying their use by children who are not visually impaired. The pedals needed to be large with a prominent top part to simplify their location and use (not too much pressure). The small children were not capable of controlling two pedals, an accelerator, and a brake at the same time. It was more advisable to have one pedal that activated the vehicle when pressed and stopped the vehicle when the foot was removed, without the need to brake. It also was considered necessary to include safety systems (e.g., belts) and to improve the vehicle's stability. Specially suitable for children with visual impairment was the inclusion of coherent and realistic activities in the toy vehicles (i.e., accessories that could be found in a real one). A suitably realistic design (not incompatible with the world of imagination and fantasy) that enables the child to recognize and identify it would be the best option. It was recommended, for instance, that the inclusion of a telephone among the accessories of a car be avoided. Instead, it was deemed advisable to include raised labels so that visually disabled children could recognize the different parts of the vehicle by touch.

The optimum design of the toy vehicles could vary slightly according to the age group for which it is designed. As stated earlier, the research established, according to the evolutionary stages of infancy, two fundamental intervals during which these differences could be identified: ages 1 to 3 years and ages 3 to 6 years. Some specific requisites for each age were established.

Children 1 to 3 years old handled the triscooters especially well. The scooter with two wheels was not sufficiently stable, and the double-pedal car had an activation system that was too complicated for them. Thus, the triscooter was selected for children this age.

The most suitable dimensions also were established. It was determined that the triscooter should measure 36 to 40 cm high and 55 to 69 cm wide. Furthermore, it was concluded that the ease of access could be sacrificed for security reasons. Doors easy to open and access to the vehicle could be sacrificed to guarantee the safety of children, making it impossible for them to open the doors while driving. One nonreverse gear that did not exceed 3 km per hour was recommended.

For the older children, the car was deemed the most appropriate vehicle, and the double-seater was considered to be very attractive because it enables two children (visually impaired or not) to share the play experience, which starts to be a fundamental activity at this age. It also was concluded that at this age children already are capable of using two pedals, although it was recommended that the system be simplified in this case as much as possible. The doors of the vehicle did not present any danger in the use of the product by children 3 to 6 years old. For this reason, it was recommended that opening and closing doors be included because it gave the car more realism, something that is always positive. It also was recommended that sounds related to the toy and illuminated indicators be included because they were considered to be fundamental elements for the attractiveness of the product and for the playtime capabilities of this age group.

Teachers

According to teachers, the vehicles currently on the market may be used without serious problems by children with visual disabilities. However, they considered that children who are completely blind were not able to benefit as much from these products because they always had to be under adult supervision as a result of their disability. They also believed, without the conclusions obtained in the test with children, that the suitable age for using these products is 3 to 7 years of age. Therefore, given that the fundamental problems involved spatial orientation and control and independence during play, a brainstorming session took place for new ideas and solutions. In this session, it was concluded that technological research would be necessary for incorporation of new products with an obstacles and position detection system as well as a remote control that could help adults to control the product in case of risk.

The imaginative conclusions reached by the visual handicap experts during their brainstorming sessions gave to the research its most creative component, suggesting very innovative solutions to the design representatives for the new products in question. In this way, high technology could be incorporated into playtime activities, whereas, until then, it had never been applied.

Parents

From the interviews with the participating parents it was concluded that parents with disabled children should buy electric vehicles for them, as do parents of children without disabilities. However, the parents expressed the view that their children were not particularly compelled to use such vehicles after encountering many difficulties in their use, and that on several occasions the toy remained for long periods without being used. This helped to justify again the sense of this research.

In relation to the purchase criteria, both the parents of visually impaired children and the parents of nondisabled children valued the security and stability of the vehicle in deciding what to purchase. The parents with children who had disability gave high consideration to the usability of the products, whereas the parents of nondisabled children gave special importance to the price and their size. The main disadvantage the parents found with this type of toy was that in their view it did not encourage shared play or interaction with other children, and that it did not help overall motor development. This opinion does not coincide with that of the play experts participating in the research, as has been previously pointed out. The parents of the children with disability also showed their concern for excess noise produced by toy vehicles, which limited the child's reception of sound stimuli, making orientation difficult. That also was a fundamental idea to consider in the design of the prototypes.

PROTOTYPES

The information obtained from the children, the parents, and the eyesight handicap specialists allowed the design representatives from FAMOSA to begin creating electric toy vehicle prototypes accessible for children with visual handicaps. Two prototypes were developed initially, each one destined for one of the age groups indicated since the beginning of the research: 1- to 3-year-olds and 3- to 6-year-olds.

The FPS System

Responding to the opinions of parents and eyesight handicap experts and to the results obtained from the testing sessions with the electronic toy vehicles, the coordinators of the research began evaluating the possibilities offered by new technology for solving the usability problems detected. The final conclusion consisted of incorporating a system of guidance into the toy vehicles on the basis of GPS technology, called the Famoplay Position System (FPS) in this project.

The system enables detection of obstacles and identification of vehicle's position through vibration stimuli and sound signal provided by the incorporated headphones. The vehicle comes with a pivot that functions as a finishing line. This pivot is situated in the final point of the trajectory. The child can locate the finishing line from the vehicle by turning a button, and the vehicle memorizes the position during play. At this moment, the vehicle can be put into action immediately. While moving, the user receives different stimuli. If the vehicle, through its obstacle detection system, discovers an object that obstructs its path, the vehicle vibrates, informing the child to change direction. By a change in direction the vehicle may divert from the finishing line. If this happens, the child will receive sound signals. The left headphone will sound if the vehicle needs to go left, and the right headphone will sound if the vehicle should turn to the right. Currently, the research proceeds by checking how the system works, determining whether it increases the motivation of disabled children to use electric vehicles, and whether this use contributes to improving the skills mentioned in the first lines of this article.

Prototype for Children 1 to 3 Years Old

Of all the products that were tested, the Scooty model received the most positive response at these ages. It worked using one pedal; its maximum velocity was suitable; its seats were of an easily recognizable texture; its lateral protection made it especially safe; and it was a very stable vehicle. Both the children with visual impairments and the nondisabled children were able to use it comfortably. Some problems detected in the product have been solved for the new prototype: The level of pedal sensitivity has been increased; a new color scheme has been elaborated for maximum contrast; the design has been adjusted slightly to make it more stable; and the Famoplay Position System has been incorporated.

The following picture shows the details of this prototype:

Prototype for Children 3 to 6 Years Old

For children of 3 to 6 years old, a new accessible vehicle has been designed, which is a very attractive product. Its six wheels make it an extremely stable product, capable of overcoming big obstacles. The six wheels, which turn the full 360°, also allow better maneuvering. Its driving wheels are the central ones so that the axis of turning the vehicle coincides with the axes of the child. Thus, by turning, the child knows that he or she will be exactly in the same position but facing a different direction. This vehicle also incorporates the FPS system.

In this model, high-contrast colors (white, black, and red) have been used. Although it was known that children of this age group can handle two pedals simultaneously, it was considered more appropriate to stay with a system of "one pedal" because this simplifies its use. The maximum velocity does not exceed 3.3 km/hr, as was determined ideal in the testing sessions with children. For manufacturing purposes, this model has been designed with one seat. However, the manufacturer currently is working on the design of a version of this vehicle with two seats.

In conclusion, it is important to emphasize the creation of these first accessible toy vehicles. It is crucial to realize that through this research, the first step has been taken to create products that enable children with different levels of capabilities to play together. In the near future, both the re-

searchers and FAMOSA intend to perform new investigation along the same line, hoping to incorporate solutions of this type to other types of toys. Soon new conclusions will be available.

REFERENCES

Almonacid, V., & Carrasco, M. J. (1989). *El juego en los niños ciegos y deficientes visuales.* Madrid: ONCE.

Blakely, K., Lang, M. A., & Hart, R. (1991). *Getting in touch with play: Creating play environments for children with visual impairments.* New York: The Lighthouse.

Bruner, J. (1978). *El proceso mental del aprendizaje.* Madrid: Narcea.

Gómez, F. (2003). *No boundaries: Visions of design today.* Diputación Provincial de Aragoza. Zaragoza, Spain.

Lucerga, R. M., Sanz, M. J., Rodríguez-Porrero, C., & Escudero, M. (1992). *Juego simbólico y deficiencia visual.* Madrid: ONCE.

Ludwig, I., Luxton, L., & Attmore, M. (1988). *Creative recreation for blind and visually impaired adults.* New York: American Foundation for the Blind.

Martín, J. (2001). Learning to play, playing to learn: Fostering play development patterns in deafblind children. *Integración, 37,* 8–25.

Martinez, J. J., & Muñoz, J. A. (2002). Accessible educative games: Learn and play with . . . , an example of good practice. *Integración, 37,* 18–25.

Ochaíta, E., Rosa, A., Alegría, J., & Leybaert, J. (1988). *Alumnos con necesidades educativas especiales.* Madrid: Editorial Popular.

Ramsey, C. (1990). *Juegos adapatados para niños con necesidades especiales: Estrategias para intensificar la comunicación y el aprendizaje.* Madrid: Ministry of Social Affairs.

Rivière, A. (1991). *Juego simbólico y deficiencia visual.* Madrid: ONCE.

Rosel, J. (1980a). El preescolar ciego. *Infancia y aprendizaje, 10,* 37–48.

Rosel, J. (1980b). Orientación de la familia sobre la estimulación del niño ciego. *Infancia y Aprendizaje, 12,* 37–47.

Schneekloth, L. H. (1989, April). Play environments for visually impaired children. *Journal of Visual Impairment and Blindness, 83,* 196–201.

Author Index

Subject Index

247